D0058101

WASHINGTON'S GOD

Washington's GOD

Religion, Liberty, and the Father of Our Country

———◆·◆·◆———

MICHAEL NOVAK
and
JANA NOVAK

BASIC
BOOKS

A Member of the Perseus Books Group

New York

Dedicated to
Gay Hart Gaines,
friend, inspiration, catalyst, and
Regent of the Mount Vernon Ladies Association

and to
the visitors in person and in spirit
to Mount Vernon

Designed by Brent Wilcox

Library of Congress Cataloging-in-Publication Data
Novak, Michael.
  Washington's God : religion, liberty, and the father of our country / Michael Novak and Jana Novak
      p.   cm.
  Includes bibliographical references and index.
  ISBN-13: 978-0-465-05126-7
  ISBN-10: 0-465-05126-X
  1. Washington, George, 1732-1799—Religion.   2. Presidents—United States—Religion.   I. Novak, Jana.   II. Title.
E312.17.N68   2006
973.4'1'092—dc22

                                                                    2005030381

06 07 08 / 10 9 8 7 6 5 4 3 2 1

CONTENTS

Part 3
THE FRUIT

May the same
wonder-working Deity,
who long since delivered the Hebrews
from their Egyptian oppressors,
[and] whose providential agency
has lately been conspicuous,
in establishing these United States . . . ,
make the inhabitants, of every denomination,
participate in . . . the blessings
of that people
whose God is Jehovah.

—to the Hebrew Congregation of Savannah
Undated (Spring 1789?)

PREFACE

An October Invitation from Mount Vernon

A glorious October moon still lit up the sky long after dusk, and under it a grand curve of the Potomac River lay silver in the valley below. The pillars of the portico were illuminated by candles on the laden table. Next to me, speaking in eighteenth-century turns of phrase, was a tall white-haired actor, the spitting image of a Gilbert Stuart portrait of George Washington. He was, as Washington is reputed to have been, an amiable, reserved, and kindly man, slow and sober and yet quite warm in his responses to my questions. Across the table, at its head, sat James Rees, the careful, scholarly, yet bold leader of Mount Vernon. He had said earlier he had a question for me at the end of our elegant dinner, which was attended by just over a dozen guests. Meanwhile, the conversation was lively, the Virginia wine light and tasty, and the October air balmy, fresh, and exceedingly soft upon our faces. One felt a little of the thankfulness George Washington must have felt as he sat on this very patio with his friends, two hundred years before, a glass of port in his hand.

Inside, each of the brilliantly painted walls of the mansion had been meticulously matched with the colors found on bits of ancient paint carefully uncovered during the recent restoration. As we walked through, admiringly, the question Mr. Rees at last put to me was this: He had been looking for an author to write a book on the religious life of George Washington, and having read *On Two Wings: Humble Faith and Common Sense at the American Founding* (Encounter Books, 2002), he wondered if I might do it. He pointed out the resources that Mount Vernon offered and asked me to contact Mary Thompson, a researcher in the archives there, who was assiduously digging into the background of this very subject.

I promised Mr. Rees to think the project over but told him I was already committed to several years of work on other books; so the answer would probably be no, but I would consider it. Nearly a week later, I felt differently. My daughter Jana promised to help me with the research and writing. If I could postpone the project for two years or so, enough to assign summer interns and my regular assistant, in his free time, to begin gathering materials, maybe it could be done. The more I thought about the debt my family and I owed to George Washington for the freedoms we enjoy, and the high national standard he set for us, the more the task seemed like an obligation, not simply a pleasure. So Jana and I began the buying of books and the building of files, based upon our systematic reading plan. And I telephoned in our willingness.

Mr. Rees told me that Mount Vernon receives more than a million visitors a year and, with its new Visitors Center already under construction, was making ready for many more. One of the most frequent requests he received from visitors, he said, was for a book on George Washington's religion. The subject is a delicate one, for there has been a great deal of controversy about that subject, much of it quite passionate. Some claim that Washington asked for, and received, baptism by immersion in the Delaware River at the hands of a Baptist preacher; a few even claim improbably that, due to his closeness to the Catholic Carroll family of Maryland, Washington came to admire Catholicism and asked to be baptized by a priest from Georgetown in his last days. There are untrustworthy stories about Washington in prayer at Valley Forge, as well as one about his leaving behind hand-written copies of prayers for each day of the week, taken from an official-sounding Christian prayer book. Meanwhile, as a whole, most historians of the twentieth century appeared to be rather uninterested in religion and had more-or-less exhausted the subject by putting Washington down as a deist, at best a tepid Anglican, and little more than a practical eighteenth-century rationalist.

In fact, those who were most insistent on this last interpretation—and it was the preponderant view—maintained three distinct theses:

1. Washington was a deist.
2. In a lukewarm fashion, he kept up the appearances of being a Christian, more for public consumption than out of conviction. Essentially, he was not a Christian, or was only barely so.
3. Although he spoke often of "Providence," he meant something more like fate or destiny—an impersonal force—than like the biblical God of the Hebrews and Christians, whose Providence might act in history both in ordinary and in miraculous ways.

In short, they posited, Washington was more like a modern secular believer than like an authentic Christian.

In this book, my daughter Jana and I try to take Washington's words about God seriously. We try to understand just who Washington's God is. Our findings on all three points, we will admit, are almost the reverse of the conventional wisdom. Washington cannot be said to be a deist. He was a serious Christian, perceived to be so by many quite close to him, less clearly so in the documentary record. And as he explained to the Hebrew Congregation in Savannah after he became president, his idea of Providence was the God Jehovah, who had so often guided and blessed Israel of old.

We have written this book for the average visitor to Mount Vernon, who comes physically by the million or so every year, to enjoy the beautiful home and grounds left to posterity. (Nowadays, we must add, under the protection of the incredibly dynamic and visionary

Mount Vernon Ladies Association—which was founded in 1853 by a woman distraught over the condition of the mansion, and which originally saved the crumbling estate by purchasing it in 1858— Mount Vernon has been wonderfully restored to its original appearance, and its amenities are being constantly improved.) But we write also for those who can journey only in thought, to learn more about the man who more than any other won the independence of the United States and taught the American people by his example and leadership how one lives, if one would contribute to the vitality of a free republic.

We write for ordinary people rather than for scholars, although we admit that the subject matter requires us occasionally to haul in some twenty-five-cent theological terms, such as *natural theology* and *theodicy* and *secondary causes*—but we promise to explain these quickly, in ordinary language. For example, *theodicy* is a name for the college course whose subject is God's actions in human history, particularly as regards evil in the world. The term *secondary causes* points to all those causes that are not divine (since God is the First Cause, who brings the secondary causes into being), such as the actions of human beings and other created things, including the weather, climate, hurricanes, diseases, and so on.

We are very fortunate to have, in the late stages of our own writing, the profoundly helpful new manuscript by Mary Thompson, "In the Hands of a Good Providence" (publication forthcoming). Ms. Thompson has been exceedingly kind and helpful to us from the beginning of our work. The tremendous detail she has unearthed has changed Washington scholarship on these matters for generations to come. We are lucky to be the first to have her text at hand as we conclude our own work.

We consider, not in as much detail as Ms. Thompson, the faith of Washington's parents and ancestors, as well as the faith of his step-grandchildren, nieces and nephews, and their families (it was an abiding sorrow of his that he was unable to have children of his own). He was not alone in his faith; he was part of a great chain of tradition. We look, too, at his personal correspondence and such witnesses of his personal life as history has allowed to come down to us.

One thing we discovered—a matter of great importance—is that his private life and public life were all of a piece, seamlessly connected. What he said in public about religion he also said in private about his own life. Sadly, after his death his wife, Martha, his closest confidante on matters of religion as on all else, destroyed all the many letters they had exchanged over the years. Since the two were known to be extremely close to one another—Martha followed him despite the rigors of military life to such camp sites as she could during the War of Independence—we might have expected from that correspondence a luminous revelation of their inner life, such as one finds in the letters of Abigail and John Adams. Reserved and private to the end, clearly the Washingtons did not wish that to happen. This reticence was of a piece with the General's earlier care to be known for his public, not his private, life. He wished the focus to be on the future republic for which he had risked his life, his fortune, and his sacred honor. (How the British would have loved to hang him, the leading traitor in the insurrection.)

We attend especially, then, to Washington's public declarations, orders, and messages. We do so because these are still of most weight to the public life of the United States. They set an official precedent for all commanders of the armed forces and all presidents to follow. They themselves constitute part of the official record of the basic religious expressions, rituals, and collective religious actions of the United States, particularly in its most formative stage. Many of Washington's actions established precedents to which Washington had given deliberate and careful forethought, since in most cases the Constitution and the laws allowed the discretion to him. He cared mightily that the sacrifices from which his men had suffered so much not be wasted by inattention or carelessness.

As Thomas Jefferson testified, Washington was sometimes slow to decide, but unusually thorough and attentive to alternative chains of future consequences before deciding. Had Washington wished to set forth a purely secular, Enlightenment vision of public life, for example, he could have done so. Instead, he mixed the secular and the Judeo-Christian style, in an almost perfect balance.

A NOTE ON METHOD

Writing this book was like writing a detective story. We began with certain facts that had caught our eye—for example, the warm and convincing prayers embodied in several of Washington's public documents as general and as president. Against these facts, we knew well the existing theory of the case: that Washington did not intend those prayers in the way a truly believing Christian might, since he was actually a deist, not really a Christian at all. The existing theory of the case also admits that Washington paid homage many times to the "interpositions" of "Providence" into the course of the American War of Independence. But conventional wisdom devalues these prayers because it posits that Washington really meant by *Providence* nothing more than what the Greeks meant by *fate, fortune,* or *destiny.* We suspected that the existing theory is forcing the facts, like a blanket on a boy's bed unsuccessfully hiding his favorite things.

When a detective begins to disbelieve the existing theory of the case, common practice is to go back again to the facts, as Sherlock Holmes often advises his sidekick, Dr. Watson, to do. "The facts," Holmes will insist. "First the facts." And then, "Logic, Dr. Watson. Logic." This insistence by Holmes on "logic" has often puzzled readers of Conan Doyle. For Sherlock Holmes does not exactly employ *deductive* logic—trying to reason from a general principle to a fact. On the contrary, he *begins* with facts. But he isn't really using *inductive* logic, either—building up from a series of facts to a general principle. Holmes often discovers a single slender clue, overlooked by everybody else—and then what? He employs a logic peculiar to detectives. It is a type of logic that until a hundred years ago or so did not even have a name.

The great American philosopher Charles Sanders Peirce of Harvard was the first logician to invent for this unique logic a special name: *abductive logic*. It is the logic of working from often quite tiny concrete facts, overlooked by other investigators, until a brilliant sleuth can imagine a narrative that conclusively accounts for all of these facts. It is the sort of logic relied upon by detectives, investigators into art frauds, and wilderness guides.

For example, in James Fenimore Cooper's Leatherstocking tales, one of the Deerslayer's Mohican companions comes upon the clear imprint of a forest animal at the edge of a lake. From trained observation, he "reads" many features of the "story" that lies behind the making of that footprint. He can tell how long ago the print was made, by which sort of animal, of which particular weight and height, at what time of day, and in which probable circumstances. From his general knowledge of forest life, his imagination is fertile in conjuring up possibilities and eliminating all but a very few.

Something like this happens in solving historical riddles, too. Mason Locke "Parson" Weems tells the story of General Washington slipping away into the trees for a silent prayer at Valley Forge. Weems cites as evidence for this tale the witness of a Quaker resident from nearby, a pacifist at first opposed to the war. So moved is the Quaker from watching the piety of the general at prayer, according to Weems, that he changes his mind and contemplates enlisting in the army. This is the "story" that Weems presents, and it lies behind one of the most popularly displayed of Washington portraits (see the first page of the photo insert). The story is so vivid that it at first persuades us that the story is founded upon the account of an actual eyewitness.

Later historians, however, such as Frank Grizzard, have looked into the records of the Quaker mentioned by Weems and found that he did, indeed, exist at the required time, but that he did not just then live in the nearby cottage in which Weems places him, in the year of Washington's prayer.[1] This discovery does not completely disprove the Weems story, but it does cast considerable doubt upon it, at least as Weems tells it. Since no further corroborating witness of this story is found, historians are inclined to set the whole story aside as unfounded.

A number of other witnesses during the war years, however, did testify that Washington set aside a number of hours each week (varying as to the time of day) for private time. Part of this time, some added, was for private prayer. That testimony may tend to corroborate the plausibility of the Weems tale, if not its story about the Quaker witness. There is a second consideration to address. If Washington did not in fact pray in private, he was a hypocrite. For he urged his officers and his men to beseech Providence in prayer, that the cause of freedom might be furthered by the "Almighty disposer of all human events." If he himself did not lead the way by his own personal prayers, he would have shown a grave lack of integrity.

In brief, it is by attention to such small details that an authentic narrative is arrived at, that is, a narrative that makes sense of all the known facts about a man. It is important for such a narrative to display the man's character and habits as witnesses showed them to have been. The new solution must also avoid the anomalies occasioned by the inadequate narratives it replaces. In other words, the special logic of detectives begins with the close observation of certain facts, especially facts that others have so far missed. Next, it draws upon its large experience of the world to come up with a human narrative that makes sense of these facts. It is a movement from the keen observation of known facts to an explanatory narrative. That new narrative must simultaneously satisfy all that one knows about the character and actions of the subject of investigation and also expose the inadequacies of rival narratives, point by point. That is what one means by the special logic of detectives (and certain other kinds of investigators into concrete matters). It is not necessary to remember the technical name *abductive logic* in order to appreciate it as a type of logic as important and useful in its way as deductive and inductive logic in philosophy and the sciences.

There is one further and related point about our method that may help some readers to see what we are doing, although perhaps not all readers.

An artist and historian of art well known to the authors (mother of one, wife of the other) has pointed out to them how the fourteenth-century painter Giotto discovered the role of perspective in painting: He rendered objects farther away in the painting smaller, just as they appear to the eye. Because of Giotto's discoveries in technique, painting ceased being "flat" (like ancient icons) and acquired "depth." In this and other ways, Giotto changed the course of Western painting forever; and yet, Giotto's own discovery was only partial. In one painting, for example, the perspective he used to paint a bed runs in one direction, but the perspective he used in painting the walls of the surrounding room runs in another, and the perspectives used in painting the exterior gardens and the far-off orchards on the hills are different yet again. Only a while later did painters come to recognize the importance of the *single-point reference* that is natural to the human eye. In a painting itself, this single point is invisible, in the sense that nothing in particular may mark it. But by studying the way all the lines of the painting point, as well as the depths of perspective within it, one may imagine that point lying in space somewhere "behind" the entire painting. It is the point from which every line in the painting receives its orientation. If it is missing, the eye is puzzled and restless, for something in the painting is really amiss. Now there is something like this "single-point perspective" in a biographical study, too. If the interpretation is true, everything must point in the same direction.

For most historians in recent generations, it appears, the organizing point of reference for George Washington has been that he was not a Christian, except perhaps in some perfunctory sense, but a vague sort of "deist." He is said to have been a believer in a god who does not act in history, a god that does not favor one side in human affairs over another, a god that does not perform "miracles," or even great and wondrous deeds, a god that is indifferent to human events.

Unlike the atheist, the deist does believe in some great and "divine" force of life or energy, driving through all things. But the deist holds that the divine force in things is impersonal and, on the whole, indifferent to human life. To such a god, who is rather like nature itself, there is really no point in praying, or making sacrifice, or performing fasts and other acts of humiliation and petition. To a deist, such acts seem irrational and unworthy of persons of common sense.

Yet these are exactly the sorts of acts in which George Washington did participate, at Anglican services throughout his whole life, and in the most solemn way with his troops during the war, and with his fellow citizens on many formal occasions during his presidency. The conventional point of reference for Washington's life, therefore, seems to leave out important facts, and to falsify important aspects of his behavior.

By contrast, our own single point of reference, giving perspective to every point of our narrative, is that George Washington was a man of integrity, who meant what he said, and did what he asked others to do, and acted seamlessly between his private life and his public life. We do not believe that he was a hypocrite. We do not expect that he commended religion to the public only in the service of a "political religion" or "civil religion," in which he was for his own part too sophisticated to believe. This is, at least, our hypothesis, the point of departure at which we begin, the point of view we adopt provisionally.

A historian might well begin a study of Thomas Jefferson from the opposite point of reference, since Jefferson gave many fairly visible signs of his disbelief in orthodox Christianity, at the same time as he very publicly, marching down Pennsylvania Avenue with his red prayer book under his arm, took part in Christian services at the Capitol building in Washington.[2] (He even ordered the Marine Band to provide the music, at government expense. Where was the ACLU when we needed it, right at the beginning?) These services in the Capitol building were, during the Jefferson administration, the largest Christian services in the nation, and Jefferson quite prominently took part in them. Nonetheless, Jefferson practically admitted that he took part from a sense of duty, not from faith.

One cannot, we think, begin with the assumption that Jefferson's double vision about religion (public versus private) was also operative in George Washington. Our method, at least, was to begin with trust in Washington's integrity. All the facts fall far better into place if we expect to find integrity of public and private in Washington's views and actions regarding Providence and Christian faith. Washington's virtually universal reputation for integrity among those who knew him seems to confirm what we found.

CONCLUSION

In short, the adventure of writing this book was intensely fascinating. The research was extraordinarily absorbing. It might seem impossible to come away from a study of the details of his life with an even higher estimation of Washington than when we began, since the mythic dimensions of his public image already seem too good to be believed. The truth is that the more one meets him as a human being like oneself, the closer one comes to being stunned by his sheer achievement, and not just in the public sphere, but just as much in the private sphere. How, for example, can one not admire his lifelong battle to master his own violent temper, and to lighten around the dinner table his own reserved and serious nature? From both his father and his mother, not to mention the older brother he idolized, he learned always to want to be better. As a boy, he even wrote out in his own hand 110 maxims by which he could measure his own self-improvements, if he so chose. And so, it seems, he did choose.

Washington did not lose himself in public life. He did not fly from his own interior struggles. He loved his private life even more than his extensive service to the public. The integrity, the wholeness, of his life is perhaps its most impressive feature.

Michael Novak
Jana Novak
Washington, D.C.
October 19, 2005
224th anniversary of
Washington's victory at Yorktown

THE MAN

If in the execution of an arduous Office I have been so happy as to discharge my duty to the Public with fidelity and success, and to obtain the good opinion of my fellow Soldiers and fellow Citizens; I attribute all the glory to that Supreme Being, who hath caused the several parts, which have been employed in the production of the wonderful Events we now contemplate, to harmonize in the most perfect manner, and who was able by the humblest instruments as well as by the most powerful means to establish and secure the liberty and happiness of these United States.

—Letter to the Inhabitants of Princeton,
August 25, 1783

If my Conduct throughout the War has merited the confidence of my fellow Citizens, and has been instrumental in obtaining for my Country the blessings of Peace and Freedom, I owe it to that Supreme being who guides the hearts of all; who has so signally interposed his aid in every Stage of the Contest and who has graciously been pleased to bestow on me the greatest of Earthly rewards: the approbation and affections of a free people.

—Letter to the Mayor, Recorder, Aldermen,
and Common Council of Annapolis,
December 22, 1783

Chapter 1

GEORGE WASHINGTON,
THE MAN

No man ever lived, more deservedly beloved and Respected.
—Abigail Adams,
December 22, 1799[1]

Since the integrity of George Washington is an impressive feature
of his life, and even critical to understanding his religious beliefs, our
first duty is to savor at least a little of his life, and to gain, as it were,
an overview of the man. It would be unsatisfying to pronounce on
whether he was a deist or anything more than a weak and watery
Christian without seeing the totality of his personality and his life.

THE MAN

The women of his generation were invariably excited to meet General
George Washington in person. He was tall—some accounts say six
feet four. His demeanor was grave but extremely courteous, and with
the ladies, gallant. His blue-gray eyes seemed to gaze deeply into the
eyes of those he met, and he took women seriously. With his men,
Washington stood like a Roman warrior in his dignity, serenity, and
sense of purpose. His build was tall and strong, as well a warrior's
might be; his arms were long, and his grip was forceful. He was reputed to be one of the best horsemen in Virginia, and his movements

struck witnesses as unusually lithe and graceful. Those who in various cities along the route from Virginia to Philadelphia, New York, and Boston saw him ride into town, usually on a white stallion, behind a troop of honor guards understood what the saying meant, "A man born to the saddle." The general was plainly also a man born to lead other men, a man intended by Providence to lead men into battle and out again, a man intended to be honored, admired, trusted, followed.

Such was the effect George Washington had upon his contemporaries. There was never any dispute about it, even among the very smart and ambitious men who chose him as their leader. In his favorite blue coat, white waistcoat, and buff trousers, the tall horseman among them, or the suave, usually silent, mild conversationalist, George Washington knew he was a man to be reckoned with. But he was also without pretense. Although he was a complicated man, of many turbulent passions (nearly always kept under control), and of a much-remarked reserve and sense of privacy, what you saw, for the most part, was what you got. To those he addressed, he seemed fully present, and his manner was unfeigned. Most who met him found him quite impressive, even moving, and therefore to become a loyal follower of Washington—and to want to be his friend—seemed not at all difficult.

Captain George Mercer, an aide to Colonel Washington in the Virginia militia, wrote of him in 1760 (when Washington was not yet thirty): "In conversation he looks you full in the face, is deliberate, deferential, and engaging. His demeanor at all times composed and even dignified."[2] Just months before Washington's death in 1799, while her husband John was serving as the nation's second president, Abigail Adams—who could be quite critical of other males around her, especially Thomas Jefferson, to whom at times she was particularly hostile—wrote in a private letter to her sister what she had come to think of Washington, now that she had come to know him so closely, and after so long a period of time:

No man ever lived, more deservedly beloved and Respected. The praise and I may say adulation which followed his administration for several years, never made him forget that he was a Man, subject to the weakness and frailty attached to human Nature. He never grew giddy, but ever maintained a modest diffidence of his own talents, and if that was an error, it was of the amiable and engaging kind, tho it might lead sometimes to want of some decisions in some great Emergencys. Possesst of power, possesst of an extensive influence, he never used it but for the benefit of his Country. Witness his retirement to private Life when Peace closed the scenes of War; when call'd by the unanimous suffrages of the People to the chief Majestracy of the Nation, he acquitted himself to the satisfaction and applause of all Good Men. When assailed by faction, when reviled by Party, he suffered with dignity, and Retired from his exalted station with a Character which malice would not wound, nor envy tarnish. If we look through the whole tenor of his Life, History will not produce to us a Parallel.[3]

These words seem all the more significant in that, early in their careers, John Adams had openly announced in the Continental Congress that he considered himself Washington's superior. Adams had even said (outrageously, and over the top): "That Washington was not a scholar is certain. That he was too illiterate, unlearned and unread for his station and reputation, is equally beyond dispute." Adams had even once stooped to such pettiness as this: "Would Washington ever have been Commander of the Revolutionary Army or President of the United States if he had not married the rich widow of Mr. Custis?"[4] Before Washington had married, of course, he was actually far wealthier in land than John Adams. On the other hand, Adams had earlier praised Washington very highly to Abigail, as far back as 1774, before Abigail had ever met the Virginian, when Washington and Adams both attended the First Continental Congress in Philadelphia. And his praise of Washington, in the name of the Senate, when Washington accepted the presidency, was of a very high order.[5] Both John and Abigail could be witheringly frank in their assessments of others, especially of rivals of John for international fame, and as a consequence their praise, being rarer, has higher value than most.

But it is not only his countrymen who admired Washington. King George III himself, on hearing that Washington laid down his sword after the British armies at last left the United States, and retired to private life on his farm, said with some wonderment that this act "placed him in a light the most distinguished of any man living. . . . The greatest character of the age."[6] Some years later, in 1794, the English statesman Charles James Fox wrote of Washington: "It must, indeed, create astonishment, that placed in circumstances so critical, and filling for a series of years a station so conspicuous, his character should never once have been called in question, that he should in no one instance have been accused either of improper insolence, or of mean submission, in his transactions with foreign nations. For him, it has been reserved to run the race of glory, without experiencing the smallest interruption to the brilliancy of his career."[7]

Rarely in the annals of history have as many diverse persons testified so freely to a leader's merit and praised his steady display of virtue. What was the source of his steadfastness under most bitter adversity—military reversal after military reversal, illness sweeping his troops, lack of promised funds to pay them, dejection, and low morale? What was the source of his ability to resist temptations of power and might that have turned the heads of nearly every successful savior/general in history? What kept his keel so even? These are questions we must often come back to in this study. They are the questions that logically flow out of the years of historians dismissing Washington as a deist and proclaiming him not a Christian, or at least not a strong Christian. For where did Washington himself pinpoint the source of his strength? Whom did he thank?

Of course, many were the words of criticism launched at Washington during his lifetime. He was forced to be quite self-conscious about his lack of learning. While he had attended some years of schooling as a boy, he did not receive the normal full complement.

Later, his "university" training—unlike that of John Adams at Harvard, James Madison at Princeton, and Alexander Hamilton at Columbia—consisted of four rugged expeditions into the backwoods of the Monongahela, seeking out representatives of the French and Indians, once for peace and the other times in war, when he was in his early twenties. So his only higher education consisted of the lessons he took in surveying, which was considered a prestigious career at the time, and so he was able to satisfy his own ambition and put in his possession a useful trade. On the other hand, during his lifetime he accumulated, mostly by deliberate purchase, a library of more than seven hundred books, a great many of which he perused or even studied closely. He was no dummy, and his extemporaneous writing style, although simple and direct by the standards of the time (but complex by today's standards), is often quite moving.

Well before he married Martha Custis, Washington was engaged in as much buying of land as he could afford—fifteen hundred acres in one great transaction—and he surveyed many of his new purchases himself. He earned hundreds of acres through his surveying and some timely purchases that it led to, and he received thousands of other acres from his multiple services at Monongahela. In the end, added to what he inherited of his own near Mount Vernon (some twenty-two hundred acres), his holdings, some ten thousand acres even before he married Mrs. Custis, were quite large. Although many good historians don't seem much to admire Washington's enterprise or his agricultural and commercial skills, these deserve detailed attention. Washington was one of the great business leaders in Virginia. His land holdings were vast, and his whiskey still at Mount Vernon was the largest for several states around (he produced eleven thousand gallons of alcohol in 1798).[8] Without any doubt, his skills in enterprise exceeded those of Jefferson, Madison, Adams, and most of the other famous men of his generation. His achievements in business would have made him notable even apart from his military and political exploits. He loved to discover the practical secrets of these domestic crafts and studied them assiduously.

HIS MORAL EDUCATION

Washington had been born into a Virginia family of moderate wealth (roughly the equivalent of today's upper middle class) and the traditional faith of the Church of England. In England, George's great-great-grandfather had been an Anglican pastor. The family, although not overly devout or outwardly demonstrative, was faithful: lessons in religion, regular prayers, reverence for the Almighty, observant attendance at Sunday services at least once a month. The branch of the church they belonged to was latitudinarian—rather than strictly biblical. George was a third son, and even though his father died when he was only eleven, his father paid shrewd attention to him, ensuring that he would grow up into a good, smart, and honest man. Indeed, this was the point of the famous (apocryphal) story about the young boy cutting down the cherry tree. As told by the colorful hagiographer Parson Weems, whose poetic/mythical biography of Washington sold out edition after edition, the nub of the story was that a son's truth telling is a treasure for a father's heart much more valuable than a cherry tree.[9]

As a young man, George copied out in his own handwriting 110 maxims of the moral life codified by sixteenth-century Jesuits for the worldly guidance of French aristocrats. As he had a lifelong love of maxims (and often coined his own, later in life), this task must have pricked his mind. The last of these maxims read as follows:

#110   Labour to keep alive in your breast
that little spark of celestial fire called conscience.

Washington's family believed in the idea that all were constantly under God's watchful, benevolent eye. This divine attention—at times harsh, probing, and testing, and sometimes benevolent—he was taught to call *Providence*. He referred to himself, a recent study suggests, as "in the hands of a good Providence."[10]

That hand became almost physically visible in his life when, at the age of twenty-two, he escaped from a very hot battle near what is today Pittsburgh, with four bullet holes in his coat, two horses shot out from under him, and men falling to his right and left; yet he had emerged intact, without a scratch. Even into old age, George Washington recalled those events and thanked Providence. Similar events befell him all through the War of Independence, much to the wonderment, fear, and delight of his fiercely devoted soldiers. Washington's early trust in a kind Providence was never to fail him, no matter how tested he was by hardship.

There is another apocryphal story about a lesson Augustine Washington taught his son. The father planted cabbage seeds in a plot near their house, in a pattern spelling out *G-E-O-R-G-E*. He had George water the plot, all unknowing, and much enjoyed the boy's delight when at last the pattern became visible. "How did that happen?" the boy wondered. "Do you think it was by chance?" the father asked him, leaving the boy to muse. This is a great thing, the father concluded, "which I want you to understand. I want, my son, to introduce you to your *true* father." In Weems's telling, it is the father who is the center of the story, instructing his son's head and heart at the same time.[11]

When he became a man, Washington's morals seemed visible to others in his countenance and in his bearing. For those who gazed into Washington's face, the grown man's clear eyes flashed with candor and good grace. His nose was long, in an almost straight line from his forehead, like the countenance of a Roman Caesar or of Cincinnatus abandoning his plow. The skin of his face was faintly marked by youthful smallpox, as though to add to his face masculine toughness. His natural hair—he did not wear a powdered wig— betrayed a slight reddishness (it was sometimes brown, sometimes reddish-brown), although in his later years it turned prematurely white. That white hair added dignity and wisdom to his appearance. It also gave substance to the admiring words of his officers, that he had grown gray in the defense of the republic. Here is how Captain Mercer described his young commander:

A large and straight rather than prominent nose; blue gray penetrating eyes which are widely separated and overhung by a heavy
brow. His face is long rather than broad, with high round cheek
bones, and terminates in a good firm chin. He has clear though
rather colorless pale skin which burns with the sun. A pleasing
and benevolent though commanding countenance, dark brown
hair which he wears in a cue. . . . His features are regular and
placid with all the muscles of his face under perfect control,
though flexible and expressive of deep feeling when moved by
emotions.[12]

Washington spoke gravely, others also testify, a little slowly, but
with warmth and wit. He treasured parlor conversation as well as
dinner conversation and treated them as arts a gentleman ought to
enjoy—and help his fellow travelers to enjoy along with him. He
had made it one of his rules ever since his teens to try to say no un-
kind or distressing word at mealtime, but only graceful and cheerful
things—banter, really, especially with the ladies:

#62 Speak not of doleful things in a time of mirth or at the table;
speak not of melancholy things as death and wounds, and if others
mention them, change if you can the discourse. Tell not your
dreams, but to your intimate friend.

He was, by all reports, a considerate host, friend, and companion. A man's man—and also a lady's man, at the proper time. Ever
since he had been a boy, he had tried to show respect to all with
whom he engaged in conversation:

#1 Every action done in company ought to be done with some
sign of respect to those that are present.

As for his outward bearing, Captain Mercer's eyewitness account
describes him as "straight as an Indian, measuring six feet two

inches in his stockings and weighing 175 pounds." At his death, Washington was measured at six feet three and one-half inches, and of course in boots he would have seemed even taller. Since in those days, most men were about five feet six inches or so, and women rather shorter, Washington was easy to pick out in most drawing rooms or even meeting halls. Mercer went on: "His frame is padded with well-developed muscles, indicating great strength. His bones and joints are large, as are his hands and feet. He is wide shouldered but has not a deep or round chest; is neat waisted, but is broad across the hips and has rather long legs and arms."[13]

The painter Charles Willson Peale left us a story about Washington's legendary arm strength, based on observing him in the throwing of a long heavy bar, in a game Peale was engaged in at Mount Vernon while waiting to paint Washington's portrait. This was before the War of Independence:

> One afternoon, several young gentle men, visitors at Mount Vernon, and myself were engaged in pitching the bar, one of the athletic sports common in those times, when suddenly the Colonel appeared among us. He requested to be shown the pegs that marked the bounds of our effort; then, smiling, and without putting off his coat, held out his hand for the missile. No sooner did the heavy iron bar feel the grasp of his mighty hand than it lost the power of gravitation, and whizzed through the air, striking the ground far, very far, beyond our utmost limits. We were indeed amazed, as we stood around all stripped to the buff, with shirt sleeves rolled up, and having thought ourselves very clever fellows, while the Colonel, on retiring, pleasantly observed, "When you beat my pitch, young gentlemen, I'll try again."[14]

THE INNER MAN

On the inward side, another characteristic of the man was a prudent reserve about his private opinions, personal judgments, and deepest convictions. He was especially, but for an Anglican not untypically, silent about his religious convictions. Yet, as with most people, this does not imply he did not have any. Like many Anglicans of his class and time, George Washington believed strongly in the sanctity of private opinions and felt it to be rude of one person to inflict his personal views upon others, since strongly held opinions, especially in matters of politics and religion, can swiftly disrupt otherwise amicable discussions, at dinner, in the parlor, and at peaceable meetings set aside for business, civic, or purely social matters.

With respect to religion, however, there was for Washington even more to his reserve than custom and class. His excellent recent biographer, Joseph Ellis, quipped that Washington was a "lukewarm Episcopalian and a quasi-deist."[15] Yet in this context, "lukewarm" is not so fatal an epithet;[16] for an eighteenth-century Virginia Anglican (and perhaps even today) it is almost redundant. The Anglican "way" requires eschewing "enthusiasm" and avoiding outward displays of piety in favor of understatement and even taciturnity. Anglican manners recommend the "middle way," that is, a relatively cool, commonsensical, practical way of putting things and, moreover, a way that is not divisive but aims for a maximal degree of common ground. One overriding purpose is not to give offense. Another is to keep the peace. A third is to preserve maximal space for shared sentiments. In a gentleman, "devoutness" would seem showy, even boastful; the truly devout man ought to hide his devotion.

In this framework, a gentleman tells his deepest convictions only to the closest and most intimate of friends. Indeed, even with friends—even one's spouse—a gentleman might maintain sober reserve, preferring judicious circumlocution and allusion.

Washington knew that he would have to proceed carefully step by step, taking care not to narrow his appeal in a time of controversy. He also knew well that religious passions were just then rising along the Virginia frontier (not at all far from Mount Vernon), since by 1750 more and more Baptist and Methodist itinerant preachers were lighting the fires of evangelicalism in central, southern, and western Virginia.

Washington, ever the quiet observer, noted how broad a range of religious passions and convictions were active in American life. Unitarians were regarded by Baptists as hardly Christian at all, because they did not accept the divinity of Jesus Christ. Presbyterians seemed to Anglicans a bit severe, whereas to Presbyterians Anglicans seemed lax, broad-minded, weather-vane-driven. The grave and prosperous Quaker pacifists of Philadelphia—opposed to war and, for that reason, to declaring independence—were not deeply admired by those ardent patrons of independence who were ready for war, such as John Adams and General Washington. In such an environment, Unitarians hardly respected Trinitarians, and evangelical Christians were almost as despairing of Anglicans as of Roman Catholics. There were good reasons why Washington thought it more prudent to avoid a confessional way of speaking of God.

A work of art that helped Washington to do that was one of his favorites, Joseph Addison's *Cato,* a play that Washington not only frequented many times during his life, but even had performed for his troops at Valley Forge. Addison's text of *Cato* bore the following inscription (from Seneca) as its frontispiece. This text from a Roman pagan philosopher helps us to understand how easily Washington could put together the ancient Stoic idea of God with his Christian way of thinking:

But lo! here is a spectacle worthy of the regard of God as he contemplates his works; lo! here is a contest worthy of God,—a brave man matched against ill-fortune, and doubly so if his also was the challenge. I do not know, I say, what nobler sight the Lord of Heaven could find on earth, should he wish to turn his attention there, than the spectacle of Cato, after his cause had already been shattered more than once, nevertheless standing erect amid the ruins of the commonwealth.[17]

George Washington, like other leaders of the country's founding, understood that the new republic faced a critical problem regarding an inherently proper and yet widely acceptable religious language for public use. They remembered one political touchstone of the New Testament, "Give to Caesar what is Caesar's and to God what is God's" (Mark 12:17). From this text, they learned that many matters of government—the whole U.S. Constitution, for instance, setting forth the three branches of government—can be couched in the language of Caesar. There is no need to clothe such matters in religious language.

Not at all shirking those duties that individuals (and even nations) owe to God, nonetheless, Washington, like the other Founders, insisted on speaking openly of God. They kept the functions of state and church independent of each other, but they announced clearly that republics are not likely to survive without lively and healthy religions to invigorate the mores and customs of the people. This sharp difference between the institutional issue (church and state) and the issue of moral ecology (religion and public life) confronted them with a novel problem. George Washington was the first to face it, in 1775, as general of the Continental Army. When duties of gratitude and petition require men to speak of God, the problem is how to speak of God in a way that unites—rather than divides—a religiously pluralistic people. Some individual states, which had their own established churches, did not have to confront this problem with the same urgency that the whole new nation did, and Washington first of all.

Washington's solution lay in developing a special kind of philosophical language, which used terms derived both from the philosophers and also from the biblical story of creation and the biblical conception of God—a God who is Spirit, and who wishes to be worshiped in spirit and in truth (more on this in Chapter 6). Indeed, Washington preferred philosophical words impregnated with biblical (usually Hebrew) content.

Before the War of Independence, he had purchased from London a beautifully printed thin Book of Psalms to carry in his coat pocket, and many of its descriptions of the Creator and Divine Architect seeped into his imagery. The psalms of David describe a God who *acts* in history. Washington and his men publicly prayed that God would act on their behalf, as he had done on behalf of the first Israel. Puritan preachers sometimes referred to America as "God's second Israel."

In brief, Washington's writings, as his remarks to the Hebrew Congregation of Savannah illustrate (see the epigraph to this book), show that his vision of God was in good measure that of the Hebrew prophets and the psalmist. There are many direct allusions in George Washington's writings to the Book of Amos, to Proverbs, to Ecclesiastes, and to the Psalms.[18] His was a richly informed biblical mind—informed, perhaps, by the Anglican Book of Common Prayer (which is itself saturated with biblical references), which he knew from childhood on.

We have already seen that, as he was concerning many other intimate matters, George Washington was quite taciturn about his personal religion, even in his private correspondence. In public, he spoke very often and emphatically about religion, referring to it as "an indispensable support" for republican government, a "vital" support for his armies in the field, and a primary "duty" of individuals and nations alike. He helped to create a public philosophy of American religion, a public language that on the surface combined the strengths of Cicero, Seneca, Aristotle, and other sources of public law with the vigorous manliness of the Hebrew prophets and the psalmist.

HOW HE APPEARED TO OTHERS

After first meeting him in 1774, John Adams praised Washington more than once in letters to Abigail, yet not excessively. She was in any case primed to have a good impression of him but did not finally meet him until 1775, when John was in Philadelphia. Abigail, much to her own surprise, was blown away. She wrote to John: "You had prepared me to entertain a favorable opinion of him, but I thought the one half was not told me!" She broke out into lines from John Dryden:

> Mark his Majestick fabrick! He's a temple
> Sacred by birth, and built by hands divine.
> His souls the deity that lodges there.
> Nor is the pile unworthy of the God.[19]

Taking into account how acerbic Abigail's pen could be, this swoon quite stands out in her accounts of the men of her time. Moreover, she was not alone in seeing the virtual nimbus that seemed to move with George Washington. Here is his aide George Mercer again, describing the same sorts of features that Abigail discerned on her first meeting: "His demeanor [is] at all times composed and dignified. His movements and gestures are graceful, his walk majestic, and he is a splendid horseman."[20]

And Mrs. Horace Bland, wife of a colonel who was serving with Washington, wrote to a friend of hers: "Now let me speak of our noble and agreeable commander, for he commands both sexes, one by his excellent skill in military matters, the other by his ability, politeness, and attention." Washington was generally busy in the forenoon, but "from dinner till night he is free for all company. His worthy lady seems to be in perfect felicity when she is by the side of her Old Man as she calls him. We often make parties on horseback." Then "General Washington throws off the hero and takes on the chatty, agreeable companion. He can be downright impudent sometimes—such impudence, Fanny, as you and I like."[21]

Despite all this praise, it is well to recall that for nearly a decade of Washington's life the nation was in a life-and-death battle to win its independence. Its adversary commanded the largest naval power in the world, and its army may also have been the most powerful. By comparison, the Continental Army was puny, ill equipped, virtually without uniforms, short on boots, and most often hungry, unpaid, and in large proportions too sick to march or fight. The representatives of Great Britain entertained for many years a quite low opinion of the American foe, and even of their commander. The British diplomat Edward Thornton wrote back to an undersecretary of the British Foreign Office this "description of the President of the United States":

His person is tall and sufficiently graceful, his face well-formed, his complexion rather pale, with a mild and philosophic gravity in the expression of it. In his air and manner he displays much natural dignity, in his address he is cold, reserved and even phlegmatic, though without the least appearance of haughtiness and ill nature; it is the effect I imagine of constitutional diffidence.

Hazarding this hypothesis, the diplomat gathers his thoughts, then resumes:

That caution and circumspection which form so striking and well-known a feature in his military and indeed in his political character, is [*sic*] very strongly marked in his countenance: for his eyes retire inward (do you understand me?) and have nothing of fire, of animation or openness in their expression. If this circumspection is accompanied by discernment and penetration, as I am informed it is, and as I should be inclined to believe from the judicious choice he has generally made of persons to fill public stations, he possesses the two great requisites of a statesman, the faculty of concealing his own sentiments, and of discovering those of other men.

But now he seems to be praising Washington too much and draws back a little:

A certain degree of indecision however, a want of vigour and energy may be observed in some of his actions, and are indeed the obvious result of too refined caution. He is a man of great but secret ambition, and has sometimes, I think condescended to use little arts, and those too very shallow ones, to secure the object of that ambition.

A little more balance now!

He is, I am told, indefatigable in business and extremely clear and systematic in the arrangement of it; his time is regularly divided into certain portions, and the business allotted to any one portion rigidly attended to.

Before settling in for his summation, the diplomat recalls for himself the person he is writing to and what he will want to hear—and need to hear. Then he sails in for his summation:

Of his private character, I can say very little positive; I have never heard of any truly noble, generous or disinterested action of his; he has very few, who are on intimate and unreserved friendship; and what is worse, he is less beloved in his own state (Virginia) than in any part of the United States. After all, he is a great man; circumstances have made him so; but I cannot help thinking that the misconduct of our commanders has given him a principal part of that greatness. It does not resemble (to conclude this description with a simile) that of the mid-day sun, of which we form a magnificent idea from its own irresistible brightness and invigorating heat; but it is that of a setting sun, whose magnitude is increased from the confused and misty atmosphere that surrounds it.[22]

Washington did not lack for critics. Yet it is astonishing how many virtues and claims to greatness his critics conceded to the man. The low-level diplomat Edward Thornton, just quoted, no doubt contributed to His Majesty's government's consistent underestimating of their American challenger. Yet even he paid many compliments: "natural dignity," "caution and circumspection" (the opposite of "hothead" and "reckless"), "discernment and penetration," "indefatigible in business and extremely clever and systematic in his arrangement of it," and "after all, a great man." Thomas Jefferson, an ideological rival of Washington and a rival for international acclaim, nonetheless had wise praise for Washington, even while taking care to point out his lesser educational attainments:

> His mind was great and powerful, without being of the very first order; his penetration strong, though not as acute as that of a Newton, Bacon or Locke; and as far as he saw, no judgment was ever sounder. It was slow in operation, being little aided by invention or imagination, but sure in conclusion. . . . He was incapable of fear, meeting personal dangers with the calmest unconcern. His integrity was most pure, his justice the most inflexible I have ever known. . . . He was indeed, in every sense of the words, a wise, a good, and a great man.[23]

IN THE THEATER OF POWER

Professor Edmund S. Morgan has written in *The Genius of George Washington* that few if any statesmen in all of American history had as deep an understanding as Washington of political power, its multiple shapes, and its uses.[24] Washington quietly and astutely studied public sentiment, the ways of Congress, the thinking of British generals and European monarchs, the manners of Indian chiefs and of brave and wise men, and the habits of fur trappers of the frontier and farmers and merchants, and of course the inner passions of his own fighting men. He learned how all such persons think, and what they take to be *real,* and what they fear, and what attracts them most and moves them to action. He was very near a genius in getting the best out of his own hotly rivalrous cabinet. He had enormous common sense and a wordless instinct for how things actually work in the real world. He understood the dramatics of gesture, raiment, and dress and paid precise attention to timing and symbolic surroundings. He understood the role of imagination as well as reason in politics, of passion as well as logic.

Washington took the whole public for his audience and proved himself an astute and self-effacing teacher of the habits of republican citizenship—at a time when no one had ever experienced a republic such as the one Providence had called upon him to lead. In politics as in battle, not without much hesitation, even indecision (which some saw as his chief fault as a commander), he knew—with one or two exceptions—when to advance and when to withdraw. Once he had made up his mind on timing and method, he was irrevocably decisive.

All the while, Washington knew well that the tasks he undertook were too big for him, that he was too unlearned, that he lacked some of the necessary gifts, that the odds were far too steep, that he might embarrass all who depended on his success. He truly, genuinely, feared failure.

He came very close to getting his fill of excruciating failure. He could *taste* the fear of it, it came so close—at Monongahela, on Long Island, at Valley Forge, on the icy Delaware, at the Newburgh meeting. His was not a fake humility. He knew he had many limitations. He knew the task was too immense for him. He trusted in "a kind Providence." If there is one thing faith teaches, it is that every day has trouble sufficient to the day; one need not now fear tomorrow (Matthew 6:34). Nor need one worry about the harvest, only about the sowing and the tending; the increase depends upon the Lord. That is not so far from being "in the hands of a good Providence" that Washington wrote about.

Washington had an ally to whom he often, publicly and privately, gave thanks.

Chapter 2

HIS LIFE IN OUTLINE

Born to high destinies, he was fashioned for them by the hand of nature. . . . His form was noble. . . . On his front were enthroned the virtues which exalt, and those which adorn the human character. So dignified his deportment, no man could approach him but with respect—none was great in his presence. His judgment was always clear, because his mind was pure. And seldom, if ever, will a sound under-standing be met in the company of a corrupt heart. . . . In him were the courage of a soldier, the intrepidity of a chief, the fortitude of a hero.

—Gouverneur Morris,
December 31, 1799[1]

A TRADITIONAL ANGLICAN FAMILY LIFE

George Washington was born on February 11, 1732 (which, with a change in the calendar during his lifetime, became February 22). He was born to a moderately wealthy family, landowners in the top tenth of Virginia's families, but far below the prominence and wealth of the elite.[2] His father, Augustine, came from English stock, of a family of Anglican churchmen, military men, and farmers. When Augustine's first wife died, and with three children eventually surviving from that marriage (the youngest and only girl, Jane, died when George was three), he married the "self-willed" young orphan Mary Ball and by her had six children, of whom five survived. George was the eldest child of that second marriage.

George grew up on the Rappahannock River, across from Fredericksburg, in Virginia. A port town that catered to transatlantic shipping, Fredericksburg was a relatively bustling area, so that George was by no means sheltered from the outside world during his youth, that is, except in one regard: He did not get the chance to travel abroad, except for one trip to Barbados to accompany his half brother Lawrence, who was seeking a cure for his virulent tuberculosis. Lawrence, fourteen years older, had watched over young George like a second father. The devastating experience of a trip on which he had to watch his revered older brother suffer had hidden within it one great future benefit, of which George was to learn only years later. While in Barbados, George also became ill with smallpox, and that brief affliction later made him immune from the single greatest killer of the War of Independence. (At times, more than half the men in his army lay stricken with it.) All in all, the trip was an unhappy memory. Not too long after Washington returned on his own, Lawrence was to come home, uncured, to die.

It had been intended that George would attend school in England, following in the footsteps of his father and two half brothers, but to his lifelong regret, his father died when George was only eleven, and it was not to be. Instead, the older boys received their portion of the estate, and Mary Ball Washington was obliged to struggle with what was left while caring for five small children. Young George was now the titular head of the household—and under the watchful, domineering, and possessive eye of his mother. Mary Ball Washington was a strong-willed and independent woman who quickly focused all her attentions—positive and negative—on her eldest son: Throughout his life, he could never please her or succeed in her eyes. In fact, as biographer James Thomas Flexner noted, "Even when he was Commander in Chief, even when he was President, she objected to his occupations, complaining violently that he was ungratefully neglecting his duties to her."[3]

Perhaps the fact that she had earlier been an orphan, and was now a widow, left her feeling vulnerable. One of her daily rituals was to find a secluded spot a short way from the house, to which she took a book of religious readings and spent time in reflection. We have no records from George about such moments, but two from her grandchildren, whom she often took with her to her favorite rock.[4] As the oldest son, George was the one most to bear the expression of her fears and concerns for the future, and to receive her recitation of chores to be done.

George had earlier found relief from this constant presence through his half brother Lawrence. Lawrence had been his protector, teacher, and role model. In fact, it was Lawrence's enrollment as captain in an American regiment, attached to the British regular army, that first got George interested in military matters. And it was due to Lawrence's foray to Cartagena, Colombia, with the British army that Mount Vernon acquired its name—for when Lawrence inherited the property, he christened it Mount Vernon in honor of Admiral Edward Vernon, who had commanded the doomed Cartagena expedition. (Admiral Vernon, outfitted with a splendid fleet, had been so certain of victory that he sent home a packet ship with the news in order to have a commemorative medal struck in advance, but in the jungles surrounding the huge fortress city, carved out of a rock mountain and known as "Unconquerable Cartagena," whole units of his army came down with malaria, and he had to retreat, without his much-desired triumph.) Lawrence's tales of the British army's treatment of the colonials was to stay with George throughout his own interactions with the British.

George first intended to join the British navy, but thanks to his mother's complaints, he early turned to surveying instead. Bitterly upset throughout her life that her son, in her opinion, was constantly deserting her and neglecting her, Mary did what she could to keep him closely under her control. But George was able to elude her grasp at times: When he was sixteen, he accompanied a group that was surveying land on the frontier for Lawrence's wealthy neighbor, Lord Fairfax, and from that moment on, the frontier became a huge part of his heart and life. It also became his means of income as a youth, for at seventeen, he became a professional surveyor of the lands on the other side of the Blue Ridge Mountains. He used what he could save to buy land, both in the wilderness near his lands in Virginia and near the Ohio Valley once he got the chance.

It was during this time that George made his aforementioned trip to Barbados to accompany his dying brother, Lawrence. This event, though he was never again to mention it, was the first turning point in his young life. For his brother's death opened up for him a career in the military. Lawrence had been slated to be named Adjutant General of Virginia, the officer who served as a leader and instructor of Virginia's voluntary militia. Lawrence's death created an opening for which young George decided to fight—and with all the weapons a gentleman could summon. Even though he had no military training, only the skills of a true horseman and a knowledge of backwoods life on the frontier—whereas the main role was to train the militiamen in military skills—he called upon influential members of the House of Burgesses, some of whom he knew from his parish and its surroundings, to secure the position for him. Although Virginia ended up being divided into four military districts, Washington was still successful and was appointed adjutant of one of the districts (the smallest). He thus found himself, at the age of twenty, a major in the Virginia militia.

THE YOUNG MAJOR IN THE VIRGINIA MILITIA

Having tested his political muscle for the first time, young George now found himself chosen to become the British envoy to the French army then operating in the areas to the west of Virginia. The so-called Ohio Company had laid claim to half a million acres in this territory, and its officers (his half brother Lawrence had been president before his death) were horrified to learn that the

French were trying to seize this very land for themselves. Lieutenant Governor Robert Dinwiddie, a member of the Ohio Company, as well as the highest crown official in Virginia, quickly complained to King George II, who ordered a fort to be built, once an envoy had been sent out to discover the French position. With his wilderness experience surveying in the Shenandoah Valley, as well as his connection with Lord Fairfax, Washington was an ideally situated candidate.

This trip in October 1753 and his several return trips, in April 1754, April 1755, and fall 1758, to the wilderness of the Ohio Valley were to have a profound impact on his life and were to become the stuff of legend. Through his experiences on the Monongahela, about which we will go into greater detail in the next chapter, Washington learned an incalculable—and invaluable—amount about the military, the Indians, the British, and, most important, about the character of men and of Providence. This experience was to shape his beliefs—proving to him without a doubt that an intervening force was at work rather than a simple predestined fate, knowledge that was to sustain him through the rest of his life.

Finally, after the last foray into the wilderness, when the British finally succeeded in forcing the French to abandon the land and the fort they had built, Washington again resigned from the army to return to his life as a gentleman farmer. He was again roundly praised by his fellow men and the legislature; his reputation, both nationally and internationally, certainly well known. Rewarded for his military service with large tracts of land in the Ohio Territory (most of which he simply held for investment purposes) he retired to his Virginia farm, cultivating the land, purchasing additional property nearby every chance he got (although still in his twenties, he had become a significant landowner, with nearly ten thousand acres of his own), and mentally distilling his experiences in the military.

On January 6, 1759, Washington married Martha Dandridge Custis, a widow with two small children and a large estate, embracing some thirty-five thousand acres, lots of slaves, and, unusual for that time, a great deal of sterling silver. According to James Thomas Flexner:

> The future Mrs. Washington, being about five feet tall, came up only to her suitor's chest. She was plump, with small hands and feet. Her large eyes, wide brows, and strong, curved nose would have created bold beauty had not timidity imposed a gentle charm. Despite her grand first marriage, her own family background had been modest; she preserved simple manners, uninsistent dignity. She was not given to startling ideas or brilliant talk; her intelligence and imagination ran to relations with other people. Down the long years, when her husband was so often embattled, no man or woman ever wrote of her with enmity. She proffered appreciative friendship to all. Washington was to find her such a companion as he had dreamed of when a boy under the whiplash of his termagant mother: "A quiet wife, a quiet soul."[5]

Washington gladly took on the responsibility of stepfather to Martha's two small children: John Parke Custis, known as Jackie, and Martha Parke Custis, known as Patsy. They were only four and two, respectively, when Washington married their mother. Unfortunately, Patsy was found to be epileptic at twelve, dying after a seizure at age seventeen, in 1773. Both children had already been surrounded with great affection by their mother, and now Martha became even more possessive of Jackie, spoiling him even more than before. As for George, he loved having Martha at his side, and they shared every aspect of each other's lives. In later years, he often called her to join him for the long months at his military headquarters during the War of Independence. They were soul mates. Abigail Adams once wrote, while serving with them as the vice president's wife during Washington's presidency, that their affability, dignity, and ease together and with others touched her in human terms far more than she had ever felt with the royal family in Britain, when John had been ambassador to London.

THE FARMER AND THE CONGRESSMAN

Meanwhile, for sixteen years, Washington kept himself busy as a planter and businessman. He was an active and involved farmer, overseeing his land in Virginia regularly, reading agricultural manuals, experimenting with planting and fertilizing, trying his hand at tending grapes for wine, even inventing a plow that automatically dropped the seeds into the furrows. He loved learning about the land and about the implements of everyday work. He loved the science and the art of it. Eventually, he decided that tobacco was a poor crop and a worse business proposition, and by 1766, he was concentrating solely on wheat and corn, which could be sold locally. This choice allowed him to end his dependence on England, as he no longer had to rely on selling his tobacco crop abroad, and he turned his interests inward, to American goods. Most wealthy Americans made large household purchases from England, particularly the tobacco farmers, who often ended up in deep debt to their British dealers. Soon, his main business in England was simply to pay off his debt, and only sometimes to order household goods he could not yet obtain in America.

Eventually, Washington also built the large whiskey still mentioned in Chapter 1 and was quite pleased with the blends he developed and the profits obtained. His mind was always restless for new arts to learn and new businesses to create.

During this time, Washington was also a member of the House of Burgesses and a vestryman of Truro Parish, among other neighborhood offices. He was elected vestryman in 1762, his active service continuing basically until 1775. He did not officially resign, though, until February 1784. His duties as vestryman could be quite heavy; he and his colleagues were responsible for repairs to the church, obtaining the salary for the preacher, instructing the youth, and caring for the poor. There were at times many details to take care of.

In the mid-1760s, the colonists and the British crown began to quarrel openly over taxation: England tried to levy one tax after another, in part to pay the costs of sending troops to protect the colonies from the French, but the colonists replied that was unfair and illegal without their having representation in Parliament. Washington was no firebrand, but he did follow closely the ban on importing British goods (which he judged was good policy for the Americans and for the local economy). As early as April 1769, he began to consider the eventual necessity of armed rebellion. He was reticent on this subject, but his general sobriety and good sense made him attractive to the property owners of Virginia, who kept electing him to the House of Burgesses. That House in turn, when it elected seven delegates to the First Continental Congress, scheduled to meet in Philadelphia in the fall of 1774, gave Washington the third highest vote. The purpose of the convention was to demonstrate to the king that all the colonists were united in a desire for peace; they swore their loyalty to him as the source of colonial power, as distinct from the Parliament, which had nothing to do with the legal status of the colonies. The convention's aim was to avert war.

During the official sessions in Philadelphia in September and October, Washington largely remained silent, allowing the others present to make the arguments and debates. He was a focal point of much interest in the populace and the other delegates, nonetheless, since his military reputation had preceded him, and most delegates were already fearful about the possibility of war.

COMMANDER IN CHIEF

Then, during the Second Continental Congress in May 1775, after the opening Battles of Lexington and Concord and the taking of the British fort at Ticonderoga on May 10, Washington chose to wear his military uniform. Yet, when rumors began to fly that he might be appointed not just commander in chief of the Virginia forces, but actually commander in chief of a continental army, he was horrified. He had never been in charge of large armies in the field. He was uncertain about how to command large maneuvers and give appropriate orders. He urged some of his friends to stamp out the movement to draft him. Despite his best efforts, he was elected unanimously. He accepted on June 16, 1775, declaring himself unequal to the command. After refusing to take a salary, he promised to keep "an exact account" of the expenses for which he could be reimbursed.

At this time, Washington was the only one on the continent with sword in hand since no "Continental Army" yet existed—and to British eyes clearly stamped "traitor" and violator of his oaths to the king. For the colonists, independence now rested on his shoulders. Thus, on June 23, 1775, Washington set out to join the forces in Cambridge, Massachusetts, where they were already encircling Britain's army in Boston.

Since the two opposing forces were at a standstill, basically locked into a long-term siege, his first battle (see Chapter 4) did not come until much later, on March 5, 1776. During the previous night, he had built fortifications on Dorchester Neck, a hill above Boston, and pulled many cannons into place. A fierce storm that day prevented both Britain's massive attack on Washington's position and Washington's planned counterattack on Boston, which was perhaps providential, for the colonial army discovered later that it could never have breached Boston's impressive fortifications. Days later, the British decided it was foolish to remain in range of the newly positioned colonial artillery and decided to abandon Boston. By March 17, they were completely gone. Washington had scored an early victory.

Unfortunately, the rest of the war did not prove to be so easy, nor the British so quick to run. The long war ended up being fought as a campaign of retreats by the Continental Army—basically, a defensive war, in which Washington mostly focused on escaping from the British maneuvers and only occasionally made his own attacks. One of the most difficult maneuvers in warfare is to keep up the morale of young men during retreat after retreat, not to mention humiliating losses. So Washington's campaign required patience, steadiness, determination—and a firm belief that the fledgling nation was "in the hands of a good Providence." Proportionately, the Americans lost more lives per population than in any war the nation was later to fight. The decisive battle, that of Yorktown, did not conclude with General Cornwallis's surrender until October 19, 1781. The "interim" peace treaty itself (and even then the actual terms of peace were not yet agreed upon) was finally signed on November 30, 1782—the official text of this pact did not even reach the Second Continental Congress until the next year, on March 12, 1783.

During this time, Washington offered much evidence of his beliefs in religion and its importance, by taking very seriously his duties as leader and role model, even teacher and, in the idiom of the day, "nursing father." (The last was a biblical phrase, used of magistrates who nourished their people; it appeared often in tributes to Washington after his death.)[6] As he had as leader of the Virginia forces earlier in life, he requested and put in position chaplains throughout his army and had the government pay their salaries—eventually one chaplain per regiment, paid a monthly salary of forty dollars. In addition, he issued many orders commanding ("enjoining") his troops to pray; to attend divine services; to observe days of thanksgiving; to spend days in fasting, humiliation, and prayer; and to respect the free exercise of religion and conscience among the citizens of the land. Despite urgings from the Congress to live off the land, using force where necessary, to save expenses for the Congress, he ordered his troops to go hungry rather than force citizens to part with victuals at bayonet point. As John Adams explained, Washington preferred his troops to suffer a little but win the loyalty of their fellow citizens, while allowing the British and the Hessians to reap hatred for using their bayonets to extract food from civilians. Washington grasped intuitively that if his men lost the people, they would lose the war, and if his men lost the war, they would never be paid and, in fact, might be hanged in the bargain. So far did he go in trying to win the esteem of the citizenry that he forbade his troops under pain of death to utter blasphemies, even profanity. They must live among the people, he explained, and not offend them. They must conduct themselves as Christian soldiers, because the people demanded it.[8] They must demonstrate the moral character of the American cause, to make it worthy both of the people in whose name they fought and the Providence whose favor they implored.

Washington also endured many painful defeats, such as the loss of Philadelphia to the British in the fall of 1777 and, more painfully, the duplicitous behavior of several of his generals during the so-called Conway Cabal, which tried to undermine Washington before the Congress in order to replace him in command. That plot backfired spectacularly. But what pained Washington most was the flagrant treason of Benedict Arnold, one of the greatest military commanders on either side and a particular favorite of Washington's. Washington called it a providential design that Arnold's plan was discovered just in time, in late September 1780, right before Arnold turned over to the British free entry into one of the most important forts on the Hudson River. As Washington wrote: "Happily the treason has been timely discovered to prevent the fatal misfortune. The providential train of circumstances which led to it affords the most convincing proof that the Liberties of America are the object of divine Protection."[8]

Thereafter, Washington was less trusting and directed some persons closest to him to bring their reports confidentially and only to him. Worst of all, for almost eight years, month after long month, his most pressing concern throughout the war was getting the Continental Congress to pull from the states the money they had pledged for the war, and in which most were in deep arrears. This delinquency left his beloved soldiers in desperate straits, unable to send money home to their needy families, unable to obtain medical care for their own wounds and wasting illnesses, hungry, meanly clad, short of ammunition, and often bleeding in the snow for want of boots. The whole nation teetered on the edge of bankruptcy from the long war. Until the very end, it was unclear who would be forced to quit first, the colonies or the faraway seat of empire. The war was more than either could afford.

There were, of course, several highs for General Washington as well: the nearly miraculous deliverance of his army from the Battle of Long Island in August 1776 (also discussed in detail in Chapter 4); his resounding victory at the Battle of Trenton against the British-hired Hessians on Christmas Day 1776, with the follow-up surprise attack on Princeton a week later; his introduction to, and then close friendship with (as if father-to-son), the Marquis de Lafayette, who served as a trusted aide and confidante; France's decision both to recognize the independence of the United States, which Washington learned of in early May 1778 (and its previous decision to discreetly send supplies and munitions to the American army), and, finally, to join the war on the American side, with four French regiments arriving on July 10, 1780; and the arrival offshore of a great French fleet just in time to close the trap on the British and help secure the final victory at the Battle of Yorktown on October 19, 1781. In a glorious scene, hugely satisfying for Washington, an entire British army surrendered en masse to his troops. This grand blow, although it did not end the war, and the skirmishes continued, clearly signaled the beginning of the end, which came in 1783. After seven long years, Washington would finally be able to return to Mount Vernon and rest under "his vine and fig tree"—to employ here, as he often did, one of his favorite biblical sayings.

First, though, just to survive—and to avoid hanging by the British—Washington had to demonstrate day after day the type of man he was: the indispensable man who was nonetheless modest and circumspect. As the country roiled in the throes of political crisis while the war drew to a close, as the proud individual states struggled to unite under one national government, financiers and creditors worried about huge and unfunded debts. A bruised and unpaid army, at any moment liable to flare into rebellion, might all too easily be led into seizing power and so satisfy the basic needs of its soldiers for at least some recompense. To say the least, the future of the United States was most uncertain. In fact, many influential patriots became convinced that the United States now needed for its own survival a strong, one-man government, at least for a temporary period.

TURNING AWAY FROM POWER

In fact, in May 1782, Washington received a letter from one of his colonels, Lewis Nicola, urging him to become king. Washington was shocked and horrified. He replied,

> With a mixture of great surprise and astonishment I have read with attention the Sentiments you have submitted to my perusal. Be assured Sir, no occurrence in the course of the War, has given me more painful sensations than your information of there being such ideas existing in the Army as you have expressed, and I must view with abhorrence, and reprehend with severity. For the present, the communicatn. [*sic*] of them will rest in my own bosom, unless some further agitation of the matter, shall make a disclosure necessary. I am much at a loss to conceive what part of my conduct could have given encouragement to an address which to me seems big with the greatest mischiefs that can befall my Country. If I am not deceived in the knowledge of myself, you could not have found a person to whom your schemes are more disagreeable.[9]

Washington turned aside from the ultimate temptation set before him. A little later, he had to go a step further, putting himself on the line to quell a possible coup by the army, of which word had been brought to him. Appearing by surprise at a meeting of officers on March 15, 1783, held specifically to discuss getting long-delayed justice for the suffering troops, Washington quashed the potential civil discord with a carefully calculated use of theater. He spoke peremptorily and clearly, forbidding his men from throwing away everything for which they had so long sacrificed. Then after his speech, fumbling for eyeglasses to read a letter from a congressman, he excused himself by saying that he had "grown gray in your service and now find myself growing blind."[10] He quelled the mutiny, as many of his officers ended up in tears at his words.

As Thomas Jefferson was later to remark, "The moderation and virtue of a single character probably prevented this Revolution from being closed, as most others have been, by a subversion of that liberty it was intended to establish."[11]

Crisis averted, Washington could return to his favorite of all refuges, Mount Vernon, and finally retire from public life. As he wrote to his friend and former colleague, Major General Henry Knox, soon after retiring, in words reminiscent of Christian in John Bunyan's *Pilgrim's Progress:*

> I feel now, however, as I conceive a wearied Traveller must do, who, after treading many a painful step, with a heavy burden on his shoulders, is eased of the latter, having reached the Goal to which all the former were directed; and from his House top is looking back, and tracing with a grateful eye the Meanders by which he escaped the quicksands and Mires which lay in his way; and into which none but the All-powerful guide, and great disposer of human Events could have prevented his falling.[12]

Of course, a man such as Washington was not the type to truly retire. He left public life, but he did not leave the working world. He quickly reestablished his hardworking schedule of tending his lands and experimenting in agriculture. He also ended up as a prodigious host, as everyone flocked to Mount Vernon to be near the great man, especially artists, forcing Washington to sit through hours of being stared at, sketched, drawn, and painted. Though he hated being the object of their interest, Washington believed strongly that "to encourage Literature and the Arts, is a duty which every good Citizen owes to his Country,"[13] and so, as in everything else, he felt strongly his responsibility to others.

This responsibility especially included family, and Mount Vernon found itself once again filled with the laughter of little children.

Upon stepson Jackie's early death, the Washingtons adopted his two youngest children, George Washington Parke Custis and Eleanor Parke Custis (Nelly).

Despite Washington's fairly grim financial situation after the war—he lost a great deal of money during the hostilities by paying many things out of his own pocket when Congress could not, by accepting as a duty the new continental currency that in reality was not worth much, and by refusing a salary and receiving his promised reimbursement for expenses in nothing more than certificates of indebtedness—he still never accepted any public help for doing his necessary entertaining of foreign and other official visitors. But Washington did enjoy the gratitude he was given from all sides. Even that, of course, he might have been willing to forgo, if Providence had withheld it. He made it his practice to steel himself (as more than once his letters advised others to do) for whatever Providence might have in store. In this case, it was a very happy period for the Washingtons, perhaps the happiest of their lives. They had each other, and they lived in peace on the spot above the Potomac that they loved the best in all the world. This idyll, all too quickly, came to an end in the spring of 1787, when the Constitutional Convention convened in Philadelphia. Though deeply worried about blotching his own unsullied reputation if he got involved in the messiness of congressional debate, for which he felt himself ill suited, and of which his experiences during the war left him with a sour taste, Washington at last decided that he simply must risk his entire lifetime reputation once again, lest everything he had sacrificed so much for during the war come to naught. He soon was elected president of the convention, and his personal prestige kept the assemblage on even keel, as his eminence as focal point of the war brought disparate delegates together. The compromises necessary to crafting the Constitution most likely would never have occurred apart from his influence, and the confidence of the people in the convention's proceedings, especially the confidence of his beloved veterans, would not have been nearly as high. On September 17,

1787, the twelve present states (Rhode Island had boycotted the convention) unanimously voted to accept the draft constitution.

The debate over ratification began, and Washington eagerly read all the pamphlets that were then being quickly produced to argue pro and con. Although initially hesitant over the draft constitution, believing it not perfect, his reading and reflection led him to whole-heartedly endorse it. Yet he did not do so publicly. In public, he maintained silence, worried about the impact of any meddling by someone of his stature. He finally heard the result he had been wait-ing for in late June 1788, when news came to Mount Vernon of states nine and ten voting to ratify. The goal was met; the measure had received the approval of the people. The people had their Con-stitution—and their nation.

SHOULD HE ACCEPT THE PRESIDENCY?

The next challenge was now staring Washington in the face—the presidency. How he dreaded that. He had already sacrificed so much for his country. Must he again push his personal life aside? And for what? For the arguments, rivalries, divisions, and pure *politics* of a government office? Especially the highest office? Besides, he was a general, a military man.

On February 4, 1789, Washington was picked as president by the unanimous vote of the Electoral College. Not surprisingly, though, there was yet another delay: The vote needed to be counted in front of both houses of Congress and thus formally ratified. It took over a month to bring every delegate from the distant states to form a quorum, and so it was not until April 14 that Washington was fi-nally and officially told of his election. Once again, he headed north to an unknown future. And on April 30, 1789, wearing a rare suit made of American-woven cloth, and speaking passionately about religion and Providence, he gave his inaugural address to a joint meeting of both houses of Congress. (See Appendix 1 for selections from the text.)

The next months were spent working out the details of the new government: The role the vice president, John Adams, and a general concern to have one strong executive, would play (due to personal tension between Washington and Adams, this position was given very little responsibility); the creation of "great departments" and the selection of their heads (what we now know as a president's cabinet); the day-to-day interaction between the president and Congress; and so on. Virtually all of the decisions that Washington made during these days became tradition—the unwritten law of the land. He also assembled around him a very talented group to be his heads of the great departments. Henry Knox remained as Secretary of War; John Jay, by his own choice, switched from Secretary of Foreign Affairs (under the "Articles of Confederation" government) to chief justice of the Supreme Court; Edmund Randolph became Attorney General; Alexander Hamilton became Secretary of Treasury; and Thomas Jefferson became Secretary of State (though he delayed his acceptance for months). With a minimum of conflict and strife, our government had been established.

Few, if any, presidents in our history turned out to be better than Washington in getting these many rivals and great talents in his cabinet to produce at their highest levels, and to achieve higher than merely tolerable cooperation. The new president turned out to have a deft touch, with strength and yet affability, firmness in his own role, modesty toward himself, and deference toward others. He understood how to use power, almost effortlessly, better perhaps than all but a few presidents in our history. He did so precisely because he understood power so well—he knew that involving himself in the partisan fray (as Hamilton and Jefferson eventually did) would undermine his role as a disinterested, fair, and ultimately unimpeachable actor on the national stage. He gave slack to a lively cabinet to fight out issues among themselves, without pulling on the reins sharply himself.

During the spring of 1790, the new government moved to address some of its most pressing issues, the foremost being that of the national finances. Through a last-minute compromise between northern and southern interests, engineered by Jefferson, Hamilton's three-part plan passed (which was favorable to the North), and the new capital city was to be located on the Potomac River (which made the South happy), with Washington himself to pick the exact spot.[14] In the meantime, Philadelphia was to serve as the capital for the nation's first ten years.

The next issue, when Congress reconvened that December, was Hamilton's plan for a national bank, to remove the issue of money from the vicissitudes of government interference. The Virginia contingent—James Madison, Thomas Jefferson, and Edmund Randolph—opposed this move, arguing under "strict interpretation" of the Constitution (a reversal of their earlier support for "implied powers") that Congress could not incorporate institutions. Hamilton recognized the danger in some uses of strict interpretation, in that they would eventually make the federal government obsolete when it could not respond to new situations, and his argument won the day. The debate, though, highlighted the regional conflicts that were to continue to buffet the new nation. It also created our first political parties, with Jefferson's supporters, more agrarian and pro-French, calling themselves "Republicans" and Hamilton's, more capitalist and pro-British, claiming the title "Federalists" (though Jefferson derisively termed them the "Monocrats").

Alas, Hamilton and Jefferson developed an intense and profound hatred for each other, and their rivalry spilled out into public view and complicated government business. Its intensity surprised Washington, who believed that most men had his own outlook, doing what was "best for the nation." The Jefferson-Hamilton rivalry, and also the Jefferson-Adams rivalry, were often to roil the republic over the next fifteen years.

In the meantime, Washington focused on the pressing matters at hand: the Indians' constant guerrilla warfare and Britain's continuing hostility toward the new nation (now with respect to trade regulations). To the south, the Indians were encouraged by Spain, but

Washington was able to calm this region by obliging Georgia to draw back from annexing a huge number of acres between the Mississippi and Yazoo Rivers. To the north, the British were much more persistent and harmful in their efforts to stir up the Indians, as they tried to secure their lucrative fur trade in the Ohio region and up toward Canada; Washington's first term ended with him still trying hard to negotiate with the Indians.

During his two terms as president, Washington made long, arduous, and bumpy tours of the new nation, north and south, both to acquaint himself with the countryside, and to permit his new citizens to examine their president close up. He was already well known in New England from his campaign to liberate Boston, and that tour consisted of great and glorious ceremonies and parades. The South, though, was another matter. There, he found a less populated landscape, less than adequate roads, and large tracts where he could move about in virtual anonymity. At each city, he would attend religious services, sometimes as many as three in one day. Through these arduous tours, Washington learned of a basic satisfaction with the federal government, and a basic pride in it, that left him well pleased.

Meanwhile, Washington made it a point to respond to all the letters he received from congregations of each major religious group in the nation. He wanted church leaders of each community to feel as though this republic belonged to them, and that their activities were crucial to its health, and that each of them had a clear channel to address their president. It was as though he had recognized, before Alexis de Tocqueville, that religion "is the first political institution of democracy."

THE DIFFICULT SECOND TERM

The election of 1792 became a battleground between Hamilton, Adams, Jefferson, and still others. Fortunately, they all agreed on one thing: that Washington needed to be persuaded to stay on.

Washington was concerned with setting a precedent for a peaceable turnover of government—he did not want to die in office, thus creating a kind of monarchical succession to his vice president—and really did not want to run. He would rather have seen a new election and a peaceful, lawful succession. Once again, though, the logic of the situation came home to him and he was, fortunately, convinced to stay in office for another term.

Meanwhile, the French Revolution had taken Europe, and America, by storm. The initial news of the defeat of the French king's armies in December 1792 led Americans to believe that the "Spirit of '76" was sweeping Europe and would destroy aristocracies as it went. Pro-French fervor swept the United States, carrying Jefferson on its crest. Even the initial news about the bloodlust of the Terror did not dampen enthusiasm. Washington, who was worried that this new sentiment would drag America into foreign affairs it did not need to be entangled in, was reserved and troubled. Eventually even he was caught up in the argument, since Jefferson's "mouthpiece," the *National Gazette,* in its faux "egalitarian" spirit began attacking Washington directly for behaving aristocratically. In other words, Jefferson wanted Washington's job and did not scruple to use the language of the French Revolution to mark out the terrain of the next campaign.

The French Revolution was also fated to become the defining upheaval of Washington's second term. Its spirit came to America in bitter attacks, both rhetorical and physical. As England and France went to war, their partisans in America began to take sides, and America's trade ships became popular targets for British and French naval vessels and privateers. Officially America remained neutral, although Washington had chosen to recognize the new French Republic. Then a war of words erupted, and seizures of American ships increased in numbers, from both sides. Thus, from all sides, foreign and domestic, Washington became the target of bitter attacks. This was Washington's reward for setting aside his deep misgivings and agreeing to stay on for a second term.

In fact, Washington's second term was quite a nightmare for him: Much of his cabinet turned over, including Jefferson, who resigned at the end of 1793, freeing himself to become the vocal leader of the opposition, and Hamilton, who resigned in the beginning of 1795. Washington could see that the wartime focus on American interests rather than on party interests was no longer operative. Newspapers became more pointedly critical and vitriolic; and foreign affairs threatened to entangle U.S. shipping, interests, and alliances, as it struggled merely to establish itself as a new nation among nations. Meanwhile, the excise tax on whiskey fomented the so-called Whiskey Rebellion in 1794, forcing Washington to raise an army to contain it. He did not shrink from using force. The alternative was too awful to contemplate. He acted decisively.

Then, the gravest crisis took over his presidency: Former Supreme Court justice John Jay had been sent to England to negotiate a treaty and had returned with one in the spring of 1795 that was unfavorable to the United States—but to reject the treaty was to court war with Britain, and to accept the treaty was to court civil discord within the United States. As he, Congress, and the public argued over the treaty, Washington was to receive another blow.

His remaining confidant, Edmund Randolph, who was the new Secretary of State, was privately accused of treason by several of his colleagues in the cabinet. When confronted, Randolph's reaction seemed to confirm his guilt; he resigned in a fury and set about attacking his former patron. Washington, wishing not to destroy Randolph, refused to respond publicly by releasing the proof of Randolph's complicity (a secret French dispatch) or by giving any response at all. Randolph, for his part, published a long *Vindication* in December, which though confused, self-pitying, and not as damaging as he intended, still attacked Washington as indecisive and gave evidence of failing mental powers.

This cannonade burst the dams of criticism. Whereas previously any attacks on Washington had caused the people to rally round him, this time many restless citizens jumped on the bandwagon.

Everything Washington did or said was cause for complaint, with examples true and false put forth to accuse him of monarchical tendencies. This was the premise that Jefferson had long ago planted.

The House, the more Republican of the two bodies, since it was popularly elected, decided to take advantage of this situation to reopen the question of the Jay Treaty. Although Washington declared the treaty the law of the land in February 1796, the House immediately voted to reconsider it and demand all papers relating to the treaty and its negotiations. The United States was at the crux of a constitutional crisis. If the House succeeded, the Constitution would be overridden. For the Constitution had empowered only the Senate to advise and consent regarding treaties. Thus, the president's prerogative would be overturned, and no foreign power would be able to trust American treaties again. Washington, who had so carefully never encroached upon congressional power, and who desperately wanted to ensure that no governmental conflict would prevent the powers of the presidency from being handed over intact to a new president, refused the House's demand.

Although the Republican leadership was incensed, their bitter attacks and the president's typical silence finally created a backlash. The public protested the House's action, and the majority withdrew their demand. Still, the rancor among the Republican politicians was personal, destroying any last vestiges of affection they had for the president. Washington and Jefferson stopped speaking. Washington's hope of leaving behind a unified nation was dead. He was deeply hurt and now even more firmly committed on his retirement. On September 19, 1796, a Philadelphia newspaper published (it was never actually spoken) Washington's now-famous Farewell Address (see Appendix 1 for excerpts).

With criticism of parties or factions and of "permanent Alliances, with any portion of the foreign world," and strong praise for unity and the Constitution as an instrument thereof, for financial credit, and for "religion and morality" as "indispensable supports" of political prosperity, Washington made plain his views on government, the United States, and its future direction. He was widely praised around the nation. He even managed to get a disguised dig at Jefferson into his text when he wrote "whatever may be said of men of a peculiar character," in speaking of the need most humans have for God as the backbone of their moral lives. It was a profound document, and one which seems to address quite directly any questions regarding his own views on religion. Like virtually all presidents, Washington had help in drafting texts like this one but signed his own name only when satisfied.

Although several months of his presidency remained and included further aggravations from France and the pro-French/anti-Washington Republican camp of James Monroe, Madison, and Jefferson, Washington was finally able to see sunlight ahead. Scrupulously honoring his belief in allowing a truly elected, republican government to flourish, he steadfastly stayed out of the campaign to replace him. Thus, in the spring of 1797, Washington happily watched his vice president John Adams become inaugurated as president and then made his way home to Mount Vernon.

AGAIN TAKING UP THE PLOW

Washington returned home in March 1797, to an estate falling apart from a lack of competent supervision. Although his current manager had made a success by introducing whiskey distilling on a large scale, in all other ways the farms were a mess. Although Mount Vernon alone was never a profitable—or even self-sustainable—farm, its present situation was a financial disaster. If it had not been for Washington's astute business acumen and success in land speculation in the West, he would now have been penniless. As it was, he was cash-poor and land-rich. (Six months before his death, he assessed his own unsold land at the optimistic but not unrealistic value of $488,137[15]—although it is impossible to compare eighteenth-century financial values to those of today, suffice it to say that it would probably be worth tens of millions of dollars.)

Of course, Washington was not allowed to retire quietly. When, in the spring of 1798, Adams's administration became embroiled in the XYZ Affair, which aroused the belief that France was readying an expeditionary force to invade America, Adams again called on the old war hero. Without advance notice, Adams appointed Washington lieutenant general and commander in chief. Unfortunately, Washington created a small crisis when, against President Adams's wishes and judgment, he insisted on having Alexander Hamilton as his second in command, followed by Charles Cotesworth Pinckney, and then, third, his old friend Henry Knox (who had already informed Washington that he would not serve under Hamilton)—or else he would publicly resign. Adams had no choice but to accept, even though he had serious reservations about Hamilton's intentions. Fortunately, all came to naught, as Adams belatedly recognized that the army was unnecessary and stopped its organization.

Washington was able to turn to his personal pursuits again. In his remaining time, he still performed several "revolutionary" acts. The most far-reaching was his decision to free his slaves after his death—the only Founding Father to do so. He had already made several decisions regarding slavery, based on his conscience: He would not sell or even move slaves without their permission (rarely, if ever, given), he urged promises of freedom to blacks who had enlisted during the war, he freed several of his house slaves based on Pennsylvania law at the end of his presidency, and he encouraged slave marriages. He finally did what he could in the face of Virginia law, which required that all freed slaves be supported by their former owner. Half the slaves at Mount Vernon were not George's, but part of Martha's estate (which meant that they belonged to her children and not him), so in his will he freed all of his slaves, upon Martha's death, with instructions on how to support them (clothe and feed the old and infirm, and educate and apprentice the young). Martha, upon advice, freed them instead at the end of 1800, and his heirs supported all the freedmen who needed help (not just the old and infirm), their last payment being recorded in

1833. Unfortunately, Virginia passed laws preventing the education of blacks, so that wish of Washington's to prepare his newly freed slaves for the wider world was not possible.

As we shall see in Chapter 11, Washington's end came quickly, though much in the manner of his life. Nearing midnight on December 14, 1799, surrounded by Martha; his secretary, Tobias Lear; his friend and longtime doctor, James Craik; and several house servants, Washington felt his own pulse and then, peacefully, died, just short of the New Year—and the new century. He had reached very near the end of his sixty-eighth year.

Hundreds of eulogies were preached to mark his passing. Few men in history have been so generously praised. Most noted that Washington had made the guidance of Providence the lodestar of his life.

In the next two chapters, we shall recount two sets of his early experiences of Providence, the first during his adventures in the Monongahela Valley in the 1750s, the second during that roller-coaster year 1776, in Boston and on Long Island. After that, we shall reflect on his special relationship with his beloved army, the first army of free men of democratic habits in the world.

Chapter 3

THE PROTECTION OF
PROVIDENCE

Heroism on the Monongahela

I now exist and appear in the land of the living by the miraculous care of Providence.

> —Letter to John Augustine Washington,
> July 18, 1755[1]

TO THE DEPTHS OF THE WILDERNESS

The shot rang out suddenly, with no warning, whistling across the bright clearing as it sought its target, threatening a nation's very existence. "Are you shot?" called out the tall, young man, worried about his guide and only companion. "No," came the answer. Within moments, the two men were upon the Indian and had thrown him to the ground. The Indian, gun dropped, could do nothing but struggle under their weight. Although breathing heavily, young George Washington was unscathed.[2]

The young major had originally embarked on this journey with high hopes and ardent ambition. He had been the logical choice to serve as the British envoy on this diplomatic mission into the wilderness, where the French army had put down roots—much to Britain's dismay. He had had earlier wilderness experience, from his several years of surveying in the "new" lands to the west of established

47

Virginia, and he had the right political and social connections. Thus, at the ripe old age of twenty-one, Washington found himself leading a small party over the Allegheny Mountains into the vast wilderness beyond. It was an experience that would have a pronounced impact on Washington—not just in a professional capacity, but also personally, shaping his understanding of the world around him, and especially the force guiding him through that world. Fortunately for us—and for historians ever since—Washington kept a careful diary of his trip, leaving us a wealth of information about his experiences.

The autumn leaves falling around him, young George Washington made his way across the land he had already come to love, in search of an enemy that one day would be his indispensable support. Already, he was wise enough to understand the political and military ramifications of his task. This land had already been claimed by the Ohio Company, a British company, which numbered among its members wealthy Virginia gentry, as well as Virginia lieutenant governor Robert Dinwiddie, the highest-ranking crown official in Virginia. Any incursion by the French would be violating British property. Even King George II had come to see it this way and had ordered that a fort be built to protect what was at least half a million acres of land. Of course, first the French had to be located, their intentions discovered, and the site for a fort scouted out.

It was already fall 1753 when Washington and his group of two interpreters (one for the French and one for the Indian dialects) and four "servitors" made their way into the Ohio Valley.[3] Carefully recording his observations, Washington began the first of his tasks: scouting a location for a new fort. Although he had no real background in such decisions, he proved to be more than adequate to the task. The location he chose for a fort not only ended up being in the exact spot where the French eventually located their fort, after their occupation of the territory, but also where the city of Pittsburgh stands today. Using common sense, since in actuality the only real fort he had ever seen was the one in Barbados, he chose the one site with "absolute Command of both rivers,"[4] the Monongahela and the Allegheny, where they join to form the Ohio.

Moving forward in hopes of finding the French, he reached Logstown, an Indian village where he could enlist several Indians to serve as his escort. He was delayed while the "Half-King" was summoned back to the village. The Half-King, an Iroquois (Seneca) chief, was the most important chief in this area, and it was critical to be introduced to him, especially since he had already allied himself with the British. While waiting for the Half-King's return, Washington also met his first enemy troops—a group claiming to be deserters from the French army.

After holding a private meeting with the Half-King, Washington gained a crisper understanding of the situation. Though he had been led to believe these Indians were firmly pro-British, he discerned they were in fact chiefly concerned with their own interests—and whichever side could help them to achieve these interests was all that mattered. Although Washington had no understanding of, and therefore routinely violated, Indian diplomatic mores, he was still able to elicit the information he needed, namely, that the French did have designs on the land. It appeared they wished to build a chain of forts from Lake Erie to the Ohio River—connecting Montreal to New Orleans.

After three long days of waiting for the Half-King to be ready to accompany them, Washington's group, which now included a small handful of Indians, though only one was a warrior, traveled on to the first French fort, located where the Allegheny River meets French Creek. There Captain Philip Thomas Joncaire, Sieur de Chabert, who not only looked half Indian but had been raised by the Senecas, was commander. During dinner, Washington pretended to drink at the French officers' pace but instead made careful mental notes about their conversation. Although he was unaware that the French routinely practiced making threats to frighten the Indian tribes into compliance, he was able to glean much important information about French fortifications all the way up and down the wilderness line to Montreal. Unfortunately though, his "diplomatic" letter was not addressed to Captain Joncaire, but to the commander at Fort Le Boeuf, another fort some sixty miles further along French Creek. His journey must continue.

Delayed once again by the Indians—who chose to linger with Joncaire and got drunk on his proffered brandy[5]—the little party eventually reached Fort Le Boeuf just shy of a week later. With as much magnificence and official propriety as could be mustered in the deep wilderness, Washington then held his meeting with the French commander, Legardeur de St. Pierre. While the French officers discussed Lieutenant Governor Dinwiddie's pronouncement of prior claim, Washington was left free to explore, and note down, the fort and its fortifications.

Soon, though, St. Pierre had a response ready—mostly that he needed to pass the British letter further up the chain of command and that he would not leave his post in the meantime—and he gave Washington two canoes to ease his return. Unfortunately, with the snows of winter already upon them, the freezing water quickly became nearly impossible to travel, and even the trails were slow going. Eventually Washington concluded that he must set out on his own. So, with the company of only the Indian interpreter, Christopher Gist, they "set out with our packs, like Indians."[6]

Through the almost unbearable cold and snow, Washington and Gist trudged toward home. First reaching a small Indian village, Murthering Town, Washington decided that the most direct route home, though it meant leaving the trail, made the most sense. He convinced an Indian brave whom they met at the village to be their guide, and once again, they marched off. Soon the two companions began to distrust the Indian, who did not seem to be leading them in the right direction. Their unease proved well founded: Suddenly, as the three men walked into a clearing, the Indian raced ahead, turned, and fired. As noted above, fortunately both men were untouched. They took the man captive and, though Gist wanted to kill him on the spot, Washington insisted on releasing him, never having killed a man.

Washington and Gist then spent a panic-filled night, racing to avoid the strange Indian—or his friends, in case the latter were following in pursuit. The two men eventually made it safely to civilization. Their adventures included their makeshift raft's spilling them in the freezing Allegheny River and their spending a long, bitterly cold night on a small island in midstream, but Washington persevered, and by early January 1754, he finally reached Williamsburg.

HIS FIRST MILITARY ENGAGEMENT

Lieutenant Governor Dinwiddie rushed to print up Washington's journal, which eventually came to be published not just in Williamsburg, but in London as well. It quickly prompted debate on both sides of the ocean, resulting in the British rousing themselves to do something about the French situation. Under Dinwiddie's ever-insistent direction, money was offered by the legislatures of New York and Virginia. In Virginia, a small group was sent ahead to fortify the location Washington had scouted out, and an army of three hundred was authorized. Washington, acknowledging his military limitations, requested and received the post of second in command and found himself freshly minted a lieutenant. Thus, in April 1754, Washington was once again heading out into the Ohio wilderness, with the approximately 150 men he had been able to recruit. Simply forming the expedition was a difficult task in and of itself, since Washington needed to deal with all the details of recruiting men, enlisting them, feeding and clothing them, and paying them. It was a small taste of the unpleasant experience he would have to repeat many times during his long military career.

This time, Washington found a much harsher trip through the wilderness, since the troops had to work hard to cut a road for the wagons—creating, for the first time, a cleared route into the Ohio

Valley for future wheeled vehicles.[7] During this slow going, Washington met up with the garrison stationed at the Forks, now in retreat. They reported that a huge French force had arrived at the Forks and told them to leave. Though the Half-King had been defiant, the British troops happily departed with their lives.

Washington decided that action was needed, and disregarding his instructions that his was to be a purely defensive operation, he forged ahead. Finally creating a base of sorts at Great Meadows, he prepared for the encounter with the French that he believed to be inevitable. Summoned by a message from the Half-King, who had espied an attachment of French troops, Washington headed out to rendezvous with the Indians.

Coming upon the French troops' location, Washington determined he would attack them and take them by surprise. With the Indians directed to come up on the French rear, Washington organized his troops to attack from the right and left. This first experience in real battle was quickly to turn into an easy victory for Washington and his men, with ten French killed, one wounded, and twenty-one captured. Washington exultantly wrote his brother, John Augustine, known as Jack, "I heard the bullets whistle, and, believe me, there is something charming in the sound."[8]

But there was nothing charming about the situation Washington had just created. The surviving French troops claimed that they had been on a diplomatic mission, much like Washington's earlier foray into the wilderness. They protested further that one of the French dead was the commander and diplomat, Joseph Coulon, Sieur de Jumonville. The Jumonville Affair was to create a serious stir in both France and Britain, and in later years, historians were to label this action the first blood drawn in the Seven Years War.[9]

Washington returned to his base at Great Meadows and hastily erected a rudimentary fortification, labeling it "Fort Necessity." The Half-King scoffed at this attempt at a fort, but Washington refused to listen to his criticisms. In the meantime, the titular head of the

Virginia troops died, never having caught up with his command, and Washington was promoted to colonel of the Virginia Regiment.

The impatient colonel headed out once more for a council with several of the local Indian tribes. The end result of that council was that most of the tribes had been ordered by their "national" leaders to stay neutral—even the Half-King no longer seemed to be a reliable ally. Hearing that a large French force was on its way to make a stand against his few troops, Washington's war council elected to return to Fort Necessity, where Washington exhorted his troops to further fortify their little fort. The Indians, meanwhile, foreseeing a disaster ahead, quietly slipped away.

The French troops arrived en masse on July 3, 1754—and they quickly wreaked their revenge on Washington for the Jumonville Affair. Within hours the little fort was blood-soaked, and the situation was only made worse when a tremendous downpour started in the late afternoon. The fort, which was built on the low ground, quickly became flooded, and most of the stores of ammunition and powder were rendered useless. As night began to fall, the French signaled for a conference. Washington sent an emissary, his interpreter, Jacob Van Braam. Though Washington's situation was beyond hopeless, Van Braam returned with incredible terms: If they surrendered, they could go home.

After some back-and-forth over the specific terms, an agreement was reached—one that was more than satisfactory in Washington's mind. Unfortunately, he overlooked an important part of the agreement, a short explanation attached by the French commander, Coulon de Villiers, who happened to be the brother of Jumonville, which stated that this action was not to disturb the peace between the two nations, but simply to avenge the assassination of a French officer. When this agreement was published, it caused a spectacular uproar—and England and France took a large step closer to what would become the Seven Years War in Europe and the French and Indian War in America.

Yet even more important to Washington's life was the monumental impact his failures would have upon the future of this nation. In fact, he had failed several times over: bungling not only his first command, by wounding British relations with France, but also his second command, by weakening British (and future American) relations with the Indians. In England, "Washington's name became synonymous with the long-assumed incompetence of Colonial military officers."[10] Yet, in Virginia, with its parochial outlook and inexperience in military matters, Washington became a hero. He had proven he could lead men and inspire them. And at the tender age of twenty-two, he had already made a name—an international name!—for himself.

THE CARE OF A GOOD PROVIDENCE

Unfortunately, the ambition that welled up in Washington after this battle was not to come to fruition. He had hoped that the Virginia Regiment would become part of the British regular army, and that he would become an officer in that army. Instead, the regiment was disbanded, it was decreed that there would be no colonial officers higher than captain, and all colonial ranks would be lower than British regular army ranks. In disgust, not wanting to be demoted, Washington resigned from the army.

He returned home to Ferry Farm but quickly decided it would not do to remain there. With his imperious mother well ensconced in his late father's home, he wanted his own place. Since Lawrence's widow had remarried, Mount Vernon now stood empty. Washington arranged to rent the place (the house, the lands, and the resident slaves) from her. He now had a home of his own. Meanwhile, he was also the owner of several thousand acres of land awarded him for his services on the Monongahela, plus his earlier purchases.

Shortly after Washington settled at Mount Vernon, Major General Edward Braddock arrived in Virginia with orders to take the new French fort at the Forks, Fort Duquesne. Washington immediately sent the general a letter of welcome, hoping his military career was not yet over. It was not: The British general's staff quickly realized the wealth of knowledge that Washington could offer, and an invitation was tendered for Washington to join the general's personal staff as an aide-de-camp, with the courtesy title of colonel. And in April 1755, Washington headed to Frederick, Maryland, to join General Braddock and his troops.

This time, the progress into the wilderness was even slower than Washington's last trip, for the British army insisted on creating a good road—slowing the advance to barely two miles a day. Though Washington argued for a more mobile army, he was sharply rebuked by Braddock and quickly forgot his arguments after he came down with a serious illness (probably dysentery). By mid-June, Braddock finally relented: He called a council of war, and they adopted some of the steps that Washington had earlier proposed. The army was divided in two, with a smaller number—twelve hundred troops with thirty carriages of artillery and supplies on horseback—sent ahead, and the rest continuing at the slow pace. Being ill, Washington was to remain with the slower elements in the rear.

Finally, after three weeks, Washington was able to catch up with the advance division, reaching Braddock on July 8, 1755, only twelve miles from Fort Duquesne. Though still sick, the next day, Washington tied pillows to his saddle and mounted his horse to join the general and his officers as they moved out toward the fort. After crossing the Monongahela River successfully for the second time, the main column moved forward, only to hear shots ahead, from the point where Major Thomas Gage was leading the advance guard. Booming sounds of war made clear that this was an intense engagement—and, just as quickly, the main column was suddenly faced not only with the panicked arrival of fleeing British troops from the advance guard, but also with a tightening of hostile Indians firing rifles into their ranks from all sides. Frightened British regulars fired wildly, often hitting their own colleagues; officers on horseback were easy marks, as one after another fell; and finally, even Major General Braddock lay wounded in the dirt.

Washington, himself, was later to write his brother Jack:

> As I have heard since my arriv'l at this place, a circumstantial acct. of my death and dying speech, I take this early oppertunity of contradicting both, and of assuring you that I now exist and appear in the land of the living by the miraculous care of Providence, that protected me beyond all human expectation; I had 4 Bullets through my Coat, and two Horses shot under me, and yet escaped unhurt.[11]

An anecdote, perhaps a legend, recounts that others that day also were amazed by the situation. According to the story, a great Indian chief had watched the young Colonel Washington in this battle near the Monongahela. As the chief told Washington fifteen years later, from that time on he had predicted to those who would listen that young Washington would one day become a great leader of his people: "A power mightier far than we shielded you. . . . Washington was never born to be killed by a bullet! I had seventeen fair fires at him with my rifle, and after all could not bring him to the ground."[12]

Most of the officers were dead or wounded, leaving Washington the only senior man with his wits about him. Loading the general, who by now had slipped into a coma, into a cart, Washington organized those troops who would listen into a semiorderly withdrawal. When the general regained consciousness, he ordered the still ill, woozy, and feverish Washington to ride to the second division—some forty miles back—to ask for provisions and to request cover for the army's retreat. This ride, which took the exhausted and ill young Washington the whole night, became a recurring nightmare. Washington was later to describe it, in notes written to David Humphreys, who had begun work on a biography of him:

The shocking Scenes which presented themselves in this Nights March are not to be described. The dead, the dying, the groans, lamentation, and crys along the Road of the wounded for help (for those under the latter descriptions endeavoured from the first commencement of the action, or rather confusion to escape to the 2d. divn.) were enough to pierce a heart of adamant. the [sic] gloom and horror of which was not a little encreased by the impervious darkness occasioned by the close shade of thick woods which in places rendered it impossible for the two guides which attended to know when they were in, or out of the track but by groping on the ground with their hands.[13]

Unbelievably, considering his illness and the trials of the last twenty-four hours, Washington arrived at the camp and was able to arrange for provisions to be sent out toward Braddock. Once Braddock finally arrived at camp, swaying on horseback because none of the soldiers would carry his litter, and barely alive, he ordered an immediate and complete withdrawal from the wilderness. Everything that could not be moved was to be destroyed. It was one of the general's last orders. Somewhere near the spot where Fort Necessity used to stand, General Braddock died. Although still quite ill, Washington was one of the few aides still active, and intelligently, he ordered the general be buried in the middle of the road, and then to have all the wagons run over the location as the train moved forward. He thus destroyed any evidence of a fresh grave, in order "to guard against a savage triumph."[14]

Washington again, finding himself in circumstances beyond his control and in a predicament beyond his experience, not only persevered but in fact proved his mettle and leadership. Against the odds, he survived the gun battle unscathed and was able to organize the withdrawal, ride out for reinforcements, and even bury his commanding officer, all virtually without instruction. He had also seen firsthand the workings of Providence. As he was to later write a friend, "Its [sic] true, we have been beaten, most shamefully beaten, by a handful of Men! who only intended to molest and disturb our March; Victory was their smallest expectation, but see the wondrous works of Providence! the uncertainty of Human things!"[15]

In the meantime, Washington had now cemented his role as a hero in Virginia and was slowly increasing his national and international reputation. That August, a local minister in Virginia gave a sermon about religion and patriotism in which he pointedly lauded Washington: "As a remarkable instance of this, I may point out to the public that heroic youth, Colonel Washington, whom I cannot but hope Providence has hitherto preserved in so signal a manner for some important service to his country."[16] A reputation indeed!

SUCCESS IN THE WILDERNESS

Alas, this reputation did not persuade the British to turn further to Washington. Instead, they abandoned the area west of Virginia, leaving Virginia to figure out for itself a way to patrol this wilderness and protect its settlers. In this vacuum, the Virginia Assembly decided to create an Army of Virginia and turned to the one man they could rely on: George Washington. He was elected "Colonel of the Virginia Regiment and Commander in Chief of all Virginia forces." Having learned some bitter lessons from experience, Washington insisted that he be able to control all the disparate factors involved with raising an army, such as choosing his own officers and having full support to discipline the troops. This fresh work was a new eye-opening experience, which shaped his ideas, actions, and opinions throughout his life. It was excellent preparation for his assignment during the War of Independence. Very quickly he had come to recognize that he could not rely upon the "good nature" of men or the generosity of the people he was protecting, or even the competence of those around him. His men lacked discipline, training, and manners. Supplies came fitfully, if at all—and those that did arrive were often spoiled or broken down. He was to protect a thinly settled frontier almost four hundred miles long with only seven hundred "soldiers." It was a trying—but very valuable—experience. He learned to expect endless disappointments.

It was also a waiting time. As Washington tried to man the "forts" he erected along the border, he also had to deal with the politics and discussions back home. Not only in Virginia, but in all the colonies affected, there was debate back and forth over how to handle the frontiers, and how to rid themselves permanently of the threat of the French and the Indians. He busied himself trying to keep abreast of political developments and training and disciplining his men. He even spent time trying to get a minister assigned to his army, to bring a modicum of religion and morals to the camp.

Eventually the political discussions stopped: Great Britain decided that yet another British commander would lead an expedition into the wilderness to secure Fort Duquesne. The relationship between the young colonel and the British commanding general, Brigadier General John Forbes, was not as close as with Braddock, still Washington found favor—even though he had argued with Forbes, perhaps a bit too vehemently, to use the road out of Virginia (now known as Braddock's Road) rather than a more direct route out of Philadelphia. Though Forbes found young Washington to be a bit of a thorn in his side, he also had to acknowledge that Washington was more knowledgeable about the area in which he was about to lead a campaign. In the end, Washington was temporarily promoted to the rank of brigadier general and was put in charge of the advance division in the assault on the fort.

Soon though, Washington once again faced death, later referring to the danger—in 1784, even after all he had experienced during the War of Independence—as a time when his own life was "in as much jeopardy as it had ever been before or since."[17] While the entire British force was waiting for the next move at Loyal Hannon (today's Loyalhanna, a river in southwestern Pennsylvania), scouts reported a large French reconnaissance party nearby, and General Forbes immediately sent out five hundred men, a portion of Washington's Virginia Regiment. Within a short period of time, the entire Forbes camp heard the sounds of a fierce engagement echoing off the woods. Washington asked for permission to lead a rescue mission.

With a small group of volunteers, Washington followed the sounds of battle, until the firing abruptly stopped. Suddenly his fresh troops seemed to be surrounded, as men filtered past amid the trees in the gathering darkness. His men and their opponents engaged. Through slight pauses in the action, Washington heard a familiar voice on the other side and caught a glimpse of a familiar face: they were surrounded by their own advanced party from the Virginia Regiment, which had been sent ahead to investigate. Both sides were firing on their own comrades! Dashing down the line of his troops, dodging bullets, Washington used his sword to knock up their weapons, trying to halt the bloodbath. Understanding came too late: Fourteen men were dead and twenty-six wounded. Despite his reckless action, Washington came out at the other end of the line unscathed. Another chapter was added to the stories of his instantaneous courage.

With the vanguard division, Washington spent days cutting the final miles of forest for the new road. By the time the army reached Fort Duquesne, there was nothing but ash left: The French had run, burning the fort behind them. Forbes's plan had met with success, despite Washington's frequent and vehement disagreements with it. For the time being, Virginia's frontier was safe. Once again, Washington was free to return home. Despite the unhappiness of his men, who had come to respect and even love him, Washington resigned his command. Somewhat disillusioned and bitter after his putdowns by the British military, Washington had nonetheless been able to prove to himself, and his fellow colonials, that he was a brave and capable leader. He returned to a grateful colony, filled with awe for this man who had defied death several times and seemed marked for greater things. He then turned from war to the pursuits of peaceful commerce.

Washington himself gladly embraced the next seventeen long, but exceedingly happy, years of his newfound domesticity with his wife, Martha. Despite his wonder at Providence's care for him during his military career, he did not foresee a return to arms in his future. But as he himself was to remark many times throughout his life, we are at the mercy of Providence's interpositions. Or, as he so succinctly stated in the midst of the War of Independence, "No Man has a more perfect Reliance on the alwise [*sic*], and powerful dispensations of the Supreme Being than I have nor thinks his aid more necessary."[18]

As we will see in the next chapter, Washington would rely repeatedly upon Providence throughout the many victories and losses he and the Continental Army were to suffer during the defining year of 1776 and, indeed, during the whole of the War of Independence. It would be the rock upon which he was able to center himself as he endured severe trials and celebrated wondrous successes.

Chapter 4

1776

A Year of Providential Interpositions

The hand of Providence has been so conspicuous in all this, that he must be worse than an infidel that lacks faith, and more than wicked, that has not gratitude enough to acknowledge his obligations, but, it will be time enough for me to turn preacher, when my present appointment ceases; and therefore, I shall add no more on the Doctrine of Providence.

—Letter to Brigadier General Thomas Nelson,
August 20, 1778[1]

We have, as you very justly observe, abundant reason to thank providence for its many favourable interpositions in our behalf. It has, at times been my only dependence for all other resources seemed to have fail'd us.

—Letter to Rev. William Gordon,
March 9, 1781[2]

These are the times that try men's souls. The summer soldier and the sunshine patriot may, in this crisis, shrink from the service of his country; but he that stands it now deserves the love and thanks of man and woman.

—Thomas Paine, *The Crisis*,
December 19, 1776[3]

A TRANSFORMATIVE TIME

As author David McCullough has so skillfully related in his own book, 1776 was a year of transformative political events, both for George Washington and for his beloved country. Yet McCullough focuses more on the military and political events, not the personal transformation that would take place in this all-important period for General Washington himself. It was a year in which Washington's belief in "Divine Providence" was severely tested and found sturdy enough to absorb the searing ups and downs of these twelve eventful months.

Washington knew that after he had taken up command in 1775, nothing would ever be the same. He was, officially now, a rebel and a traitor to his king. Yet even he was not sure exactly what this meant. How would it all end? With his head through a noose, his country in ruins? Or with the sweet sounds of success and bells tolling for liberty? Washington did not know and had much to fear.

As Washington had written his wife, when he informed her of his election as commander in chief of the Continental Army, "I shall rely, therefore, confidently on that Providence, which has heretofore preserved and been bountiful to me, not doubting but that I shall return safe to you in the fall."[4] He repeated the same reluctant acceptance of his commission in a letter written the next day to Burwell Bassett, his brother-in-law on Martha's side: "May God grant, therefore, that my acceptance of it, may be attended with some good to the common cause, and without Injury (from want of knowledge) to my own reputation."[5]

Clearly Washington knew that he faced an uphill struggle, but he was not completely without hope. He knew his soldiers, if he could even call them that yet, were rough, untrained, undisciplined, and even uncouth. But he also knew what strong leaders and discipline—especially moral discipline—could accomplish. He had learned this lesson very early, while still a colonel with the Virginia militia during the French and Indian War. He commented at the time on the need for chaplains by remarking to officials back in Virginia that "as touching a chaplain, if the government will grant a subsistence, we can readily get a person of merit to accept of the place, . . . as it is highly necessary we should be reformed from those crimes and enormities we are so universally accused of,"[6] and yet again later that "common decency, Sir, in a camp calls for the services of a divine, and which ought not to be dispensed with."[7]

He remembered this lesson when he took command of the Continental Army, ensuring that he not only would have chaplains in the army, but that there would be enough chaplains to minister to all the men and that they would be paid sufficiently. He repeatedly ordered (or, his favorite locution, "enjoined") his men to pray and to attend divine service. In fact, one of his early orders as commander in chief, less than a month after he was elected, was quite straightforward: "And in like manner [the General] requires and expects, of all Officers, and Soldiers, not engaged on actual duty, a punctual attendance on divine Service, to implore the blessings of heaven upon the means used for our safety and defence."[8] Among many other "General Orders," just a short time later he made his conviction even more explicit:

> The Commander in Chief is confident, the Army under his immediate direction, will shew their Gratitude to providence, for thus favouring the Cause of Freedom and America; and by their thankfulness to God, their zeal and perseverance in this righteous Cause, continue to deserve his future blessings.[9]

In other words, Washington believed that prayer without self-reform would be hypocritical. His men must make themselves worthy of divine favor. In fact, completely contrary to any purported deist tendency, he never hesitated to be explicit about his belief in and reliance upon "Providence" and its much-needed "interpositions" in the war. In a later order, after the war had progressed, he would write that the commander in chief "has the full confidence that in another Appeal to Heaven (with the blessing of providence, which it becomes every officer and soldier humbly to supplicate), we shall prove successful."[10]

Toward the end of the war, he noted: "The Commander in Chief earnestly recommends that the troops not on duty should universally attend with that seriousness of Deportment and gratitude of Heart which the recognition of such reiterated and astonishing interpositions of Providence demand of us."[11]

His was now a life noting Providence's "astonishing interpositions." Whether in his own mind or in the minds of those who witnessed, it seemed clear that God had a higher plan both for this nation and for this self-educated Virginia planter. Though we have discussed earlier his seemingly miraculous survivals during his youth, the War of Independence only deepened his gratitude to Providence. He especially cherished the idea that Providence sustains humans through the trials and the tribulations as well as the joys and successes of life. Two key battles, early in the war, paint a vivid picture of these extremes.

THE BATTLE FOR BOSTON: MARCH 5, 1776

From what has been said upon this subject, you may see what ground there is to give praise to God for his favors already bestowed on us, respecting the public cause. It would be a criminal inattention not to observe the singular interposition of Providence hitherto, in behalf of the American colonies. . . . How many discoveries have been made of the designs of enemies in Britain and among ourselves, in a manner as unexpected to us as to them, and in such season as to prevent their effect? What surprising success has attended our encounters in almost every instance? Has not the boasted discipline of regular and veteran soldiers been turned into confusion and dismay, before the new and maiden courage of freemen, in defence of their property and right? In what great mercy has blood been spared on the side of this injured country? . . .

The signal advantage we have gained by the evacuation of Boston, and the shameful flight of the army and navy of Britain, was brought about without the loss of a man. To all this we may add, that the counsels of our enemies have been visibly confounded, so that I believe that I may say with truth, that there is hardly any step which they have taken, but it has operated strongly against themselves, and been more in our favor, than if they had followed a contrary course.[12]

And so the Rev. John Witherspoon, one of the signers of the Declaration of Independence, proclaimed on May 17, 1776, the work of God behind the early successes of the American cause, particularly noting the battle for Boston earlier that year. Indeed, that was one of the first major battles that Washington was involved in as commander in chief, and also one of his first resounding successes. Yet, were it not for "the singular interposition of Providence hitherto," as Witherspoon put it, it could have been a humiliating defeat.

Washington had arrived outside Boston as the newly appointed commander in chief of "the army of the United Colonies" in early July 1775. Since then he had tried to gain his bearings, to learn what kind of "army" he actually had and what quantities of supplies, and to instill some sort of training and discipline in his men. He soon realized that the lengthy siege of Boston had to be ended—action, and hopefully a victory, was needed. The men were restless in their makeshift camp, and the enlistments ended in December—and very few men were reenlisting.

The first bit of good news to arrive came on November 29. A privateer sent out by Washington as a substitute for his lack of a navy had captured a British supply ship weighted down with war matériel. Suddenly Washington had at his disposal arms, cannon, mortars, and, above all, desperately needed ammunition. It was an amazingly good sign, and Washington immediately noted, "We must be thankful, as I truly am, for this instance of Divine favour; for nothing surely ever came more apropos."[13]

As the New Year came and went, and the army itself came and went, since old enlistees returned home and new recruits arrived, Washington felt sure he had to act quickly, while he still had at least some resources. Against orders, departing soldiers had walked off with their guns, depleting the supply dangerously, and the freezing weather and smallpox had rendered half his army unfit to fight. Gunpowder was still rare, and money (for food, medicine, pay, and other necessities) rarer still. He wrote to his secretary and friend Joseph Reed, "If I shall be able to rise superior to these and many other difficulties, which might be enumerated, I shall most religiously believe, that the finger of Providence is in it, to blind the eyes of our enemies; for surely if we get well through this month, it must be for want of their knowing the disadvantages we labour under."[14]

Dismal news—the American army's attempt to take Quebec had been badly defeated—was quickly lightened by critically important good news: Colonel Henry Knox had successfully retrieved the guns at Fort Ticonderoga and had brought them, during an arduous month-long trek over land, to just outside Boston. This feat was Herculean, as the heavy guns (said to weigh more than 120,000 pounds total) needed to travel hundreds of miles, in the bitterness of a nasty winter, across lakes, mountains, and, when Knox's men were lucky, barely passable roads. The achievement was amazing, and the timing of the guns' arrival perfect. Quite suddenly, with these guns, the Americans had the upper hand. The whole British army lay vulnerable under their barrels.

Counseled by his generals, Washington developed a bold plan: Rather than directly attack the strongly fortified town of Boston itself, the Americans were going to seize the hill of Dorchester Heights overlooking Boston Harbor and lure the enemy out to attack them. Then, as the enemy attacked, a portion of the army would flank their troops, crossing over into Boston to seize the town. The key was this: The Americans would take control of Dorchester Heights on one night, without alerting the British. With a frozen and quite high hilltop and a steep slope to climb before reaching that top, getting the guns on the Heights and building defensive fortifications seemed foolhardy and impossible.

Washington had his men build fortifications in the main camp, which could then be erected up on the Heights. Then they prepared barrels filled with earth to be rolled down upon the enemy, and finally they built a "wall" of hay bales to conceal their trek to the Heights across a low-lying causeway. As a final subterfuge, Washington ordered those guns from Ticonderoga that were placed elsewhere to begin a nightly bombardment of the British positions—both to distract and to cover any noise. Late Saturday night the cannons began firing, continuing intermittently each night until the target date of Monday night, March 4. That night, under the covering fire, some four thousand men quietly trooped over to Dorchester Heights, along with hundreds of carts and wagons filled with fortifications and, of course, some of the guns from Ticonderoga.

The night was beautiful: clear, mild, and with a full moon—perfect for the work that needed to be done. As one patriot minister noted, "It was hazy below so that our people could not be seen, though it was a bright moonlight night above on the hills."[15] And again, a British brigadier general was informed about the Americans' actions—and yet chose to ignore the report. No alert was sounded. The next morning, March 5—the sixth anniversary of the Boston Massacre—the British were completely surprised to wake up and find thousands of Americans and twenty cannon staring down at them. Shock and awe, indeed.

British Major General William Howe had no choice but to attack. By mid-afternoon, he had his troops gathering on Castle Island, preparing for battle. Meanwhile, Washington's four thousand troops were standing by to cross the bay in counterattack and begin their invasion of the city. At nightfall a furious storm blew up, pounding the area through the next day. American Brigadier General William Heath "concluded that 'kind Heaven' had stepped in to intervene."[16] Washington himself agreed, later writing, "I will not lament or repine at any act of Providence because I am in a great measure a convert to Mr. Pope's [the poet Alexander Pope] opinion, that whatever is, is right."[17] "Whatever is," in Washington's understanding, was often bitter defeat and near-despair.

Washington was at first bitterly disappointed and deeply frustrated by not being able to make a direct attack and provide a glorious victory for the American army. Later, after occupying Boston and gazing out at its intricate inner defenses, the Americans recognized that their attack could not possibly have succeeded without immense carnage. At the time, though, Washington swallowed his frustration and simply noted Providence's interference. General Howe, on the other hand, leaped at the providential opportunity to save face and canceled his planned assault. He also faced the inevitable—surrounded by guns, his ships in danger—and ordered Boston's evacuation. He requested a kind of truce until he could set sail. Thus, by March 17, when the winds finally turned favorable, the British ships took full sail, and Boston was free at last of British occupation. The Americans on shore were ecstatic. Abigail Adams wrote her husband, "Surely it is the Lord's doings and it is marvelous in our eyes."[18]

Meanwhile, General Washington, who allowed Major General Artemus Ward (the commander in chief of the Massachusetts troops, who had directed the siege before Washington's arrival) the honor of leading the first troops triumphantly into Boston, stayed behind in Cambridge to attend church. It was his first real victory, and he had much to be thankful for. As he commented shortly afterward: "To obtain the applause of deserving men is a heartfelt satisfaction, to merit it is my highest wish. If my conduct, therefore, as an instrument in the late signal interposition of Providence, hath merited the approbation of this great country, I shall esteem it one of the most fortunate and happy events of my life."[19] Harvard gave him the honorary degree of doctor of law. On that occasion, too, he gave the glory to Providence.

THE BATTLE OF LONG ISLAND: AUGUST 27–30, 1776

The time is now near at hand which must probably determine, whether Americans are to be, Freemen, or Slaves; whether they are to have any property they can call their own; whether their Houses, and Farms, are to be pillaged and destroyed, and they consigned to a State of Wretchedness from which no human efforts will probably deliver them. *The fate of unborn Millions will now depend, under God, on the Courage and Conduct of this army*—Our cruel and unrelenting Enemy leaves us no choice but a brave resistance, or the most abject submission; this is all we can expect—We have therefore to resolve to conquer or die: Our own Country's Honor, all call upon us for a vigorous and manly exertion, and if we now shamefully fail, we shall become infamous to the whole world. *Let us therefore rely upon the goodness of the Cause, and the aid of the supreme Being, in whose hands Victory is,* to animate and encourage us to great and noble Actions—The Eyes of all our Countrymen are now upon us, and we shall have their blessings, and praises, if happily we are the instruments of saving them from the Tyranny meditated against them. Let us therefore animate and encourage each other, and *shew the whole world, that a Freeman contending for LIBERTY on his own ground is superior to any slavish mercenary on earth.* [Italics added.]

—George Washington, "General Orders,"
July 2, 1776[20]

Washington had long understood the importance of the political and military war he faced when he became commander in chief, and he tried hard to impress his men with what was at stake. The Declaration of Independence had been the first official statement by the fledgling "government" on its struggles. Washington had been heartened to hear cheers when he read the Declaration to his men. Now, the war took on an entirely different meaning—it was truly a revolutionary war. Would the people—and his soldiers—respond the right way? No other people had *ever* broken away from an established foe, an empire—in modern times—and won their freedom. It was now six weeks past that historic declaration of July 4.

Washington knew the next attack by the British would be upon New York City. Therefore, he had marched his troops, numbering twenty-three thousand, from Boston to New York. It was the middle of August and hot and miserable. Worse yet, on their arrival the American army faced a British army 30 percent larger—thirty thousand men, including ten thousand hired Hessians. (The Prince of Hesse regularly rented out his army, to raise much-needed foreign currency.) Not only was the British army larger; it was also better trained and better supplied. Its thousands of guns would beat a ragtag collection of pitchforks, rifles, and muskets, any day. The Americans also faced an army that could rely upon a strong and swift supporting navy—a navy that allowed the British to have easy mobility, so they could strike wherever they willed. They held virtually complete dominion over the seas.

There was one bright spot for Washington to contemplate though. The American army was truly American—the men came from all over the colonies; it was no longer just a New England war and a New England army. It was truly a Continental Army. They lacked discipline, uniforms, sufficient powder, money, a navy—almost everything. But they were fighting to be free and independent.

Now, the guessing game began. Washington was absolutely convinced that British Major General Howe planned an assault on New York City. Of course, with the British navy standing by, Howe could attack virtually anywhere along the New York or New Jersey coast. Washington, therefore, vigilantly prepared as best he could, trying to imagine what Howe might do. Building and improving his fortifications, requesting more arms and more ammunition, anything that might hold off the impending attack. Yet the endless days passed quietly, and still he waited. He was totally perplexed by the delay, commenting on August 19 to his cousin, Lund Washington, the caretaker of Mount Vernon in his absence, "There is something exceedingly misterious [*sic*] in the conduct of the Enemy."[21]

Then, finally, movement. On August 21, a large detachment of British regulars advanced to the western tip of Long Island, landing at Gravesend Bay on August 22. In response, Washington fortified Brooklyn Heights, a location across from the tip of Manhattan, which controlled the East River. He also placed 3,500 of his most skilled men in the forested hills blocking the British advance. In command of these men Washington placed Major General John Sullivan. Though he was not fond of or particularly impressed by Sullivan, he had no choice. His favorite, General Nathanael Greene, was incapacitated with a fever, probably malaria. The rest of his men, some 4,000, he stationed in Brooklyn Heights.

Though it was estimated that 8,000 British soldiers were now ashore on Long Island (eventually the number would be closer to 20,000), and marching toward the American lines, still Washington was erroneously convinced that the main thrust would be at New York City itself. With no way to counter the British navy, he had no choice but to be prepared on all fronts. He waited in Manhattan, not traveling to Long Island until the afternoon of August 23. From then on, he traveled back and forth continuously, inspecting the defenses that Sullivan, who was responsible for the outer defenses, and General Israel Putnam, the overall commander, had established.

The 3,500 men under Major General Sullivan's command were thinly stretched out along the nine-mile line of the wooded hills. Since he did not have enough men to cover the entire span, Sullivan opted to leave his left flank lightly defended, if at all. He was confident that his troops had the British covered on the right and in front, with Manhattan behind them. After all, in Sullivan's mind, his men had covered the three main roads that led toward the American positions. The much smaller "Jamaica Pass," to the north and much farther east, seemed to him inconsequential. A field commander looking at Sullivan's deployment now would recognize the danger inherent in Sullivan's position, but at the time, neither Sullivan nor Washington commented on it. In fact, the only person to worry at all was Lord Stirling, Sullivan's senior commander, and he had to use his own money—fifty dollars!—to pay five young officers to patrol Jamaica Pass at night: five solitary men to block any potential British flanking movement through the pass.

Unfortunately, whereas the American generals discounted the possibilities of an attack through the Jamaica Pass, British General Henry Clinton saw a golden opportunity. Despite his unpopularity at headquarters, he finally managed to convince General Howe to outflank the Americans via the Jamaica Pass. Stealthily, the British troops moved forward on the night of August 26, leaving their tents pitched behind them to give the appearance of the camps' still being in place. By midnight, some two-thirds of the British army was traveling up this road. By 3 A.M., the advance force had quietly seized Stirling's five helpless young guards. By dawn the entire British force was together at Bedford, north of the American lines and behind them, and poised to cut off Sullivan's entire forward line.

The battle itself finally began that night, early on August 27, sometime just after midnight. A British regiment first attacked the American right flank, along the Gowanus road, at the opposite end of the American line from the Jamaica Pass. Sullivan rushed a battalion there to reinforce Lord Stirling. Meanwhile, he kept an eye on his center, the Flatbush road, and his immediate left, the Bedford road. General Howe had placed the Hessians facing the front center of Sullivan's line, and though they were not yet advancing, Sullivan knew their cannon were targeting his roads. Neither Sullivan nor Putnam saw any cause for concern though, believing the battle well within their means, and so no emergency message was sent to alert Washington.

It was not until morning, approximately 8:30 A.M., that Washington once again crossed back to Long Island to oversee the first real battle in New York. Aware of the seriousness of the situation facing the troops, he was nonetheless confident that their response so far showed they'd put up a good fight—at worst, they'd make a slow retreat to the safety of Brooklyn Heights. Instead, disaster soon struck from the unprotected flank to the north.

Sometime around 9 A.M., the British snapped the trap: They moved up behind the unsuspecting American troops fighting on the right and center, many of whom initially assumed these were American reinforcements, until the British began firing from behind them. The Hessians were then ordered to attack from the front, and a horrible slaughter began. The Americans were trapped between the anvil of Hessian and British troops at their front and the incoming hammer of British troops behind them, blocking their retreat to the fort. Their only possibility of escape, and it was hardly a reasonable option, was the marshy and rapidly rising Gowanus Bay. Trapped in desperate straits, many of the American troops fought bravely and valiantly—Washington himself is said to have exclaimed, "Good God! What brave fellows I must lose this day!"[22]—especially Lord Stirling and his Maryland "Old Line." Unfortunately, only 10 of Stirling's 500 men made it safely to Brooklyn; the rest were either killed or taken prisoner, and Lord Stirling was reported missing, as was Major General Sullivan.

Washington, from the vantage of the fort at Brooklyn, could do nothing but watch and wait as his men were slaughtered, and few, very few, survivors made it safely to the fort. Meanwhile, British regulars quickly marched up to the fort and, staying just beyond musket range, stared down the fearful men within. With their officers gone (missing, captured, or dead), and their friends gone (dead or taken prisoner), these men were virtually useless. Although some still obeyed Washington enough to strengthen the fort's defenses, the army was a shambles. And worried still that New York was a target, Washington felt he could not reinforce Long Island too much. He could do not much more than wait for the oncoming attack, which would utterly destroy his troops and end the nation's fledgling hope for independence not yet two months after the Declaration.

Yet, based on their belief that all they needed was a show of force to get the rebels to back down, the British turned back and moved beyond range of Washington's marksmen. Then they made camp. Convinced the British had the American army trapped in Brooklyn Heights, British General Howe was more interested in winning "cheaply," with a minimum of British lives lost, than in making an attack that, although it would shatter the American army, he was certain would be a costly repeat of Breed's Hill, better known as the Battle of Bunker Hill. On that occasion, a straightforward British assault up a small hill cost Britain more than a thousand dead. It was a cost that Howe was convinced the British public would not bear again.

So Howe sat patiently outside the fort, making small advances every night, sending out his soldiers to dig closer and closer, and instigating small skirmishes here and there. He knew the American army had nowhere to go. When a downpour moved in the next day, Howe knew the American guns and ammunition would most likely be useless. He was confident he was in absolute control. However, on the morning of August 30, Howe awoke to an abandoned fort. The American army (what was left of it)—as if by magic—had escaped.

AN UNUSUAL FOG

Washington had decided he had to save his army from certain doom, and the only hope was a swift, organized retreat across the East River. The technical difficulty of this idea was overwhelming: how to get thousands of men, supplies, horses, cannon, and more, quietly, across a wide river, without the British discovering them and annihilating them.

By 10 P.M. on August 29, Washington had done all the preparations he could do: His plans were made, the subterfuge that the wounded men would be transported back to Manhattan and that the others would be "under arms with packs and everything"[23] had been spread throughout the American ranks, and every possible boat had been gathered. The American troops were at alert at their positions, thinking a possible—and brazen—counterattack was about to commence. All signs of life were kept up, from campfires burning, to snipers taking shots at the waiting British. Then, slowly, one by one, American regiments were ordered from their trenches and sent down to the riverfront. Their dread turned to relief, then near panic, as they realized what was happening and began pushing and shoving to get on the first boats, afraid of being left behind. Washington, who had not slept for forty-eight hours and yet was overseeing the embarkations himself, insisted on order and, most of all, silence.

To no avail: The noise of the Americans at the river awakened a woman who lived nearby—a woman who had no fond thoughts for the "rebels." Swiftly, she sent a black servant to alert the British. Coming upon a German officer who spoke no English, the poor servant was immediately arrested, and no message reached the British commander.

The worst crisis of the evening was yet to come. As the night progressed, and more troops made it to the river's edge to be loaded onto waiting boats, all seemed to be going as planned. Even the prevailing winds, which had prevented the first boats from reaching Long Island at all, shifted suddenly around 11 P.M. Unfortunately, one aide's careless misunderstanding almost ruined everything. At 2 A.M., as the evacuation was slowly continuing, and not even half the men had made it to safety, Washington spotted Colonel Israel Hand approaching him. But Colonel Hand and his Pennsylvania troops were supposed to be the last ones on the boats—they were to be the final line of defense, the final decoy to the slumbering British camp that all was well and unchanged at the American camp. Now, the front lines were unprotected!

Colonel Hand explained that General Thomas Mifflin had ordered him to the boats; Mifflin explained that Washington's aide-de-camp, Alexander Scammell, had given him orders, supposedly coming from Washington himself. Washington was furious. His hot temper, which he always struggled—and usually successfully—to control, flared. He roared, "Good God! General Mifflin, I am afraid you have ruined us by so unseasonably withdrawing the troops from the lines."[24] But the anger lasted for only seconds. Washington recognized quickly the grave danger resulting from this blunder. All could be lost; it could be another slaughter. He ordered Hand back to his position, until summoned. Though they were understandably reluctant, Colonel Hand was able to lead his men back, and to hold the line.

Washington watched the men depart and then turned to face the river again. There was much left to do. As he sat on his handsome steed watching the transport, hours passed, and day began to show its first signs. Washington realized with dread that he had only half his troops safely across the river. The British would surely discover their movement as soon as the sun rose! Yet, just as dawn began to stretch its colorful fingertips across the horizon, a heavy fog rolled in. Suddenly, all was gray and yellow, an unforgettable fog. No one could see far in front of him—movements ahead were entirely obscured.

Washington had much reason to be grateful, for within hours, still under the cover of fog, Washington was finally able to step onto one of the last boats, with his gray charger beside him, and set sail for the safety of Manhattan. Less than an hour after the last boat landed in New York, the last of the yellowish fog dispersed. Washington had not left one living man behind. His army was secure. They had been spared an ignominious defeat. Washington and his men would live to fight another day.

A YEAR OF TRIALS

In his gripping tale of the events of 1776 in the life of George Washington, author McCullough makes many mentions of the faith of Washington and others in his company in the guidance and succor of Divine Providence on behalf of the American cause. But McCullough does not focus specifically on the richness and significance of these acts of faith. In fact, Washington devoted quite a lot of energy during 1776 attending to the religious life of his troops, which he considered indispensable to their success. Although a full analysis of the complexities of Washington's view of Providence must be put off to later chapters (see Chapter 10 especially), in this chapter we have highlighted some of Washington's actions in connection with religion: instructions to his troops and expressions of gratitude, on the one hand, and, on the other, the resolute trust during one of the many severe trials of the year, which began with the disaster at Long Island and lasted until late December.

Most interesting to note is that by *Providence* Washington understood both the total sovereignty of God over concrete contingent events and the benevolence of God, even when his dispensations plunged mortals into the most severe trials and difficulties. In the one case, the doctrine of Providence reminded people in moments of success and glory that, in the words of the psalm sung by Henry V's victorious troops at Agincourt, "Not to us, not to us, O Lord, but to thy Name be the glory." In the other case, it was not only in exultation that humans needed equilibrium, but also in temptations to despair. In cases of defeat, failure, and seeming hopelessness, so taught the doctrine of Providence as Washington understood it, Providence tests and tempers the character, seeing how far a person's ultimate faith will stretch, how much pressure it can withstand. In bitter suffering, too, the committed Christian must maintain an equilibrium, urging herself, "Be not afraid!" She must trust that the Lord is with her always, and especially in the dark.

It was from such convictions that Washington found the inner strength to maintain a relatively even keel during the horrible rollercoaster events of 1776—the amazing, almost bloodless victory in Boston in the spring; the humiliating defeats in and around New York from August through November; and the crushing retreat down through New Jersey, in which his now-divided army lost three-quarters of its original strength (down to some four thousand or so), with the enlistments of another two thousand set to expire on December 1. Meanwhile, scores of thousands of New Jerseyans were rushing to sign the loyalty oaths to the king that would buy them amnesty for their prior support of independence. Only at the very end of the year came the exultation of a surprise attack and complete victory at Trenton at Christmas. As Washington was to note later in the war, "But ours is a kind of struggle designed I dare say by Providence to try the patience, fortitude and virtue of Men; none therefore that are engaged in it, will suffer themselves, I trust, to sink under difficulties, or be discouraged by hardships."[25]

Indeed, 1776 was a year of trials for the newly minted commander in chief. Yet, with the composure and confidence born of an abiding faith in Providence, by the end of the year he had a better handle on his responsibilities and his skills. It would be a long, tough struggle, but Washington had an unshakable but much tested belief that independence could, eventually, be won. Here is what he noted shortly after the disastrous defeat at Long Island:

> The General hopes the justice of the great cause in which they are engaged, the necessity and importance of defending this Country, preserving its Liberties, and warding off the destruction meditated against it, will inspire every man with Firmness and Resolution in time of action, which is now approaching—Ever remembring [sic] that upon the blessing of Heaven, and the bravery of the men, our Country only can be saved.[26]

He was like a rock.

His army was not always so steadfast. But he loved them anyway and nudged them along. In return, many loved him and lived long to boast that they had fought under him and, on occasion, seen him with their own eyes.

Chapter 5

HIS BELOVED ARMY

*The General . . . hopes the officers . . . and the men will re-
flect, that we can have little hope of the blessing of Heaven
on our Arms, if we insult it by our impiety, and folly.*

—General Orders, August 3, 1776[1]

*They were indeed, at first, "a band of undisciplined Hus-
bandmen," but it is (under God) to their bravery and attention to their duty, that I am indebted for that success which
has procured me the only reward I wish to receive; the affection and esteem of my Countrymen.*

—Letter to the President of Congress,
April 18, 1776[2]

A PEOPLE'S ARMY

It is one of the less celebrated of Washington's accomplishments that
he forged the first national people's army in the world, whose structure and spirit had, as *The Federalist* (Number 14) later said of the
structure of government itself, "no parallel in the annals of human
revolution . . . no model on the face of the globe."[3] The general had
to forge out of unruly and independent citizens an entirely new sort
of army, not in all parts commanded by the whip, the prison, and the
gibbet (which as a young commander in the western territories

twenty years earlier he had not been at all hesitant to employ),[4] but, as he slowly learned, persuasion, compromise, and constant personal attention. His would be the first army in the world in which men were not expected to act under severe discipline as slaves, automatons, or robots, but as free men—under discipline, yes, but freely so.

Further, to an extent shared by very few other men of his time, in any nation, Washington understood—or learned quickly—the secrets of acquiring and wielding power, in both its old and its new combinations.[5] His experiences in the West had taught him much about the small events that could alter the strategic balance between great powers. He learned quickly the secrets of silence, distance, and earning respect, even fear, from his men. He grasped the symbolism of equanimity and instant decisiveness under fire. He knew how to exercise command, even to make men willing and eager to be commanded by him. He was constantly studying how to do it better—and more effortlessly. In his eulogy in New York on December 31, 1799, Gouverneur Morris caught Washington's instinct for power, even in his physical posture and bearing:

> His form was noble—his port majestic. So dignified his deportment, no man could approach him but with respect—None was great in his presence. You have all seen him, and you have all felt the reverence he inspired. It was such, that to command seemed in him but the exercise of an ordinary function, while others felt a duty to obey.[6]

Far more deeply than others, Washington understood that it had fallen to him, not by his own choice, to set the pattern by which a new kind of army would be molded, an army of free men. In their wake, an entire new nation had to be given a distinctive set of habits, traditions, and codes of conduct. He knew from attention to history and experience that patterns and precedents and symbols, once established, have great and abiding influence upon subsequent generations. Well begun, the new republic had a chance of success. Badly shaped, its probabilities of failure approximated certainty. He could not foresee the shape of later trials and troubles, so in their regard he put his faith, as always, in a benevolent Providence, whose care for the United States had been so abundantly manifested that he (and others) thought it criminal not to be grateful.[7] He felt amply invited to trust the same Providence in the dark times yet to come. He said so in his first inaugural address as president and in his Farewell Address, too, and in any number of letters to his friends and associates.

But there was another dimension to Washington's tie with his beloved army. He loved them. They loved even looking at him and gave him enthusiastic *"Huzzahs!"* each time he appeared among them, usually on horseback. In early 1776 in Cambridge, Massachusetts, as recounted by David Hackett Fischer, a full-fledged fistfight over racial matters broke out between a mixed-race regiment from Marblehead, Massachusetts, and a regiment of white Virginians, numbering at the peak of the melee a thousand men.[8] This nonsense infuriated Washington, who with his aide, a black man named William Lee, rode speedily to the very center of the fight. There, Washington fearlessly dismounted, lifted two central protagonists, one from each side, off the ground by their necks, and "spoke" to them—no doubt shouting some sense into them. In moments, the fighting ceased and the square was emptied. Washington inspired awe and, from that, love. And by both, he taught the lessons of union in liberty.

Finally, a deeper dimension to Washington's bond with his army is revealed by his powerful sense of the recalcitrance, self-love, sloth, and rebellion native to the human heart, flaws not adequately explained by the mere flux of interest and passion, although profitably looked at even from that viewpoint. Humans are not in practice the idealists that many would like them to be. Patriotism alone, Washington warned Congress, would not be enough to carry an army through years of campaigning—although, thank God, he saw plenty of patriotism in his men. The Congress would have to make it in the men's interest to persevere; the Congress must concentrate on incentives and rewards. And for God's sake, it should begin by paying up what the states had already promised in wages, but not yet forwarded for disbursement. The men's families could not live by promises alone. Without their breadwinners at home, whole families—whole communities—would suffer too much. Again and again, Washington had to beg for bare subsistence for his suffering men, writing constantly to the president of Congress, begging for higher incentives for his men in the field—some had already served for three years, for far too little pay, in acute insecurity about their farms and families, and often waiting through months of delay for the arrival of the pay already due them:

> To reason otherwise, and suppose that public virtue alone will enable men to forego the ease and comforts of life, to encounter the hardships and dangers of War for a bare subsistence, when their companions and friends are amassing large fortunes, is viewing human nature, rather as it should be, than as it really is.[9]

And yet he, and his men, persevered.

THE MEN THEMSELVES

It was the orneriness of the men themselves that most frustrated him and impressed him. Having an understanding of the Anglican doctrine of original sin, as well as a commonsense understanding of self-love and self-interest, Washington was a Christian realist, not much given to illusions about human nature. That was a good thing, for he saw a wide array of human nature in the raw, among the many varieties of men he was trying to discipline into becoming a potent army, able to stand against a crisply trained foe. He understood the power of a thousand disciplined rifles firing at once, sending forward a withering wall of hot lead. He also knew how quickly unorganized men turn to run, in the face of oncoming blazing guns that seem unstoppable.

Beginning with his service in western Virginia and Pennsylvania, Washington came for the first time into regular close contact with the "lower classes" of American life. Surly, unused to being given orders by anyone, antagonistic to those of the higher classes like him, independent, willful, and tempestuous, as soldiers they seemed to him most difficult material. He knew from the British and the French what a well-organized military force looked like, how it acted, how it obeyed. What could possibly make Americans competitive? Out of one roll of 400 volunteers, he had to send away all but 140 as wholly unsuited, and those who stayed gave him the tussle of his young life. He had, after all, become their major sheerly by dint of his social standing, at the unripe age of twenty-one. He had a reputation for bravery already, and he was nearly six feet four inches tall and strong as any man among them. Those qualities probably saved him. In the meantime, he tried throwing the least disorderly into dark jails, ordering lashes to be applied to others (which hurt these proud men worse than death), and building a forty-foot gibbet on which to hang those whose offenses, by common usage, merited it.

But Washington was then a young officer. The fate of his own small units in the field may have seemed to require such draconian efforts to win sufficient discipline for their survival in battle. But by the time of his taking command of the Continental Army (not yet called that) in June 1775, he found himself commanding groups of a quite different character from the Virginian backwoodsmen he had led as a young officer. And they posed for him new problems that compounded the problems he already knew. As David Hackett Fischer makes plain in a brilliant chapter on the diverse forces assembled under Washington in Massachusetts, the social background of the regiments assembled from different regions brought together Americans who had never been in close social commerce before.[10] Often they did not like each other. In dress, comportment, and manners, each of them offended some others.

This is not the place to attempt the thorough job that Fischer does, but a few comments must be made. Each of the distinctive American regions represented in Washington's army meant something different by the battle cry "liberty." For instance, the Marblehead regiment mentioned above had a very strong sense of community, including men of mixed race, Negroes, and Indians, many of whom had all gone to sea together and all depended on each other. When they shouted "liberty" they meant the freedom to form their own communities, with their own ideas of equality and inclusiveness. By contrast, when Washington and the other Virginians and some other southern aristocrats huzzahed for liberty, they had in mind the vivid contrast between freemen and slaves. About this, they knew a lot; many had seen or ordered slaves whipped with the lash for insubordination. They did not want to be slaves—that is the most vivid contrast they had for "liberty." They thought property an important condition for liberty, and the freedom to acquire it sacred. They thought material equality was, as James Madison put it, "a wicked project." They valued social standing, class, good manners, and the high skills and moral seriousness of good soldiering.

Meanwhile, the rough yeomen in their heavily dyed hunting shirts from western Virginia, around Culpeper, had a still different idea of liberty, an idea that was deeply individualistic. Their distinctive white flag, bearing upon it an aroused rattlesnake, bore the warning in black: "*Don't tread on me!*" In that slogan, as Fischer adroitly points out, the warning was based on *me*. Theirs was not the covenanted community of New England, nor the aristocratic liberty of the gentleman patriots, but the "keep off our backs" of the common people of the burgeoning Middle West.

In Pennsylvania and New York, the primary meaning of *liberty* seemed to be liberty from central government—liberty meant at the very least minimal government. Partly this idea was fed by the Whig tradition of liberty in Britain, with a strong component of commercial and market liberty. In part it was fed by Adam Smith and others of the Scottish commonsense philosophers who, combined with John Locke, saw in human nature a "system of natural liberty." In Maryland, where Catholics were forbidden to hold civic office or even to seek higher education for their sons, the first expectation from liberty was—as Charles Carroll explained to Washington as

Catholic negotiators traveled to Canada to seek French support for independence—freedom from "religious tests" for public office.

"Liberty" was the unifying cry, all right. But the new commander in chief had to learn the hard way just how many different meanings of that term were vital to different sections of his army. His gentleman regiments from the South found the northern commoners a dirty, nasty, and unpleasant lot, totally hostile to any corporal punishment for insubordination, stubborn and hard to work with—but they certainly learned to admire them as fighting men. The Marblehead regiment proved itself to be one of the very best in the entire Continental Army, as also did the glistening red-coated, silk-ruffled Maryland regiment of gentlemen, at first made fun of and mocked by the northerners. Their fierce bravery under fire saved the army from a complete rout on Long Island in August 1776.

A REALIST RATHER THAN AN IDEALIST

Washington had enjoyed learning about the rough edges of life from his first adventures on the Monongahela in his twenties. He listened and carefully observed the manners of his guides and companions, not least the friendly and the hostile Indians he dealt with. He early acquired a realism about what he ought to expect from human beings. The Anglican Book of Common Prayer, in every Sunday's liturgy, would have given him a start on such knowledge. For it taught a balance between avoiding too much pessimism in bewailing human depravity, on the one side, and taking its affirmation that God had also given humans a certain nobility, making them "a little less than the angels," too far to the other extreme, on the other hand. Here is how Washington put the argument in a letter to the Congress in his role of commander in chief in the middle of the war:

> A small knowledge of human nature will convince us, that, with far the greatest part of mankind, interest is the governing principle; and that almost every man is more or less, under its influence. Motives of

public virtue may for a time, or in particular instances, actuate men to the observance of a conduct purely disinterested; but they are not of themselves sufficient to produce a persevering conformity to the refined dictates and obligations of social duty. Few men are capable of making a continual sacrifice of all views of private interest, or advantage, to the common good. It is vain to exclaim against the depravity of human nature on this account; the fact is so, the experience of every age and nation has proved it and we must in a great measure, change the constitution of man, before we can make it otherwise. No institution, not built on the presumptive truth of these maxims can succeed.[11]

And a few months later, to John Banister, Washington wrote on the same theme. The language is that of an observer of facts rather than that of an idealist. It is based in part on his broad reading in the literature on warfare and in part on his experience of life:

Men may speculate as they will; they may talk of patriotism; they may draw a few examples from ancient story, of great achievements performed by its influence; but whoever builds upon it, as a sufficient Basis for conducting a long and bloody War, will find themselves deceived in the end. We must take the passions of Men as Nature has given them, and those principles as a guide which are generally the rule of Action. I do not mean to exclude altogether the Idea of Patriotism. I know it exists, and I know it has done much in the present Contest. But I will venture to assert, that a great and lasting War can never be supported on this principle alone. It must be aided by a prospect of Interest or some reward. For a time, it may, of itself push Men to Action; to bear much, to encounter difficulties; but it will not endure unassisted by Interest.[12]

This background structure of his own mind served Washington in good stead in the field. He was often deeply frustrated and frequently almost in despair over the behavior and attitudes of "men as they are," as he witnessed them all around him under conditions of stress and trial. But these behaviors did not finally drive him off balance, for deep down he had learned to expect no more. He was determined to work with reality, not against it. He and many of his fellows absorbed quite broadly and deeply ideas based upon human nature as it is, not exactly a philosophical (speculator's) vision of human nature, but the view of a realism steeped both in daily experience and the experience of history. The Bible itself afforded them many examples of what they saw around them, even among the good and the "chosen."

Washington summarized this well when he was writing to a leader in Congress: "Experience has taught us, that men will not adopt and carry into execution measures the best calculated for their own good, without the intervention of a coercive power. . . . We must take human nature as we find it: perfection falls not to the share of mortals."[13]

THE CHRISTIAN SOLDIER

Still, the general was most intent on making his fighting force worthy of God's favor by cleaning up their behavior, so that worship would be supported by right action:

That the Troops may have an opportunity of attending public worship, as well as take some rest after the great fatigue they have gone through; the General in future excuses them from fatigue duty on Sundays (except at the Ship Yards, or special occasions) until further orders. The General is sorry to be informed that the foolish, and wicked practice, of profane cursing and swearing (a Vice heretofore little known in an American Army) is growing into fashion; he hopes the officers will, by example, as well as influence, endeavour to check it, and that both they, and the men will reflect, that we can have little hopes of the blessing of Heaven on our Arms, if we insult it by our impiety, and folly; added to this, it is a vice so mean and low, without any temptation, that every man of sense, and character, detests and despises it.[14]

And again:

Let Vice, and Immorality of every kind, be discouraged, as much as possible, in your Brigade; and as a Chaplain is allowed to each Regiment, see that the Men regularly attend divine Worship.[15]

And still again:

All Chaplains are to perform divine service tomorrow, and on every succeeding Sunday, with their respective brigades and regiments, where the situation will possibly admit of it. And the commanding officers of corps are to see that they attend; themselves, with officers of all ranks, setting the example. The Commander in Chief expects an exact compliance with this order, and that it be observed in future as an invariable rule of practice—And every neglect will be considered not only a breach of orders, but a disregard to decency, virtue and religion.[16]

He was even more explicit as the war dragged on:

While we are zealously performing the duties of good Citizens and soldiers we certainly ought not to be inattentive to the higher duties of Religion. To the distinguished Character of Patriot, it should be our highest Glory to add the more distinguished Character of Christian. The signal Instances of providential Goodness which we have experienced and which have now almost crowned our labours with complete Success, demand from us in a peculiar manner the warmest returns of Gratitude and Piety to the Supreme Author of all Good.[17]

We think it not too much to observe that Washington's reflections here not only show an explicit dedication to Christian behavior but also, although they are those of a man who never attended a university, reveal a Christian realism not so far removed from that of the greatest American theologian of the twentieth century, Reinhold Niebuhr (1892–1971), who wrote:

> Human egotism makes large-scale co-operation upon a purely voluntary basis impossible. Governments must coerce. Yet there is an element of evil in this coercion. It is always in danger of serving the purposes of the coercing power rather than the general weal. We cannot fully trust the motives of any ruling class or power. That is why it is important to maintain democratic checks upon the centers of power.[18]

And again:

> A theology which fails to come to grips with this tragic factor of sin is heretical, both from the standpoint of the gospel and in terms of its blindness to obvious facts of human experience in every realm and on every level of moral goodness.[19]

The language of sin was not Washington's daily language, but the language of human experience certainly was. Experience had taught Washington that it is wrong to expect too much from virtue alone, without attention to passions and interests, and that it is wise not to be surprised by failure, poor performance, or even disgraceful behavior, for these will most assuredly occur from time to time. Equanimity and perseverance depend on a realistic assessment of what can actually be expected of human beings. A great commander must aim his men high, to draw more from them than seems humanly possible. Yet he must also maintain his composure when, from all sorts of causes, their courage wavers, they break ranks, they run. Leading a nonprofessional army, Washington tasted often that bitter cup. Yet he also knew how to pick his men up again, lead them on, and inspire them with the hope that they might do better on another day. Between the lines of his "Farewell Orders" to his beloved army (November 2, 1783), one senses his love for them:

A contemplation of the compleat attainment (at a period earlier than could have been expected) of the object for which we contended against so formidable a power cannot but inspire us with astonishment and gratitude. The disadvantageous circumstances on our part, under which the war was undertaken, can never be forgotten. The singular interpositions of Providence in our feeble condition were such, as could scarcely escape the attention of the most unobserving; while the unparalleled perseverence of the Armies of the U States, through almost every possible suffering and discouragement for the space of eight long years, was little short of a standing miracle.

It is not the meaning nor within the compass of this address to detail the hardships peculiarly incident to our service, or to describe the distresses, which in several instances have resulted from the extremes of hunger and nakedness, combined with the rigours of an inclement season; nor is it necessary to dwell on the dark side of our past affairs. Every American Officer and Soldier must now console himself for any unpleasant circumstances which may have occurred by a recollection of the uncommon scenes in which he has been called to Act no inglorious part, and the astonishing events of which he has been a witness, events which have seldom if even before taken place on the stage of human action, nor can they probably ever happen again. For who has before seen a disciplined Army form'd at once from such raw materials? Who, that was not a witness, could imagine that the most violent local prejudices would cease so soon, and that Men who came from the difference parts of the Continent, strongly disposed, by the habits of education, to despise and quarrel with each other, would instantly become but one patriotic band of Brothers, or who, that was not on the spot, can trace the steps by which such a wonderful revolution has been effected, and such a glorious period to all our warlike toils?

In this realism, he did not fall short of acting as a Christian general ought to act.

Part Two

THE FAITH

You do well to wish to learn our arts and ways of life, and above all, the religion of Jesus Christ.

These will make you a greater and happier people than you are.

—Speech to the Delaware Chiefs, May 22, 1779

The General commands all officers, and soldiers, to pay strict obedience to the Orders of the Continental Congress, and by their unfeigned, and pious observance of their religious duties, incline the Lord, and Giver of Victory, to prosper our arms.

—General Orders, May 15, 1776

Chapter 6

WHAT'S A DEIST?

The Deist Tendency

I also give it in Charge to you to avoid all Disrespect to or Contempt of the Religion of the Country [Canada] and its Ceremonies. Prudence, Policy, and a true Christian Spirit, will lead us to look with Compassion upon their Errors without insulting them. While we are contending for our own Liberty, we should be very cautious of violating the Rights of Conscience in others, ever considering that God alone is the Judge of the Hearts of Men, and to him only in this Case, they are answerable.

—Letter to Colonel Benedict Arnold,
September 14, 1775[1]

$\mathcal{I}$n a wonderful little book on the War of Independence, the great historian Gordon Wood presents the most common view today:

It is true that many of the distinguished political leaders of the Revolution were not very emotionally religious. At best, they only passively believed in organized Christianity, and at worst they scorned and ridiculed it. Most were deists or lukewarm churchgoers and scornful of religious emotion and enthusiasm. Washington, for example, was a frequent churchgoer, but he scarcely referred to God as anything but "the Great Disposer of events," and in all his voluminous papers he never mentioned Jesus Christ. [2]

That last claim is almost perfectly true, but not quite. In actual fact, Washington advised the chiefs of the Delaware tribe that they would do well to study and adopt "the religion of Jesus Christ."[3] Indeed, Washington took a lifelong interest in Christian missions to the indigenous tribes of North America and even tried to secure government support for missionary efforts.[4] Yet, that omission noted, Wood's is a widely accepted historical account of the religion of the Founders.

It leads to the question asked by millions of visitors to Mount Vernon over recent years: What exactly were the religious views of George Washington? Was he really a deist? How did he actually picture God or think about him? Our examination of the evidence in preparing this book convinces us that Wood (along with many others) is not on target. But his is an understandable error. There does seem to be a mass of conflicting evidence.

CONFLICTING EVIDENCE

Toward the end of this chapter, we will want to look at Washington's strong position on religious liberty. That position required him to seek a language at least a step removed from Christian language, in the direction of a more-or-less universal philosophical language of human nature, character, and virtue. Simultaneously, however, it required him to draw upon a specifically Jewish-Christian concept of God as Spirit and Truth, who most highly values liberty of conscience and the uncoerced worship of the heart.

Beyond that, from his Anglican pastor's point of view, Washington was one of the most regular, reliable, and generous of parishioners, a real leader of the parish over a great many years. And yet Washington was so loath to give any public signs of his confessional commitments that many ministers (who did not know him well) were suspicious that he was harboring a secret commitment to a broad latitudinarianism, which might even be construed as deist. Some *craved* a more visible sign of his Christian faith, which he consistently withheld.

That, then, is the major puzzle. On the one hand, George Washington was a leading member of his parish church, serving as a warden or a vestryman over a period of more than fifteen years. This freely chosen service imposed demanding responsibilities. It was not without some rewards, but it nevertheless required significant expenditures of time, energy, and money.[5] Moreover, on the Sundays on which a minister was able to show up at Pohick Church (sometimes only once a month, so severe was the shortage of Anglican clergy), Washington and his family traveled some seven miles from Mount Vernon (a total round trip of about three hours) to attend divine service.[6] Less often, they drove the carriage nine miles to their second parish, in Alexandria, which Washington also supported with time and money.[7]

On the other hand, some note that Washington did not regularly receive the sacrament of communion—but neither did many others at that time.[8] Some object that he was a member of the Freemasons for many years (although his attendance at lodge meetings was extremely rare),[9] and that that is incompatible with Christian belief. (Roman Catholics, even today,[10] are forbidden to belong to the Masons; in Europe, unlike in the United States, Freemasonry has been rabidly, sometimes violently, anti-Catholic.) But many American Christians then and now have found nothing incompatible between Freemasonry and Christianity and have looked at the former as a kind of service arm of the latter.[11] Indeed, in Washington's day many bishops and clergymen were active members of their local Masonic lodges.[12]

Many historians simply write Washington off as a deist. On the other hand, in not a few households around the land, even today, the following "Prayer of George Washington," with which George Washington concluded his Circular Letter to the States at the end of the war, hangs on a family wall. It is a very real prayer, as well as a public document:

> I now make it my earnest prayer that God would have you, and the State over which you preside, in his holy protection, that he would

incline the hearts of the Citizens to cultivate a spirit of subordination and obedience to Government, to entertain a brotherly affection and love for one another, for their fellow Citizens of the United States at large, and particularly for their brethren who have served in the Field, and finally, that he would most graciously be pleased to dispose us all, to do Justice, to love mercy, and to demean ourselves with that Charity, humility, and pacific temper of mind, which were the Characteristicks of the Divine Author of our Blessed Religion, and without an humble imitation of whose example in these things, we can never hope to be a happy Nation.[13]

Although we will discuss this prayer in greater detail in Chapter 7, many of its features make it clearly Christian, not deist. It is fitting to say "holy" ("in his holy protection") of the Jewish-Christian God, but not of the impersonal deist God. "Divine Author of our Blessed Religion" does not fit deism either. But it is a familiar locution among Christians, and it fits the God of Abraham, too.

Deist? Christian? Is it any wonder that people have trouble putting all these seemingly contradictory elements together?

Was Washington a kind of hypocrite, that is, privately a deist, while hiding his private deism from the public? Was he, as some writers insist, a devout Christian believer?[14] Or was he, as others allege with equal fervor, a consciously dissenting man of the Enlightenment, a rationalist, with no trust whatever in miracles or in prayer?[15]

THE RELIGIOUS CONTEXT OF THE TIME

These questions are often complicated by the powerful cultural conflict generated in the first decades of the nineteenth century by the tumultuous Second Great Awakening. A hint of that conflict is found in Wood's toss-away phrase above, "scornful of religious emotion and enthusiasm." Sober, reserved New England Puritans, Anglicans,

Unitarians, deists, and others had a deep distrust of—and, yes, scorn for—the rising evangelical use of emotion in religious discourse. On the other hand, evangelicals positively sought to evoke feelings, enthusiasm, and the vivid experience of being "born again," through a life-changing embrace of one's Lord and Savior. Besides, evangelicals prized the "certainty" their faith gave them, guaranteed by the blood of Christ. On the other side, the more traditional Christians preferred the marks of a certain detachment and skepticism.[16]

Both sides in this cultural dispute had a certain mistrust of, and dislike for, the other. This was especially so because those who shared the "northeastern" style—"the cool, rational ones"—exuded a sense of superiority. But so, from a different point of view, did those of the warmer, more emotional style, who thought of themselves as the only "true" Christians. Still, it would be quite wrong to believe that just because a person was not emotional or enthusiastic, but calm and laid back in matters of faith, that that person lacked true religion. The Anglican style, especially, eschewed enthusiasm. Every effort was made to appear commonsensical and down-to-earth. Among the Massachusetts descendants of the Puritans, the Congregationalists, many in the 1776 generation (John Adams, for one), found greater satisfaction in a latitudinarian interpretation of Christian doctrines than in the strict Calvinism of their parents.

Much has been made of the fact, for example, that Washington wrote very seldom of Jesus Christ, whether in his public statements or, more strikingly, even in his private correspondence. Yet the same is true of Martha Washington, devout Christian though she is known to have been, in her private correspondence. It was not common for laypersons of the Anglican communion to write or speak the name of Jesus very often.

Of course, the practice was quite otherwise among the new evangelical Christians. Evangelicals spoke often of Jesus—tenderly, intimately, openly.[17] Quite steadily and dramatically, the new evangelicals were forging a new definition of what counted as

"Christian" in America. In 1740 there had been only 25 Baptist houses of worship in the Congregationalist stronghold of New England, for example, but by 1790 the number had increased more than tenfold, to 266. And in Virginia alone, 218 new Baptist churches were established, in effect challenging the privileged status the Anglican church had enjoyed for more than a century.[18]

For the Anglicans, as for the many fewer Roman Catholics (about twenty-three thousand communicants)[19] and Jews (fewer than three thousand)[20] in America in 1770, being religious meant being born into a community, into a tradition with roots that reached faraway to the Old World and back across many centuries. For Anglicans, Catholics, and Jews, faith came with one's mother's milk, so to speak, and only gradually did an adolescent make the inherited religion his or her own. The sensibility learned in such a tradition is that of a "church" rather than a "sect"—the sensibility of being born into habits, attitudes, customs, responsibilities, and duties far larger than oneself, and far beyond personal "choice." Even though, at the appropriate age, a Christian born into a church was expected to "make the tradition one's own" (or to reject it, quietly), the sense of breaking from or confirming oneself in the community is quite different from the sense of being "born again."

For the experience of joining a sect was intended—and is still intended—to shape a quite different sensibility: springing from a personal, intimate decision, face-to-face with Jesus Christ, to accept him as one's Lord and Savior. In this experience, Jesus becomes an intimate presence, closer to one's own ego than anyone else in life, closer to one (and more compelling) than one's own self. In the sensibility of the sect, expressions of love and hope in Jesus come frequently and openly to lip and pen. The whole experience is intended to be highly personal.

These two sensibilities often clashed. Not simply theology was at stake, but also a whole way of feeling and seeing. The intimacy with which evangelicals spoke of Jesus embarrassed those who had been brought up to be much more restrained and taciturn, and who accepted religious matters as part of a cherished but quiet tradition. (One did it gladly enough, but one did not go on about it.) To evangelicals, who identified religion with the vivid, immediate, intimate experience of the person of the Savior, an electrifying experience that had transformed their lives, the taciturn people who belonged to "churches" seemed to be simply plodding along by rote, without ever having come to experience real religion.

Each group disliked being judged by the other's standards.

This great transformation of American religion—in which the center of gravity for the religious sensibility shifted from church to sect—began not long before the War of Independence, accelerated steadily, and crested by about 1820. In other words, it washed right over the final thirty years of Washington's life. Indeed, this cultural transformation altered the very terms in which Washington's religion came to be interpreted and classified by others. After it, American religion was never again what it had been before.

Before the Second Great Awakening, the whole nation from Pennsylvania southward was governed, more or less, by the Anglican sensibility of the large landowners. Pennsylvania itself was predominantly Quaker, and New England to the north was predominantly Puritan. Both Quakerism and Puritanism presented a far more formal, stylized sort of evangelical tradition than that of the newcomers, the Baptists and Methodists who were sweeping southward through all the states.

After the Second Great Awakening, the predominant form of American religion was no longer Anglican or Puritan, but Baptist and Methodist—intimate, expressive, experiential, gregarious, friendly, extending a hand, and yet maintaining the discipline of small, morally watchful congregations. To be a Christian came to mean to feel much—and not to be inhibited in saying so.

Extroverted religion of this sort put to a test Washington's long-practiced taciturnity. Indeed, he seemed to resent (without showing visible offense) being asked to declare his feelings, even in relatively small groups. Politely, he would change the subject.[21]

ON THE ROAD TO *SOLA RATIO*

Already in our opening chapters we have seen much evidence that George Washington was a lot more than a deist, yet we are still in need of a rather more exact idea of what deism actually was, especially in practice. What sort of God counts as a deist god? During the past hundred years, historians have not been especially interested in theology, and few have addressed this question in a serious manner. Most have contented themselves with rough approximations.

The story is a long one, and a bit complex. Consider this stimulating bit of history by the American Jesuit scholar Avery Dulles:

As Christianity spread throughout the Greco-Roman world, it became apparent that the biblical doctrines concerning God, morality, and future retribution had similarities with the philosophical speculations of the Platonists, Aristotelians, and Stoics. The Fathers and medieval theologians had no difficulty in admitting this; on the contrary, they saw it as a confirmation of the truth of revelation. Human reason at its best, they explained, is able to discover [from nature] some of the doctrines that God revealed through the prophets and Jesus Christ.[22]

Far from Jewish and Christian faith being opposed to reason, Anglicans such as Richard Hooker and many other Christians who studied the early fathers of the church learned to think of God as eminently reasonable, the very fount of law and intelligence, the Creator who understands all the things he created, finds them good, and loves and blesses them. The Creator is the source of all the intelligence that infuses the world, the *Logos*, the progenitor both of reason in human beings and of the intelligibility in things. As a matter of fact, the first name for Christ that St. John used in his gospel is *Logos*.

Both Judaism and Christianity call humans to follow the truth, to inquire, and to differentiate truth from falsehood. Both hold that those who do not know of God through the direct revelations made by God himself to the prophets can know a great deal about him from the works of creation. Further, as Alfred North Whitehead once wrote, the rise of modern science is inconceivable apart from five millennia of teaching that all things in the universe were made by a Creator who suffused them with intelligibility. Otherwise, why would people believe in the future?[23] Bottom line: If humans apply their reason to inquiring into the cause of things, they are likely to advance from insight to insight, in cumulative understanding down the ages. And this is not contrary to faith, but an outgrowth of it. Thus, Christianity has encouraged the use of "natural theology" (the use of reason alone) and "revealed theology" (the investigation of God's revelations about himself) to explore, e.g., "theodicy," the study of how God can coexist with evil.

For many centuries, many great philosophers among "the pagans" (that is, those who had not heard of Moses or Jesus Christ) believed in the need for human beings to live a moral life; in immortal life; and in punishment or reward after death for actions performed during an individual's time on earth. To believe such things, one did not have to be a Christian or a Jew. Greeks and Romans and most other peoples also believed them. Jews, Christians, and "the Greeks" shared huge swathes of intellectual background. (As children of one Creator, made in his image as intelligent beings— they explained to themselves—how could it not be so?)

Thus, St. Paul was able to begin a famous sermon in Athens, in front of a statue to "the Unknown God," by calling attention to the things his hearers already knew about the nature of God, through reflecting on the works of nature they saw all around them (Acts 17:22–24). Then he added complementary materials that God had revealed through Moses and the Prophets, showing us more about God's inner life than we could possibly have learned without the revelation to the Jews. St. Paul finished by speaking of what Christ had revealed about his Father: his love for human beings, the distinctive love that constitutes the divine nature.

Paul's formula became the normal scheme of Christian preaching over the next sixteen hundred years. Begin with what the listeners already know; then add the "good news" from God himself, sealed by the blood of his witnesses. One finds this formula used in Origen, St. Cyril of Alexandria, St. Cyprian, St. Athanasius, St. Augustine, and countless others down the centuries. Reason and faith were pictured as complementary to one another. They were said to be like the two wings by which the human mind ascends to God. Each wing has its proper role. Both together are necessary for the full and steady flight of the human mind.

It was one of the great consolations of early Christians (and of Jewish writers, too) that what people who knew nothing of the Scriptures learned about the meaning of life, simply by the use of reason, comported so well, in its large lines, with what the Scriptures revealed. And how could matters have been otherwise? Do not reason and faith come from the same Creator?

Those who have seen the Sistine Chapel painted by Michelangelo see a celebration of that very harmony in the paintings above them and on every surrounding wall. They see the pagan seers and philosophers and lawmakers of Greece and of Rome, and Moses and the Prophets, and Jesus and the Apostles—all three sources of our civilization—in a kind of continuing debate and inquiry, century after century.

Looking at the world through orthodox Jewish or Christian lenses, then, as it appeared at the time just before the Reformation, when the Renaissance was already well under way, it is the same God who created human reason who also revealed himself in the Scriptures. In fact, it would be a very odd sort of God who gave utterly contradictory lessons through these two ways of learning about him. That the substance, degree, reliability, and precision of knowledge reached by the two methods is significantly different, even sometimes in conflict, is to be expected. But if the two methods reach contradictory conclusions, wise inquirers go back to the drawing board and start over. In principle, God the Creator and God the Revealer cannot be contradicting himself. Our knowledge of nature and our knowledge of revelation may both be flawed, and certainly our knowledge of either is at all times only fragmentary and incomplete. The tension between what we know by one method and the other, therefore, should be a source of creative reexamination and deeper inquiry in both spheres. Over the generations, the neuralgic point of the tension shifts, and as some old tensions are resolved, new ones emerge. This continuing tension has given our civilization an unparalleled dynamism.

As both Protestants and Catholics see the picture, the Protestant Reformation drew up new "rules of engagement" between faith and reason. The Protestant reformers thought Catholicism had gone too far in the direction of pagan philosophy and art, and also that its yen for rigorously rational theological speculation had led it into sterile theorizing. For instance, making the point that angels are spiritual beings, like pure intellects and wills, and do not have bodies, a Catholic scholar was said to have asked, "How many angels can dance on the head of a pin?" Answer: The question is based upon a false supposition, that angels take up space, as if they had bodies. For some generations after the Reformation, this question was ridiculed, as a typical waste of energy on a useless question— and worse than useless, since it turned the mind away from the devotion due to God alone.

The great reformers, Luther and Calvin especially, denounced the way Catholics honored reason. Luther called reason "the Devil's greatest whore"[24] and the "greatest enemy that faith has."[25] Calvin emphasized that humans are saved by faith alone, and faith does not derive from one's own efforts but is the gratuitous gift of the Holy Spirit. "Faith," he famously explained, "is a firm and sure knowledge of the divine favor toward us, founded on the truth of a free promise in Christ, and revealed to our minds, and sealed on our hearts, by the Holy Spirit."[26] It is possible to reason about faith— Calvin's great systematic treatise, *The Institutes of the Christian Religion,* is one such example—but only *after* the Holy Spirit has revealed such knowledge to one's mind and heart.

None of which is to suggest that the reformers disparaged reason as such. They thought it a gift of God when applied to the things of this world, but they flatly denied that natural human powers were adequate to comprehend anything about God. Philosophy could never bring one to faith, they argued, and it is a form of self-righteousness to think that one's own petty intellect could somehow stand in judgment over the awesome revelation of God. Faith and reason were assigned to two quite separate realms. A deep split was allowed to develop. We hasten to add that this did not happen among all Protestants, or in all respects. But the mutually helpful although conflicted yoking together of faith and reason that had marked previous centuries slipped away.

But not all Protestants could live mentally by faith alone. Some craved to reason through on their own all the small steps *before* the step across to faith, and to find reasoned versions, only approximations maybe, of those parts of the faith that they found humanly attractive. Some turned to common sense, some to philosophical reasoning. Eventually, some conceived of the idea of a religion established by reason alone. From *sola Scriptura* they passed over to *sola ratio.*

FROM REASON TO PRACTICE

Certain philosophers in England especially, after Edward, Lord Herbert of Cherbury (1583–1648), began going a full step further. Lord Herbert held that in actual practice revelation is not really necessary, since human reason can learn independently all the basic practical moral truths that result in a good life in the eyes of God.[27] What really matters, isn't it, is what we do, not what we say we believe?

It makes a modicum of sense that deism was invented in England. The English are a supremely practical people, and the main move of the new deism was to set to one side all knowledge of God through revelation. The only methods thenceforward recognized (in practice, at least) would be those of reason. Some deists used this move to depart from, and some even to ridicule, Christian faith. But many others simply tried to boil Christianity down to its most practical points.

Most thinkers of this practical bent continued to believe in God and in the moral order built into human nature. They did not so much deny Christian doctrines as try to find doctrines of reason that performed the same practical work. There were not very many who were willing to renounce Christianity as mere superstition, certainly not in America.[28] It had been different in France, of course, when deism met up with Voltaire, Diderot, and the fiercely antireligious Jacobins of the French Revolution of 1789.

One such foe of organized religion among the Americans, however, was Thomas Paine, author of the deliberately shocking book *The Age of Reason*. Yet even Paine took ship to France to beg the revolutionaries of 1789 not to choose the way of atheism, lest they undercut their own human rights and come to end in bloodshed and moral nihilism.[29] Paine continued to believe in God, a natural moral law, and the certainty of reward and punishment after death, even while he was emphatic that he was no Christian. He called himself a deist. More exactly, he called himself a "theophilanthropist"—one who believed in God, and in doing good to his fellow human beings out of love (and who thus put his three favorite words together: love, God, and man).[30]

The problem is that such modern "deists" were quite unlike the "theists" of ancient days, such as Aristotle, Plato, Cicero, and Cato, inasmuch as the *deist* was vigorous in stripping away (as he thought) Christianity and Judaism, whereas the *theists* of old had not so much as heard of Judaism and Christianity. The term *theist* came from the name for God in Greek (*theos*) and lies at the root of *theology,* the science of God. The word *deist* comes from the Latin word for God (*deus*). The connotations of the first suggest a sort of reverence, and of the second a sort of rebellion.

The ancient "theists" were thought by Christians and Jews to have discovered a remarkable amount about the God of the Jews and the Christians—not nearly everything, but quite a lot—by observing the world around them. But "theists" and "deists" were moving in opposite directions. The ancient theists seemed to be moving toward Christianity in the days before it had actually arrived, whereas the modern deists seemed to be moving away from Christianity, having grown weary of it. Some may well have been Christians, trying to hold onto their faith by tossing overboard what seemed to them superfluous.

On the other hand, much that deist thinkers regarded as having come from reason alone came, in fact, from reason heavily tutored by centuries of Christianity. Indeed, the so-called Enlightenment (note the presumptive disparagement of others built into that self-identification) borrowed many themes from the Jewish-Christian past: fraternity, equality, liberty, compassion for the most vulnerable, sensitivity to the category of cruel and inhumane treatment of human beings, the moral evil in slavery, and the rest. Even Friedrich Nietzsche, who felt that Christianity had "feminized" barbarian Europe, raised the question: If you take Christianity out of the Enlightenment—take out care for the vulnerable, compassion, equality, solidarity, a call for progress—what is left?

When the first generations of deists passed on, their children drifted farther and farther from Christianity, until it was at best a dim memory, even with the many sentiments learned from Christianity that remained embedded in "reason." Yet, not surprisingly, over time there eventually devolved a very different, more secular conception of reason, morality, and life. As Dulles notes, in this generational process deism proved to be a halfway house, an unstable mix of ideas.[31] It looks in retrospect more like a movement of the imagination, such as romanticism, than like an ideology composed of one set of clear ideas held simultaneously by many.

Among all the different groups trying to differentiate themselves from Christianity, the first principle was, as the *Westminster Dictionary of Christian Theology* puts it, a belief in a supreme being who is regarded as the ultimate source of reality and ground of value, but definitely *not* as one "intervening in natural and historical processes by way of particular providences, revelations, and salvific acts."[32] We can see a physical example of this principle at work in the way Thomas Jefferson took scissors to the New Testament, to cut out from it every passage referring to miraculous acts, in order to leave behind only the practical moral teachings of Jesus, that is, those moral teachings that comport with reason.[33] This was, of course, to reduce Christianity to the teachings of reason alone. To be sure, Jefferson occasionally insisted that he was indeed a Christian, but among all the top one hundred Founders, next to Paine he appears the least doctrinally orthodox.[34]

In this context, *The Dictionary of the History of Ideas* offers a quite powerful statement of what might be called the many different "refractions" or "emanations" of the deist tendency and cautions that deism is rather like a disposition of mind than a settled body of doctrine. There was never an official, organized association or even a systematic statement that specifically defined the doctrines of deism. That deism is best understood as an attitude, a posture, a way of imagining the world may be seen in the following propositions, which flash from the many different angles of deism. We have adapted the *Dictionary* text of this tendency slightly and highlighted the most significant point for our inquiry, number five.

THE DEIST TENDENCY

Deism is the belief that by rational methods alone men can know all the true propositions of theology that it is possible, necessary, or desirable for men to know. Deists have generally subscribed to most of the following propositions, and have ranged widely from Christian rationalists to atheists:

1. One and only one God exists.
2. God has moral and intellectual virtues in perfection.

3. God's active powers are displayed in the world, which is created, sustained, and ordered by means of divinely sanctioned natural laws, both moral and physical.
4. The ordering of events constitutes a general providence.
5. *There is no special providence; no miracles or other divine interventions intrude upon the lawful natural order.* [Emphasis added.]
6. Men have been endowed with a rational nature that alone allows them to know truth and their duty when they think and choose in conformity with this nature.
7. The natural law requires the leading of a moral life, rendering to God, one's neighbor, and one's self what is due to each.
8. The purest form of worship and the chief religious obligation is to lead a moral life.
9. God has endowed men with immortal souls.
10. After death retributive justice is meted out to each man according to his acts. Those who fulfill the moral law are "saved," and so enjoy rewards; others are punished.
11. All other religious beliefs or practices conflicting with these tenets are to be regarded critically, as at best indifferent political institutions and beliefs, or as errors to be condemned and eradicated if it should be prudent to do so.[35]

Anyone today who held all these propositions would seem to be a quite religious person. That may be why even the least orthodox of the American Founders—Thomas Paine, Thomas Jefferson, and Benjamin Franklin—left behind many passages far too religious for any self-respecting secularist today. The usual contemporary method for explaining away these religious passages in the Founders writings is to dismiss them as window dressing, intended to deceive the general public. That, of course, would make the Founders hypocrites in a most sacred matter, and deserving of popular disdain. But is the charge of mere window dressing even true? Not in the case of most of the Founders, as we believe has been shown in an earlier book, *On Two Wings*.[36] This charge of insincerity in matters of religion is certainly not true in the case of George Washington.

RELIGIOUS LIBERTY

One way to see this question is to examine briefly Washington's ideas about religious liberty. Indeed, he had a powerful passion for freedom of the individual conscience; that much is undeniable. Washington was absolutely and unqualifiedly committed to the principle that every individual had the right to follow God in the manner closest to his or her heart, even writing in 1783 that "the establishment of Civil and Religious Liberty was the Motive that induced me to the field of battle."[37] Indeed, he shared with Madison and Jefferson the same ground for defending freedom of conscience, that is, that Almighty God could have made belief in him so blinding that it would be coercive but instead chose to create the mind free. "The mind is so formed," he once noted, "in different persons as to contemplate the same object in different points of view. Hence originates the difference on questions of the greatest import, both human and divine."[38] The basis of religious liberty, in other words, is theological anthropology. It is located in the way that God created human beings.

The particular kind of God worshipped by Jews and Christians— the God whose Hebrew name is Jehovah—desires to be worshipped "in spirit and in truth," by women and men whose minds are free, constrained only by the judgment of the evidence presented to them. Therefore, all who recognize that this God respects and demands uncoerced worship must find it self-evident that individual consciences stand free before him, *especially* in matters of religion. No other person, association, or community can come between the free conscience and the God who made it—not even civil society, not even father or mother, and certainly not the state.

Yet Washington did not hold, as did his neighbors Jefferson, George Mason, and Madison, that religious liberty was in any significant way infringed when the state provided monetary support for religious groups. Evidence of Washington's views is found in the great controversy that erupted in Virginia when Governor Patrick Henry attempted to raise a tax (conscientious exemptions would be recognized) to help pay the salaries of Protestant ministers. Though he had no objection to Henry's measure in principle, Washington declined to provide public support either for the bill or for Madison's "Remonstrance" against it on the ground that in practice it was religiously and politically divisive:

> Altho, no man's sentiments are more opposed to any kind of restraint upon religious principles than mine are; yet I must confess, that I am not amongst the number of those who are so much alarmed at the thought of making people pay towards the support of that which they profess, if of the denomination of Christians; or declare themselves Jews, Mahomitans or otherwise, and thereby obtain proper relief. As the matter now stands, I wish an assessment had never been agitated, and as it has gone so far, that the Bill could die an easy death; because I think it will be productive of more quiet to the State, than by enacting it into a Law; which, in my opinion, would be impolitic, admitting there is a decided majority for it, to the disquiet of a respectable minority. In the first case the matter will soon subside; in the latter, it will rankle and perhaps convulse, the State.[39]

In a brilliant essay, Vincent Phillip Muñoz demonstrates that although Washington was as early and deep as Jefferson and Madison in his commitment to the rights of conscience, he did not share their view that disestablishment was a necessary consequence of religious liberty.[40] On the contrary, Washington—like most of the Founders—held both in principle and in practice (1) that government ought to *endorse* religious seriousness in general, since a long-lived republic depends on the virtue of its citizens, and for most citizens, weak humans all, virtue can more probably be fortified by religion than by any known alternative, and (2) that government ought to *accommodate* itself to the claims of conscience in various religious bodies, in a manner consistent with the common good and public order. To these principles, we have already seen, Washington was unfailingly faithful in his own practice. Madison and Jefferson did not exhaust the range of the Founders' thinking about matters of church and state, and their views were far more narrow than Washington's.

Washington's views on religious liberty serve to differentiate him from the deists, on the one hand, and also from Locke and other mere contractarians of natural rights theory, on the other hand. We know that Washington read Cicero, and that he ordered from London "all Ciceros Works; a very neat Editn."[41] In these respects, he was steeped in Stoic philosophy, which held a deep commitment to a vision of universal human nature, founded on the inner structure of the human soul—which the Stoics divided into an ability *to reflect* on past and future courses of action and an ability *to choose* among various proposed actions, or lines of action. (These two terms, *reflection* and *choice,* are the pivotal points in "the important question" put before the nation in the first paragraph of *The Federalist* (Number 1).[42]

Washington had a more robust theory of human nature than Locke, even when he alluded to "the state of Nature" and other Lockean themes.[43] With Stoic philosophy, Washington also emphasized two other themes, the personal *character* that an individual fashions into his "second nature" and the *virtues* (i.e., habits or acquired dispositions), which together constitute character, such as practical wisdom, courage, justice, temperance, and many others. Washington held, as Hamilton did, that freedom of conscience is built into the very structure of human nature. Human beings, alone among the animals, exhibit capacities of *reflection* and *choice.* By using these over and over throughout their lives, humans freely shape their own characters and habits. Since freedom of conscience is willed by God (by the God of Jews and Christians, at least), and since God is the Creator of all human beings alike, religious liberty is a universal inheritance of every single human being on earth. All that is required is a being capable of reflection and choice. For centuries that inheritance may appear to lie dormant, out of timidity or fear, but in its own ripe time it matures and, sooner or later, seeks outward political expression.

In his theory of nature, character, and virtue as the founts of human liberty, Washington drew heavily upon Stoic philosophy—upon Cicero and Seneca, especially (whose writings Jefferson, too, listed among the "books on natural right"). But Washington was more conscious than most that these ideas were, in fact, at least on the American scene, already suffused with Christian language about God's commitment to human liberty. In this explicitly Christian infusion into the philosophy of nature, Washington was more than deist. He used more than reason alone to come to his understanding of religious liberty.

Beyond reason, he needed "the pure and benign light of Revelation," which kept stressing that humans must come to God out of their own interiority, from the depth of their own souls, without coercion or coddling.[44] On the other hand, the reach of Jehovah, the Creator, is universal, and so Washington felt the need, too, for a language that escaped any hint of sectarianism. He felt deep within himself the pull, under God, of America's universal mission: "the lot which Providence has assigned us," he says in one place and, in another, "as the Actors on a most conspicuous Theatre, which seems to be peculiarly designated by Providence for the display of human greatness and felicity."[45] Americans are called to an experiment in liberty on behalf of all humans everywhere—an experiment rooted in human nature itself. We are called to a kind of empire of liberty.

He added: "The foundation of our empire was not laid in the gloomy age of Ignorance and Superstition, but at an Epocha when the rights of mankind were better understood and more clearly defined than at any former period."[46]

It is not so often that we see Washington carried away by poetry and romantic vision, but the theme of religious liberty brought it out in him:

> Though I shall not survive to perceive with these bodily senses, but a small portion of the blessed effects which our Revolution will occasion in the rest of the world; yet I enjoy the progress of human society & human happiness in anticipation. I rejoice in a belief that intellectual light will spring up in the dark corners of the earth; that freedom of enquiry will produce liberality of conduct; that mankind will reverse the absurd position that *the many* were made for *the few*; and that they will not continue as slaves in one part of the globe, when they can become freemen in another.[47]

We see here the universal Providence to whom Washington attributed the American founding, its unparalleled experiment in liberty of immense consequence to the entire human race, and its conspicuous place on the great theater of the world. Washington located the universal fuel supply of the sacred fire of liberty in human nature itself.

The intellectual light of Washington's vision came partly from confessional sources ("the pure and benign light of Revelation"), and partly from a philosophical/universal language beyond confessional lines. Paradoxically, insofar as Providence is the Creator of all, such a universal and neutral language is called for. At the same time, the definition of liberty "in spirit and in truth" had its genesis in the God of Abraham. But its reach exceeded its genesis. Its future expansion would carry it beyond its early boundaries. Providence intends liberty to be as universal as human nature itself. Thus, Washington's internally developed faith was partly philosophical and also distinctively Christian. In brief, Washington was a more reflective thinker than he is given credit for being. Since his thinking about religious liberty is usually overlooked, it may not be amiss to isolate its core principles.

First, Washington's notion of religious liberty sprang from his reflections on human nature, especially the nature and special characteristics of the human mind. As a result, "To expect that all men should think alike upon political, more than on Religious, or other subjects, would be to look for a change in the order of nature."[48] Therefore, with the mind "so formed" as to require reflection and choice, different persons needed liberty of movement before God and conscience, both in religious and in political affairs. Each must learn not only to tolerate, but to respect these differences in others.[49]

Second, Washington held that religious liberty was the very first imperative of government, and that there were a number of things government must do, and abstain from doing, to nourish its exercise:

> Government being, among other purposes, instituted to protect the persons and consciences of men from oppression, it certainly is the duty of rulers, not only to abstain from it [oppression] themselves, but, according to their stations, to prevent it in others. The liberty enjoyed by the people of these States of worshiping Almighty God agreeably to their consciences, is not only among the choicest of their *blessings*, but also of their *rights*. While men perform their social duties faithfully, they do all that society or the state can with propriety demand or expect; and remain responsible only to their Maker for the religion, or modes of faith, which they may prefer or profess.[50]

Third, in Washington's view, government must by no means impose a coercive establishment of one religion upon the consciences of all but must, as far as it could, encourage the free exercise of religion. Government should accommodate and fortify the religious impulse, as the source of our different ideas about conscience and rights, and of the moral habits that are their bodyguard.

Washington's fourth principle of religious liberty was to predict that one fruit of the new system of religious liberty would be a greater charity among diverse groups that conducted "themselves in respect to each other with a more christian-like spirit than ever they have done in any previous age, or in any other Nation," as Washington quite pointedly told the General Convention of the Protestant Episcopal Church in 1790.[51] Three years later, speaking in Baltimore, Washington was even more clear:

> We have abundant reason to rejoice that in this Land the light of truth and reason has triumphed over the power of bigotry and superstition, and that every person may here worship God according to the dictates of his own heart. In this enlightened Age and in this Land of equal liberty, it is our boast, that a man's religious tenets will not forfeit the protection of the Laws, nor deprive him of the right of attaining and holding the highest Offices that are known in the United States.[52]

BEYOND DEISM

Washington evinced throughout his life an original and profound appreciation of religious liberty. Furthermore, Washington was painstaking in marking out its necessary principles for future generations. He did not do this in a theoretical framework, to be sure, but he did make his principles explicit enough, and in a fairly systematic way, as he corresponded with one church group after another once he became president. Although his understanding of the proper relation of church and state was not shared by the third and fourth presidents of the new nation, it has long held ascendancy since then: a passionate principle of free exercise, the absence of any kind of federal establishment, and considerable space for the individual states to promote and support religion in their own ways. This practice would continue during the first 160 years of the Republic. Then, in 1947, the U.S. Supreme Court overthrew the traditions Washington had set and made itself the tribunal of all the nation's religious disputes, treating religion as a dangerous disease to be carefully quarantined.

More to the point of this chapter, Washington showed how his derivation of these principles obliged him to reach beyond deism, even while happily borrowing from the language of truth, reason, evidence, and the individual differences between mind and mind. To the time-honored virtue of toleration, however, he added a most important new virtue: mutual respect. These are not inconsiderable achievements. He saw well enough that this new system depends upon the Jewish-Christian conception of a God of spirit and truth, who wishes to be worshipped in freedom. On any other conception of god, the principles of religious liberty lose their point.

In that respect, Washington's God is unmistakably the God whose Hebrew name is *Jehovah,* and whose Christian name, favored by Washington, is Providence. His faith in that God drove not only his practical principles, but also his actions and even his manners. In the next three chapters of Part 2, we must explore that faith in three of its facets: its differences from deism; its public expression; and its private life within his family and in solitude. Then in Part 3 we shall pause to look at some fruits of that faith.

Chapter 7

NOT DEIST, BUT
JUDEO-CHRISTIAN

*I look upon every dispensation of Providence as designed to
answer some valuable purpose, and hope I shall always possess a sufficient degree of fortitude to bear without mur-
muring any stroke which may happen, either to my person
or estate.*

— Letter to Lund Washington, May 29, 1779[1]

*O*ur task now is to keep our focus on Washington's faith, and how
Washington himself thought about God. How *must* Washington
have been thinking of God, in order to speak of God as he did? What
are the proper names he used? With what *verbs* did Washington describe the actions he attributed to God, or expected of God, or
prayed God to carry out?

AMITY TOWARD ALL

The God that Washington prayed to, and described in his public utterances, bears little resemblance to the watchmaker god of the
deists. From the watchmaker god one does not expect miracles, and
it would be quite futile (and naive) to pray for a miracle. Washington's God, on the other hand, seems very like the Lord God described in the Hebrew Torah, historical books, and Psalms, who in

furthering his own designs interposes himself in history. Indeed, so clever an artist is this Jehovah that he does not even need to perform miracles to achieve his purposes. All he needs to do is arrange contingencies so that human agents, acting under the general laws of nature, of their own free will make the decisions that accomplish his will. The enemy commander—if we may borrow an example from the sermon on the theme of Providence and in favor of independence, given by the president of Princeton, John Witherspoon, on May 17, 1776—falls ill of dysentery the morning of the battle, from quite natural causes, and for want of his leadership, the enemy suffers an unexpected defeat.[2] Contrarily, a betrayal of important secrets by a key officer may doom the Americans to unanticipated setbacks. In both good news and bad news, Washington saw, as Witherspoon did, the guiding hand of Providence. (It is likely that Washington knew this sermon, since it was distributed in pamphlet form to all five hundred Presbyterian parishes in the nation, and was translated into Dutch and widely commented on in Europe.) In the Continental Congress, Witherspoon served on committees of crucial importance to Washington, including the Board of War and the Committee on Foreign Affairs. At Princeton he had been the teacher of at least forty important figures in the founding period, including James Madison.

Although he appealed often to Providence, Washington was quite chaste in refraining from the use of more specifically Christian names for God, such as "Savior" and "Redeemer." Interdenominational rivalries were still, in 1770–1800, matters of considerable passion. Several of the individual American colonies had been expressly founded as a refuge for one group of religious believers (dissident Puritans, Catholics, Quakers) who were escaping persecution by other Christians (also represented in America). These passions were heightened by the rapid spreading of the new, enthusiastic religions from Great Britain, those of the Methodists and the Baptists.

By about 1810, these new evangelicals had doubled their numbers more than once and had dramatically transformed the religious landscape of the nation in a way that affected Washington's
later reputation. They had even altered what it meant to be
"Christian."

The new enthusiasts (for that is how they were regarded) thought
that not only the Anglicans, but even members of the recent generation of New England Puritans, such as John Adams, had slipped
away from fundamental beliefs by allowing themselves a great deal
of latitude in how they interpreted their faith. These "latitudinarians" tended to downplay the special language and creedal claims of
Christianity, in favor of the philosophical terms shared with the ancient Greeks and Romans and with the "new science" represented
by Isaac Newton and others. These latitudinarians were not quite
deists, nor did most call themselves that; they were only "broad-
minded" in the way they spoke about Christianity, especially in
public. By contrast, the newly fervent Baptists and Methodists
tended to regard the latitudinarians as missing the main point of
Christianity altogether: salvation by faith in their Lord and Savior
on the cross. The question "Washington, a deist or a Christian?"
was to receive a new meaning in this new context. In this way, the
Second Great Awakening, slowly gaining strength in the early nineteenth century, directly affected Washington's later religious reputation, by imposing on an earlier generation a new generation's
standard for defining a Christian.

This slowly surging wave of new evangelical religion, which
Washington included in his public respect for religious bodies, had
by 1787 lent powerful support to the cause of religious liberty
through opposing public establishments of particular churches,
and insisting upon their own right to worship as they felt bound
to do. This constructive effort allowed the authors of *The Federalist Papers* to note gratefully the remarkable unity among the
American people and the wonderful harmony among factions at

the Constitutional Convention, which could so easily have been at passionate variance with one another, and to describe it as a favor from Providence.[3] The variety of American denominations, obliged to live together in tolerance, were inculcating a new religious style, a new model of religious virtue: respect for one another across religious lines. Washington was particularly proud of his fellow Americans for their "liberality of sentiment toward each other which marks every political and religious denomination of men in this Country."[4] As he wrote to the General Convention of the Episcopal Church, the new nation "affords edifying prospects indeed to see Christians of different denominations dwell together in more charity, and conduct themselves in respect to each other with a more christian-like spirit than they have ever done in any former age, or in any other Nation."[5]

To encourage this amity, dear to his heart, Washington avoided unnecessarily stoking theological rivalry. He found in traditional Hebraic terms for God room for substantial common ground among Protestants, Catholics, and Jews. If we pause here to list a few of the names for God employed by Washington throughout his public career (see Appendix 2 for more), and even in his personal correspondence, we see his extraordinary effort to find language that all Americans could accept, without excluding anybody (except possibly thoroughgoing atheists, of whom at the time there were exceedingly few, if any).[6]

Almighty and Merciful Sovereign of the Universe
Creator
Divine Author of Our Blessed Religion
Hand of Heaven
Father of All Mercies
God
Great Lord and Ruler of Nations
Lord of Hosts
Supreme Being

"WHOSE GOD IS JEHOVAH"

At the first meeting of the Continental Congress, in September 1774, at the news of a sudden outbreak of war in Boston with so formidable a military power as Great Britain, the very first motion on the floor was a motion for a prayer to seek the guidance of Almighty God. Resistance immediately erupted—not because prayer was inappropriate, but because John Jay and others protested that they could not pray in the same terms as other people present (Anabaptists with Quakers, for example, or Congregationalists with Episcopalians, or Unitarians with Presbyterians). Sam Adams settled the dispute by announcing loudly that he was no bigot and could pray along with any minister so long as he was a patriot. In a deft touch, he proposed the Reverend Jacob Duché, Anglican minister of nearby Christ Church, who, Adams said, had a reputation for good judgment. The motion carried.

Wisely, the minister prayed from Psalm 35, whose verses had been chosen for that day by the Book of Common Prayer. All could pray the Psalms together. Thus he began:

Plead my cause, O Lord, with them that strive with me, fight against them that fight against me. Take hold of buckler and shield, and rise up for my help. . . . Say to my soul, "I am your salvation." Let those be ashamed and dishonored who seek my life; let those be turned back and humiliated who devise evil against me.

In a letter written to Abigail a week later, John Adams described the electrifying effect of that prayer:

You must remember this was the next Morning after we heard the horrible Rumour, of the Cannonade of Boston. I never saw a greater Effect upon an Audience. It seemed as if Heaven had ordained that Psalm to be read on that Morning. After this Mr. Duché, unexpected to every Body struck out into an extemporary

Prayer, which filled the Bosom of every Man present. I must confess I never heard a better Prayer or one, so well pronounced. Episcopalian as he is, Dr. Cooper himself never prayed with such fervour, such Ardor, such Earnestness and Pathos, and in Language so elegant and sublime—for America, for the Congress, for The Province of Massachusetts Bay, and especially the Town of Boston.

During this scene, George Washington prayed alongside Patrick Henry and Edmund Randolph, John Jay, Edward Rutledge, and Richard Henry Lee, some of whom had expressed reluctance to worship with those not of their faith. "It has had," as John Adams explained to his wife, "an excellent Effect upon every Body here."[7]

As some preachers of the revolutionary period liked to point out, even the moral language of the eighteenth-century philosophers—so insistent upon the role of desire and self-interest in corrupting the actual life of reason—confirmed, if it was not inspired by, the realism of biblical language concerning the pull of self-love, the flesh, and worldly pride upon rational man and the ravages they wreak upon reason. On the other side of the ledger, many of the ministers in the pulpits of that period cherished a keen appreciation of reason construed as common sense and practicality and utility. They often quoted Algernon Sydney, John Locke, Cicero, and other philosophers, right along with their citations from the Bible.

Thus, for example, the two names Jefferson chose for God in his draft of the Declaration of Independence—"the *laws* of Nature and *of Nature's God*," alluding to the great Lawmaker and Governor of the universe, and "endowed by their *Creator* with certain unalienable rights" (italics added)—unmistakably have both philosophical and biblical resonance. Similarly orthodox are the other two names insisted upon by the Congress, before they would sign their names to the Declaration: "appealing to the *Supreme Judge* of the world for the rectitude of our intentions" and "with a firm reliance on the Protection of *Divine Providence*" (italics added). The God identified as Divine Providence knows the name of every human being from before the founding of the world: "Before I formed thee in the belly I knew thee" (Jeremiah 1:5). For that Providence, no detail is beneath notice. "Are not two sparrows sold for a farthing? and one of them shall not fall on the ground without your Father. But the very hairs of your head are all numbered. Fear ye not therefore, ye are of more value than many sparrows" (Matthew 10:29–31).

The God to whom Washington prays, and to whom he urges others to pray, cannot be the God of deism; it is the God of the Hebrews. For Providence is the God who acts in history and interposes his power in human events. The Supreme Judge who examines the rectitude even of our secret intentions is also a highly personal God, whose actions are those of the biblical God. The watchmaker god of the deists is indifferent to human individuals and their intentions. The most extreme deist philosophers thought a judge of consciences far too human in shape. They despised such a God and ridiculed the very conception. Their hero was Newton the scientist (not Newton the Christian), and their god the god of reason, not the God of the Bible. The deist god had more the character of the ordered, indifferent, and distant stars than that of "the Supreme Judge of our intentions."

In the letter he wrote as president to the Hebrew Congregation of Savannah, Washington, for his part, was quite clear about just who Providence is:

May the same Wonder-working Deity, who long since delivered the Hebrews from their Egyptian oppressors, and planted them in the Promised Land; whose providential agency has lately been conspicuous, in establishing these United States as an independent nation, still continue to water them with the dews of heaven, and to make the inhabitants, of every denomination, participate in the temporal and spiritual blessings of that people whose God is Jehovah.[8]

Similarly, the God of many official declarations, circulars, and decrees issued by the Congress and by presidents is discernibly the God of the Bible, especially the Hebrew Bible. Americans are encouraged by their presidents and the House and Senate to pray to that God for the following (quite nondeistic) purposes: to beg his forgiveness of the sins of citizens of all ranks, to urge his intervention so as to frustrate the aims of America's enemies and to make prosper the efforts of American arms, to send a good harvest, and to spread a spirit of charity and cooperation among all citizens. As the delegates to the Continental Congress put it in the Thanksgiving Proclamation of 1781, for instance, Americans owe a duty "with grateful hearts, to celebrate the praise of our gracious Benefactor; to confess our manifold sins; to offer up our most fervent supplications to the God of all grace, that it may please Him to pardon our offences and incline our hearts for the future to keep all his laws."[9] (For a similar proclamation from President Washington, see Chapter 8.)

We saw in Chapter 4 the seriousness of General Washington's orders and exhortations to his officers and soldiers during the long years of the War of Independence. Indeed, General Washington sometimes expressed dismay that anyone could look upon the course of events without recognizing the many signal interpositions of Providence throughout the war. "The hand of Providence," he wrote to Brigadier General Thomas Nelson after two years of hard campaigning, "has been so conspicuous in all this, that he must be worse than an infidel that lacks faith, and more than wicked, that has not gratitude enough to acknowledge his obligations."[10] As we shall see, Washington never lost his sense of wonder at the "invisible workings of Providence," which had "conducted us through difficulties where no human foresight could point the way."[11]

From his orders to his troops to the somber words on religion and morality in his Farewell Address as president, Washington taught the American public that free republican government depends upon the kind of liberty consistent with self-discipline and self-mastery, and that such liberty, in turn, for the vast majority of people (but perhaps not for a few persons "of peculiar character"), depends upon the support of religion. Washington knew people—

elites, commoners, soldiers, tradesmen—as they are, especially under the extreme conditions of war. When he spoke of the need of most human beings for religion, as an adjunct to other motives for ethical conduct, he knew from harsh experience whereof he spoke.

WASHINGTON'S STRUGGLE WITH HIMSELF

Both the writings of the ancients (especially military heroes) and of the Bible were storehouses of wisdom, and so Washington studied both. When he ordered busts and portraits for the ornamentation of his parlors at Mount Vernon, he chose exemplars of the use of power from across the centuries: Alexander the Great, Julius Caesar, Charles XII of Sweden, Frederick II of Prussia. He also hung prominently on the wall of his large dining room, the most public room at Mount Vernon, two key portraits: the Virgin Mary and St. John.[12] He kept clearly in mind—and exemplified in his own speech and behavior—the twin message of the Bible: that men are capable of both brutishness and nobility.

For Washington himself, calming his own inner furies had been an arduous task. As a young man, he had been quite prone to outbursts of anger, so he well understood that there was a war within himself. When his portraitist Gilbert Stuart commented to Washington at one sitting that he saw in him a greater tumult of temper and passion than in any subject that had ever sat for him, Washington nodded in recognition. Stuart also wrote to a friend:

All his features were indicative of the strongest passions, yet, like Socrates, his judgment and self-command made him appear of a different cast in the eyes of the world. . . . Had he been born in the forests . . . he would have been the fiercest man among the savage tribes.[13]

Passionate men who strive for perfection often erupt in frustration at others and, most of all, at themselves.

His love for classical models also led Washington to be impressed by the Masons in America, who were driven as he was by classical images, not least in classical architecture, and to be engaged in activities of considerable local benevolence. In some parishes, the Masons raised more funds and real goods for local charities than the church did. (Often, of course, it was the same men who assisted in each effort.) The language of the Masons appealed to Washington—and it was not too far removed from the reasoned language of the Anglican "middle way."

Washington himself confessed to old friends that the older he became, the more he recognized the workings of the Almighty in the affairs of men, far beyond human powers to comprehend. Although he never doubted the capacity of freemen to affect the course of events, Washington wondered at the seemingly trivial events that changed the entire direction of a battle and, at times, the fate of a nation. As he argued in 1793 to his friend David Humphreys, who, at the time of his letter, was Minister to Portugal:

> If it can be esteemed a happiness to live in an age productive of great and interesting events, we of the present age are very highly favored. The rapidity of national revolutions appear no less astonishing, than their magnitude. In what they will terminate, is known only to the great ruler of events; and confiding in his wisdom and goodness, we may safely trust the issue to him, without perplexing ourselves to seek for that, which is beyond human ken; only taking care to perform the parts assigned us, in a way that reason and our own consciences approve of.[14]

Washington had witnessed many battles in which a seemingly insignificant, small deed had thrown apparent good fortune into reverse or apparent disaster into success—in one case, an intended minor ambush leading to the unexpected panic and rout of the opposing army; in another, one courageous squad standing firm against hosts; in still others, a ship laden with desperately needed munitions captured here, enemy dispatches intercepted there, the guns of Ticonderoga arriving in Boston in the nick of time. Such scattered deeds were impossible for generals to predict, impossible to control. Washington marveled at the scope of God's actions in the world, those actions that did not diminish human freedom but seemed to work around the edges of it. Providence, as it were, allowed for chains of probabilities ("concatenations of events") to cross in wholly unforeseen ways, throwing the schemes of men off their intended paths.

Many preachers of the time—some of whom Washington heard in person—described Providence in such terms. "Special Providence," the mysterious but efficacious way in which God acts within history and among humans, without acting as puppeteer or trespassing upon individual freedom, was one of their favorite themes. Providence rejoices in humbling men when they are proud in their conceits, and even in trying the good man, to test his mettle. Often in the War of Independence the Americans fared better than they expected, and they gave thanks. When things went extremely badly, and all looked dark, still they trusted in Divine Providence. If hard things befell them, they took them as intended for their instruction. When good things befell them, they accepted them as an undeserved but gratefully received blessing.

For example, on December 18, 1777, while he and his impoverished soldiers endured the cold winds and snow of Valley Forge, Washington asked his men, under instruction from the Continental Congress, to observe a day of prayer and fasting, to give thanks to God for blessings already received, and to implore the continuing favor of Providence upon the American cause. That very day, heeding his orders, the Reverend Israel Evans, chaplain to the New Hampshire Brigade under Brigadier General Enoch Poor, delivered a sermon for the occasion, in which he praised the character of General Washington, while seeking to inspire his own brigade in a manner appropriate to a day of prayer and fasting. That sermon was printed and later sent to General Washington, who did not receive it until March 12. The very next day, Washington wrote his thanks to Rev. Evans, to congratulate him for "the force of the reasoning that you have displayed through the whole," and "to assure you, that it will ever be the first wish of my heart to aid your pious endeavors to inculcate a due sense of the dependence we ought to place in that all wise and powerful Being on whom alone our success depends."[15]

Yet, however much he may have admired the force of Rev. Evans's reasoning, Washington retained a lifelong sense of the awesome mystery of Providence, above and beyond the power of reason itself. *Inscrutable* is among the adjectives that he most frequently associated with the divine, as we shall see at length in Chapter 9.[16] Providence, Washington learned, often works "for wise purposes not discoverable by finite minds."[17] A personal God, the willful Lord of Jews and Christians, is inscrutable and mysterious. An impersonal deity, the distant and limited creator of deists and skeptics, is predictable and regular. With his constant sense that "Providence works in the mysterious course of events,"[18] Washington was very far indeed from the epistemological starting point of most deists. They thought that revelation had to be judged by the standards of reason. With his powerful sense that "the will of Heaven is not to be controverted or scrutinized by the children of this world,"[19] Washington took an opposite approach. Reason could know only so much, he realized. Beyond that, there was only submission to the will of the one true sovereign.

PROVIDENCE RULES THE STARS, NOT THE REVERSE

Still, as we have seen, most historians wish to give a deist interpretation to "Providence." This is difficult, for if there is one thing unadulterated deists do not believe in, it is a God who acts in history. The deist god is not omnipotent, but only potent enough to get the world going, as it were, and perhaps to sustain it in existence. Consider for a moment the twists and turns historians take to explain away Washington's many prayers and thanksgivings to Providence. The recent excellent biography by the distinguished historian Joseph Ellis carries this sentence: "Never a deeply religious man, at least in the traditional Christian sense of the term, Washington thought of God as a distant, impersonal force, the presumed wellspring for what he called destiny or providence."[20]

Although Washington did use both of these terms, evidence obliges us to see that he understood that the concept of *destiny* is not the same as *Providence;* to him they were two quite different ideas. Synonyms for *destiny* include *fate* and *fortune,* and there is no use praying to "destiny." But *providence* in Webster's[21] is either a synonym for *God* or means "divine guidance or care." At least in the Jewish and Christian scheme of things, praying for God's guidance, care, or action on one's behalf makes a great deal of sense. But praying to "destiny" does not.

On the other hand, Providence may use a "kind of destiny" for its own purposes. It can do so, for example, in virtue of the talents it bestows on a person, her natural inclinations, and the circumstances in which it places her. In this sense, Washington wrote to Martha on June 18, 1775, "But it has been a kind of destiny, that has thrown me upon this service."[22] In his younger years, several observers noted that the young man seemed "destined" for greater things.

The key to the idea for Providence, as we shall see in Chapter 10, is its break from the ancient idea of inexorable necessity. Providence is a sovereign God, who recognizes no limits in his care for details and particulars in the unfolding of human events, a sovereign who has particular love and benevolence toward humans, beginning with his own chosen people.[23] Such is the great God Jehovah, as Washington specified in his letter to the Hebrew Congregation of Savannah.

Providence may use "destiny," as it may use "chance"—as it uses all things according to their own laws—for its own sovereign purposes. Yet in his confusion of providence with destiny, Ellis is not alone. The great Washington biographers James Thomas Flexner and Douglas Southall Freeman (and others) also try to make the two different concepts equivalent. In addition, they strike pretty much the same two notes as Ellis about Washington's state of soul: that he was not a very serious Christian but instead had the faith of a deist. Flexner and Freeman give these points a few paragraphs of serious attention, but some historians fire off that judgment without hesitation. Some have qualms about it and write tentatively. Few expend much effort exploring the issue. Most give the impression that religion, compared with other matters, is not very important.

Some historians make evident that they fear religious interpretations of Washington more than they fear secular interpretations. "The reader should be warned," writes Flexner in a footnote, "that the forgers and mythmakers have been endlessly active in their efforts to attribute to Washington their own religious acts and beliefs. Prayers have been written for him, etc., etc."[24] But the biographers have also been endlessly active in attributing to Washington instead a lack of faith in a creedal religion, a personal God, and an ethic of love, mercy, and sacrifice. They assign to Washington a Stoic but not a Christian faith. They say his life was governed by "the code of gentlemen" rather than the morality of Christianity.[25]

Biographers such as Flexner and Freeman find it odd that Washington sometimes referred to Providence as "he, she and it," as if this variation were unorthodox.[26] But do they really think that orthodox Christianity and Judaism assigned a gender to the Creator, just as they would to a human being? On the contrary, in Jewish and Christian thought, God is beyond gender, "neither male nor female." On the other hand, the Bible generally does prefer a personal pronoun for God, rather than an impersonal one. Thus, most texts in the Bible (but not all) refer to God in masculine terms, especially in the Christian testament, with its emphasis on Father and Son (rather than, say, Mother and Daughter). Christian writers—St. Augustine, for instance—write of God mostly in one gender, sometimes in another, with copious explanations as to why they do so. The Christian God is imagined to be a person (in a sense related to, but

essentially different from, the way in which humans are persons).
Yet even though the preference is almost always for a personal,
rather than an impersonal, pronoun, the Anglican liturgy does say
of the Holy Trinity, "May it be praised forevermore."

Both Flexner and Freeman also find it odd that, as noted before,
Washington speaks sometimes of Providence and sometimes of destiny. But any student of Western classics finds both terms in play, although typically in different contexts, and pointing to quite
different concepts. For example, as we saw earlier, Washington
writes of a "kind of destiny" that put him on track to be commander in chief. Here the natural term springs from the Greek and
Roman idea of destiny, rather than Providence. Much against his
own will, he expressed in a letter to Martha, it was Washington's
hope that his service "is designed to answer some good purpose."
That is, that it might serve the larger purposes of Providence.[27] If one
wishes to emphasize poignancy and sweet pain, one writes helplessly
of destiny. If one wishes to counsel trusting acceptance, one writes
of Providence. One could say that Providence assigned Washington
a unique destiny. It would be quite odd to say that destiny assigned
Washington a particular Providence.

Both Flexner and Freeman think that *Providence* is a more impersonal term than *God*. That seems exactly contrary to normal
usage, at least in the Anglican and Catholic traditions. But it may
occur because both of them, like Ellis, seem to associate *God* with
"traditional" religion, perhaps of the more enthusiastic, heartfelt,
devotional type well known in parts of America. From such religion, they are intent on dissociating Washington. For example,
Flexner concludes: "Washington's religious belief was that of the enlightenment: deism. He practically never used the word 'God,' preferring the more impersonal word 'Providence.'"[28]

Flexner's comment is puzzling. The term *god* is quite ancient,
since, in relevant philosophical contexts, we find it both in Greek
and in Latin pagan writings, and it may mean an impersonal force
such as First Cause or Final End, or Pure Act, or the name for all the

Energy from which the world comes to be, and toward which it rushes in return; it may even mean the living force in pantheism.

By contrast, to recognize the presence of Providence in every event of daily life, and in every place, requires a certain inward bowing of the head to his sovereignty. That attitude, when it is part of daily living and frequent prayer, brings Providence into a quite intimate personal relationship. This sort of personal relation was encouraged by the books available to Washington in his youth, Thomas Comber on the Book of Common Prayer as a daily guide, and Sir Matthew Hale's *Contemplations Moral and Divine*.

Washington had been taught that there is a Creator who knowingly intervened at a particular moment to create the world out of nothing and now acts as a daily Providence that intervenes regularly in history on behalf of those who turn to him, and who interposes himself in the course of events for his own ends.[29] Some of these events are admittedly tragic and the source of immense suffering (as in the long, painful exile of his people and the trials of faithful ones in all ages), but they are always on behalf of his friendship with humans. These lessons sketch the main lines of Washington's repeated mentions of Providence. The relation in which Christians and Jews place Providence and those who trust it is palpably more personal than the ancient view of inexorable necessity, or the eighteenth-century deist view.

The Jewish and Christian version would have been very familiar to Washington from the Book of Micah and the Psalms, to both of which he often alluded in his own utterances. Washington would also have known from his education and reading that Greek and Roman gods also "intervened" in historical events, but not in the way that the God of Providence does. The Greek and Roman gods were described as being moved by human envies and passions and as involved in their own dramatic necessities. In the classical stories, they manipulated human beings as if the latter were puppets on strings. The God of the Hebrews and Christians, by contrast, has an infinitely more transcendent aim: the union of humans with himself, achieved only by and through free choice. Thus, his method of operation never deprives humans of their liberty but aims to enhance it. "I am the way, the truth, and the life" (John 14:6); "And ye shall know the truth, and the truth shall make you free" (John 8:32).[30]

POSSIBILITIES OF FAILURE, DEFEAT, AND LOSS

Flexner, moreover, attributes to Washington a rather modern and panglossian view of the world: "Providence ruled the universe and, since Washington was dedicated to the conceptions of both virtue and progress, he could not but believe that virtue would in the deepest sense be rewarded, that although the means Providence pursued were often past the comprehension of humanity, everything would eventually prove for the best."[31] Flexner may possibly have in mind a passage from one of Washington's letters, quoted earlier, in which Washington stated that he would "not lament or repine at any act of Providence because I am in a great measure a convert to Mr. Pope's opinion, that whatever is, is right."[32] But this letter was composed in 1776, before the war turned truly desperate. It is telling that this tone is later moderated in Washington's writings: This was a man who, by dint of his own hard experience, learned that Providence leads into defeat as well as victory.

Washington was by no means certain that the War of Independence would automatically work out for the best, or that the courage his men showed at Valley Forge would ever be rewarded with success. Better than to gain success, he learned, is to live so as to deserve it, win or lose. To think otherwise would be tantamount to denying the sovereignty of God. And besides, it would take all the heroism and risk out of life, all the possibilities of nobility and tragedy and loss, and also true and proven faith. The ways of Providence, he came to understand, are mysterious, and far beyond the comprehension of our little human minds.

Washington was often haunted by the thought of how unlikely his successes were, and how probable his failures. He acted anyway.

He did trust Providence, but he knew that to act is by no means to be certain of success. As he instructed his estate manager with regard to a "disaster" at home:

> The first I submit to with the most perfect resignation and cheerfulness. I look upon every dispensation of Providence as designed to answer some valuable purpose, and hope I shall always possess a sufficient degree of fortitude to bear without murmuring any stroke which may happen, either to my person or estate, from that quarter.[33]

PRAYER AND FASTING

Washington's own stepgranddaughter, Eleanor ("Nelly") Parke Custis, thought his words and actions in this respect were so plain and obvious that she could not understand how everybody did not see that he had always lived as a serious Christian. As she wrote to one of Washington's early biographers:

> It was his custom to retire to his library at nine or ten o'clock, where he remained an hour before he went to his chamber. He always rose before the sun, and remained in his library until called to breakfast. I never witnessed his private devotions, I never inquired about them. I should have thought it the greatest heresy to doubt his firm belief in Christianity. His life, his writings, prove that he was a Christian. He was not one of those, who act or pray, "that they may be seen of men." He communed with his God in secret.[34]

Nelly's last sentence goes beyond the "I never witnessed" she had just written a few words earlier. Even so, the other side of this argument needs to be placed squarely on the table. The reason why Nelly Custis wrote her letter is that some people did doubt, from the taciturnity and reserve that Washington had always maintained in public, whether—and to what degree—he really was a Christian.

Public debates on this subject raged all through the nineteenth century. Washington was certainly not a showy Christian, nor a preachy one, nor a missionary, nor a frequent public expositor of exclusively Christian truths and sentiments. On the other hand, his parents were Christians, in visible practice he was an Anglican, and his descendents (via Martha's children) maintained the tradition and claimed him for it. On a few occasions, moreover, he did let slip his inner commitment to Christianity.

There was, for example, the occasion noted in the last chapter on which he offered solemn and heartfelt advice to the Delaware chiefs: "You do well to wish to learn our arts and ways of life, and above all, the religion of Jesus Christ. These will make you a greater and happier people than you are. Congress will do everything they can to assist you in this wise intention; and to tie the knot of friendship and union so fast, that nothing shall ever be able to loose it."[35]

One of Washington's descendents, the Reverend E. C. M'Guire, the son-in-law of Robert Lewis, listed a series of witnesses to Washington's prayers during the War of Independence, and earlier Colonel Temple, who served with Washington under Braddock, claimed that he saw Washington pray daily; Generals Knox and Porterfield during 1775–1783 and several orderlies, secretaries to Washington, and other staff officers saw or heard Washington in prayer. A half century later, the Anglican historian Philip Slaughter cited similar witnesses, only partly relying on M'Guire. Such witnesses claimed that the general preferred to pray quite audibly and was at times heard through the door of his quarters or the canvas of his tent. Some reported catching him on his knees when, thinking he had called out, they opened his door to deliver a communication.[36]

For the most part, though, Washington demonstrated a commitment to considerable privacy about his own deepest religious beliefs and sentiments. Such privacy and undemonstrativeness was not uncommon for Anglicans of his time and station, although some Virginian Anglicans did write movingly of their religion and their spiritual struggles, at least in letters and diaries, such as Washington's best friend, Bryan Fairfax, and the famous governor of Virginia Patrick Henry. In nearly the whole communion there was resistance to "enthusiasm" and "show," and a preference for decorum and formality, in the manner of the highly polished Anglican liturgy whose words were centuries old and allowed little room for improvisation. In feeling, the style was decidedly not Baptist, nor even Methodist. That Washington could spend a whole day in prayer and fasting, and that he frequently attended church (but not communion) with Martha on Sundays,[37] and that he was unusually faithful to his duties as vestryman (attending twenty-three out of thirty-one possible meetings during his term of office, which in part embraced his period of military service), may have said enough, in his mind, about his seriousness in matters religious: His pastor, Lee Massey, praised him highly on this account, according to Anglican historian Philip Slaughter.[38] Most laypersons are not, after all, monks. One must allow laypersons to live as laypersons, even when they are serious about their faith.

While continuing to deny Washington's religious seriousness, biographer Freeman testifies to his self-control, spotless reputation, and even chastity:

> Although there was no compelling faith in God, principles of right conduct prevailed: there is no echo of any scandal, no hint of a breach of accepted morals, no line of obscenity, no reference to any sex experience, no slur on any woman otherwise than in reference to those who might be demoralizing his troops.[39]

Yet Washington was neither prude nor hermit, but a lively man of the world, who was at the same time always aware of his duties and obligations. One of those duties entailed living as a good Christian ought to live, even to the point of not allowing his religiousness to show itself before others, but mainly in private, where, as he knew,

God was quite capable of seeing. The whole picture of his religious life is, alas, not open to the rest of us; we see only fragments.

As the dictionaries of ideas we cited in the last chapter make clear, there were many Christians who for various reasons presented themselves to the world as deists. This appearance could be a matter of attitude, style, and manner rather than a commitment to deism in its strong sense (a denial of particular Providence). A Christian might well, for instance, express in public—even when most of the public was itself quite Christian—only those commitments that lend themselves to explanation in terms of reason alone, without meaning to limit his whole life only to those tenets. There might be many reasons for so doing, in order not to exclude those of other beliefs, for instance.

Washington, however, often went beyond that, making statements whose full sense becomes clear only when one perceives their Christian provenance. His principles of religious liberty were one such instance. To interpret these principles merely in a deist way is to miss their full sense, and to misread his behavior. He was a professed Anglican and, like many Anglicans in Virginia of his generation, rather more of the "latitudinarian" than "evangelical" style.

Thus, Washington plainly ran the risk of having many persons think him less Christian than he was. Even under provocation he retained the reserve that he had early chosen about his personal beliefs. Thus, that reserve, alas, does not allow us now to call him a fully witnessing, fully expressive Christian. Yet his conduct and his words resonate with a profound appropriation of traditional Christian ethics and concepts. To be sure, these are older Christian terms with a decidedly Hebraic cast, expressed in a preference for the language of the Psalms and Micah and the other Prophets, more often than in the tender terms of attachment to Christ. The note of tenderness did appear, but more rarely, as when he commended to the governors of the states the brotherly love and the "Charity, humilty, and pacific temper of mind" of the "Divine Author" of our religion.[40]

THE PROVIDENTIAL NATION

Finally, a word must be said about the tradition of seeing Providence in the affairs of the American colonies. This tradition was as old, of course, as the Puritan colonies of New England. But it really began to go nationwide, scholars say, during the thirty years just after Washington's birth in 1732. Indeed, young Washington's own exploits along the Monongahela had something to do with this gathering sense of a providential destiny for a whole people. In the 1750s, the threat of French supremacy bearing down on the East Coast colonies from the westward forests, along with the war parties of Indians mobilized by the French against the British settlers on the frontier, alarmed Americans. Since the danger of attacks from the French and Indians affected all the frontier states, not just one, individual colonies began to sense a common need. This alarm fed the first blooming of a sense of national unity. A new sort of metastory began taking shape to explain what the colonists were experiencing, a new sense of all being in this together—not just building little communities as enclaves for their own protection, but as in need of a common defense and, ultimately, as a new national experiment for all humankind.

George Washington entered upon the public stage just as the colonies were falling under the sway, in terms spread by the evangelists of the Great Awakening (1740–1763), of a new collective story, a story of freedom, a story of suffering and judgment to come, and a story of God's blessing on a particular people. Not yet a nation, still, many Americans were beginning to sense a national call to make real in history the intention God had hidden since before the beginning of the world: the story of universal human liberty. And so Washington pointed out in his "Circular to the States" at the end of the war:

The Citizens of America are from this period, to be considered as the Actors on a most conspicuous Theatre, which seems to be pe-

The scene depicted in this engraving is one of the most popular images of Washington and is apocryphal, but Washington is reported to have prayed alone during the war. (*The Prayer at Valley Forge*, by John C. McRae, 1889)

Washington is usually portrayed in his later years, so it is wonderful to see him as a young man. (Portrait in the uniform of British Colonial Colonel, oil on canvas, painting by Charles Volkmar, c. 1874, copied from the original by Charles Willson Peale, 1772)

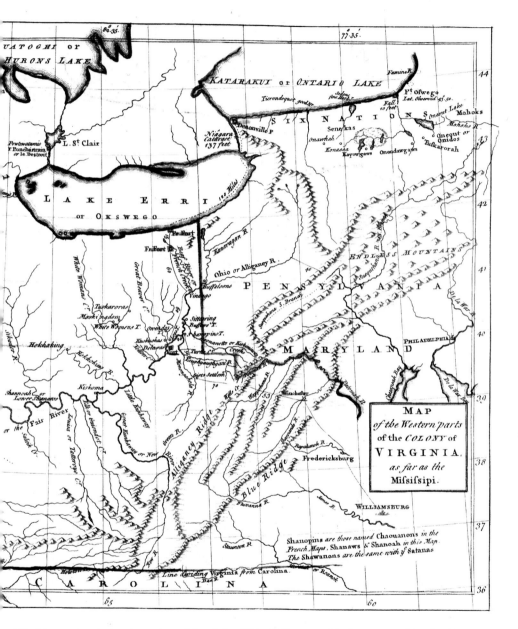

Washington's mission into the wilds of the Ohio Valley was his first taste of leadership.
(Map of George Washington's Mission to the Ohio Valley, 1753)

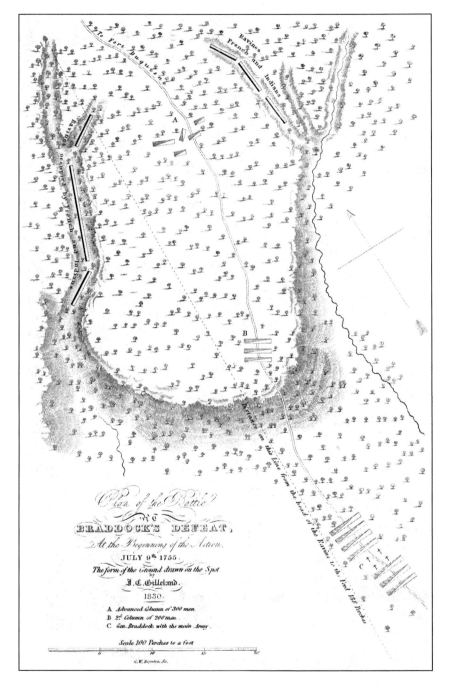

Washington proved his mettle during Braddock's Defeat, but witnessing the slaughter was to influence him for the rest of his life. (Map at the Beginning of the Action, July 9, 1755, by J. C. Gilleland, 1830)

Washington's much-loved wife, Martha, a strong woman and devout Christian in her own right, was to prove to be the "quiet soul" that he needed to sustain him throughout his life. (Miniature portrait, watercolor on ivory, Charles Willson Peale, 1776)

Artist Gilbert Stuart, who painted most of the best known portraits of Washington, always seemed to capture the serious and stern Washington, rather than the man that even Stuart once said "would have been the fiercest man among the savage tribes." (Oil on canvas, Filbert Stuart, 1796)

Washington's happiest moments were those he spent at Mount Vernon, under his "vine and fig tree," as one of his favorite biblical sayings goes, and with his beloved family. (*Washington Family in the Study*, oil on canvas, Thomas Prichard Rossiter, mid-nineteenth century)

WASHINGTON TAKING COMMAND OF THE AMERICAN ARMY.
At Cambridge, Mass. July 3rd 1775.

Washington accepted the role of commander in chief in 1775, even though he "did not think [himself] equal to the command," and knowing that it made him, at that time, the first "official" traitor in the eyes of Britain. (*Washington Taking Command of the American Army*, published by Currier & Ives, 1876)

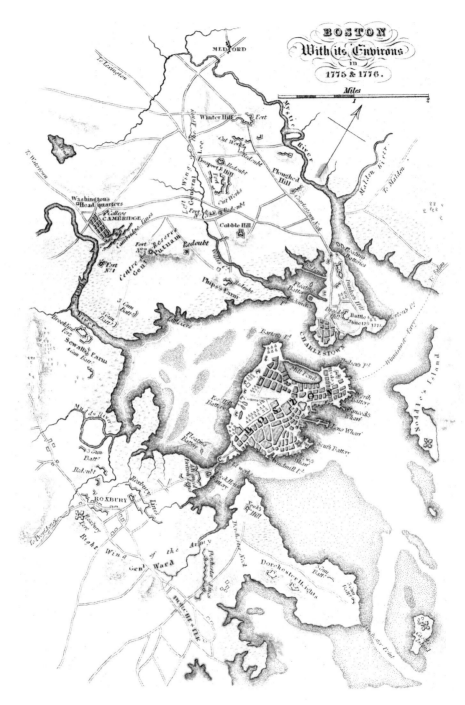

Washington's first test as leader of the new Continental Army came during the Battle for Boston in 1775 and 1776. (Map—*Boston and Its Environs in 1775 & 1776*)

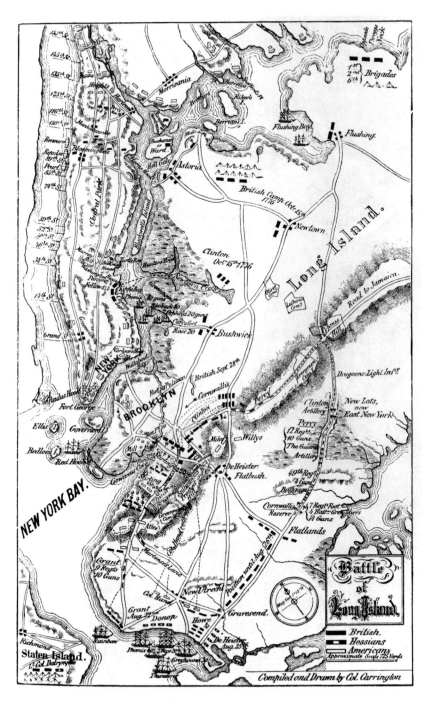

A devastating defeat for Washington and his army, the Battle of Long Island ended with the army's narrow escape across the East River under a prolonged fog. (Map of the Battle of Long Island, 1876[?], *The American Revolution: A Picture Sourcebook*, published by Dover Pictorial Archive Series, 1975)

This iconic image of Washington is also much loved for its excellent representation of Washington as a calm, steady, and determined leader, dedicated to his men. (*Washington Crossing the Delaware*, engraved by Paul Giradet, after Emmanuel Gottlieb Leutze, published by Goupil & Co., New York, 1853)

At the Battle of Princeton in early 1777, Washington, at the forefront of his lines, led his men to a convincing rout of the British—even being heard to shout "It's a fine fox chase, my boys!" as he pursued the fleeing redcoats. (*Washington at the Battle of Princeton*, engraver unknown, published by Louis Kurz, Chicago, c. 1911)

Washington's beloved home, Mount Vernon, as it was during his lifetime. (West front of Mount Vernon, oil on canvas, attributed to Edward Savage, c. 1792)

The West front of Mount Vernon, as it looks now. (Photograph by Hal Conroy, c. 1991)

The most public room in Washington's home, the large dining room, where the Washingtons entertained scores of guests over the years.

The Washingtons placed this painting of the Virgin Mary in the large dining room, one of their most frequently used rooms. (Portrait of the Virgin Mary, pastel painting, possibly after Rosalba Carriera, eighteenth century)

Washington's bedchamber at Mount Vernon, the scene of his death on December 14, 1799.

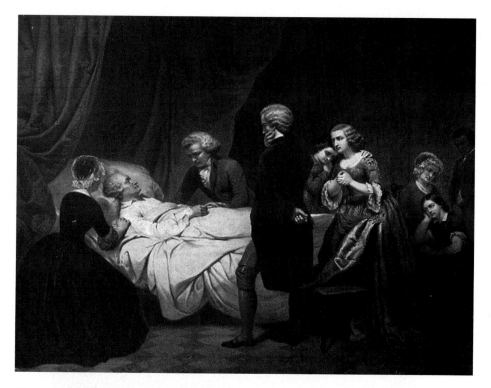

The end of Washington's life came quickly, yet he faced it with steady, calm determination and concern for others. (*Life of George Washington: The Christian*, lithograph by Claude Regnier, after the painting by Junius Brutus Stearns, 1853)

This sculpture of Washington at age 53 is considered the most accurate representation of Washington since it was created from a "life mask" shaped by applying wet plaster directly to Washington's face. (terra cotta bust of George Washington, Jean-Antoine Houdon, 1785)

culiarly designated by Providence for the display of human greatness and felicity.

In this stage, America had been favored more than any other nation with respect to its system of liberty. As Washington's eye swept the globe, it also swept back in time:

> Nothing can illustrate these observations more forcibly, than a recollection of the happy conjuncture of times and circumstances, under which our Republic assumed its rank among the Nations. The foundation of our Empire was not laid in the gloomy age of Ignorance and Superstition, but at an Epocha when the rights of mankind were better understood and more clearly defined, than at any former period.

Then Washington listed various forms of progress that had altered the world:

> ... the growing refinement of Manners, the growing liberality of Sentiment, and above all, *the pure and benign light of Revelation,* have had ameliorating influence on *mankind* and *increased* the blessings of Society. [Emphasis added.][41]

Yet the Washington who wrote these lines in 1783 never forgot the disease, misery, icy cold, and horrible wounds that his army suffered through in the long years of war. Washington's story of Providence is not solely a triumphal story. On the contrary, it is, as President Abraham Lincoln reflected on it in his own second inaugural address, far more steeped in suffering and bloodshed than any of those who were protagonists in the Civil War had earlier dreamed. The God of Providence is just, but not vindictive, and his aim is reformation and new beginning, not destruction. But his justice is far more demanding, more terrible, than many have the courage to imagine.

The Providence that ruled over Valley Forge and six years of frequent retreats and constant bloody and gangrened wounds, the Providence that ruled over Bull Run and Antietam and the Wilderness with their hundreds of thousands of fallen and shattered bodies—that Providence was not the rational God of deism but the just God of the terrible swift sword, who tramples, still today, on the vineyards where the grapes of wrath are stored. In the dark years 1776 and 1777, Washington drank from the same cup handed down to Lincoln.

The historians, we think, underestimate the depth of Washington's soul. Washington plumbed the depths of his men's capacity to suffer, in the name of liberty, under the hard judgments of the Providence that blessed them, yes, but only at the cost of blood and, for very many, life itself. This was a tough man. As his God was a tough God.

The toughness of Washington's faith, the evidence shows, was an important key to his equanimity in defeat and weary despair, as well as in victory and exultation. We shall look into Washington's idea of God further in Chapter 10. Meanwhile, we turn to the understanding of God behind his public statements (Chapter 8), and then in his private life (Chapter 9).

Chapter 8

WASHINGTON'S
PUBLIC PRAYERS

No People can be bound to acknowledge and adore the invisible hand, which conducts the Affairs of men more than the People of the United States. Every step, by which they have advanced to the character of an independent nation, seems to have been distinguished by some token of providential agency.

—Washington's First Inaugural Address,
April 30, 1789[1]

For generations, Christians have rejoiced in the private prayers attributed to Washington on his knees at Valley Forge and elsewhere. These were personal prayers, the existence of which has been disputed by later historians for lack of documentary records from verifiable eyewitnesses, and out of suspicion about the reliability of Parson Weems and other early biographers. Without relying upon those disputed accounts, however, it may be useful to consider documents of Washington that are clearly on the public record. The question we now want to ask of these documents is this: What is the concept of God that makes sense of what Washington asked from God, in public documents issued under his own name?

We think it best to go paragraph by paragraph through these public prayers, pausing each time to bring to light some of the implications of what we have just read. For sometimes words are so familiar to us that, in the light of other possible ways of understanding them, we do not grasp their whole significance. We must remember, for instance, that most historians read these texts as if Washington was a deist. But these public prayers, read carefully, cannot possibly be deist prayers, even when *deist* is meant in the broadest possible sense. On the contrary, they read as though they were prayers to the quite familiar God of the Bible.

In short, as we read these prayers, we think it wise to keep in mind the following principle of interpretation: The *names* by which Washington addressed God are nonsectarian, nondenominational names, whose high level of abstraction makes them seem deist. But the *verbs* Washington used for the actions he was asking God to perform describe an outline of God that is very like the Hebrew God, the God of the Prophets and the psalmist, as well as the God of Jesus and his disciples. It seems obvious that the nouns must be understood in the light of the verbs. The nouns may *sound* like deist names, but they must be interpreted in the light of the actions that were assigned to them.

The first of Washington's public proclamations we examine is his Thanksgiving Proclamation of October 3, 1789.

THE THANKSGIVING PROCLAMATION OF 1789

Whereas it is the duty of all Nations to acknowledge the providence of Almighty God, to obey his will, to be grateful for his benefits, and humbly to implore his protection and favor, and Whereas both Houses of Congress have by their joint Committee requested me "to recommend to the People of the United States a day of public thanksgiving and prayer to be observed by acknowledging with grateful hearts the many signal favors of Almighty God, especially by affording them an opportunity peaceably to establish a form of government for their safety and happiness."

Now therefore I do recommend and assign Thursday the 26th day of November next to be devoted by the People of these States to the service of that great and glorious Being, who is the beneficent Author of all the good that was, that is, or that will be. That we may then all unite in rendering unto him our sincere and humble thanks, for his kind care and protection of the People of this country previous to their becoming a Nation, for the signal and manifold mercies, and the favorable interpositions of his providence, which we experienced in the course and conclusion of the late war, for the great degree of tranquillity, union, and plenty, which we have since enjoyed, for the peaceable and rational manner in which we have been enabled to establish constitutions of government for our safety and happiness, and particularly the national One now lately instituted, for the civil and religious liberty with which we are blessed, and the means we have of acquiring and diffusing useful knowledge and in general for all the great and various favors which he hath been pleased to confer upon us.

And also that we may then unite in most humbly offering our prayers and supplications to the great Lord and Ruler of Nations and beseech him to pardon our national and other transgressions, to enable us all, whether in public or private stations, to perform our several and relative duties properly and punctually, to render our national government a blessing to all the People, by constantly being a government of wise, just and constitutional laws, discreetly and faithfully executed and obeyed, to protect and guide all Sovereigns and Nations (especially such as have shown kindness unto us) and to bless them with good government, peace, and concord. To promote the knowledge and practice of true religion and virtue, and the encrease of science among them and Us, and generally to grant unto all Mankind such a degree of temporal prosperity as he alone knows to be best.[2]

Washington asserted "the duty of all nations" in regard to God. Is it really true that whole nations, as distinct from the individuals who make them up, have duties? That would seem to create a number of problems for a pluralistic nation, in which various peoples see their duties in one way, and others in another. Many today are certain that *individuals* have duties toward God. Yet most have a harder time imagining how nations do, and how nations would best fulfill such duties if they did. Yet whatever we today may say, or think, Washington wrote, "It is the duty of nations." That is a very strong claim. The very same claim was also made by Lincoln some generations later and has been repeated by other presidents and public figures since.

A God to whom whole nations have duties would seem to be a very special kind of God. It would be odd to imagine whole nations having a duty toward the god of deism, for instance. Such a god is not a person or a judge or even a creator of all things. *Creator* seems too anthropomorphic a conception, too magical, for the sort of law-like, rational governor of all things—the immanent spirit in all things—that the deists had in mind. Contemplating the orderliness of the stars in the black night, the regularity of the seasons, and the beauty of mathematics, many astute minds of the eighteenth century had no difficulty sensing a kind of universal rational spirit penetrating all things. They thought of this being as the "god of nature," the rational god of mathematicians and physicists.

The laws of nature, such as the laws of geometry and mathematics, biology, and perhaps even psychology, understood in a scientific sense—these a deist might recognize, metaphorically, as "nature's laws" or even "god's will." But to imagine that god has a will independent of laws that reason has uncovered would seem to a deist more like superstition than like religion, and quite unworthy of a fully reasonable human being.

"To humbly implore his protection and favor" must also seem to a deist a childish and immature fantasy, a projection of infantile desire, such as Sigmund Freud was a century later to portray in *The Future of an Illusion*. Yet here was the practical farmer and soldier, General Washington, and then President Washington, asserting such fantasies as solemn duties to be observed throughout the land. Such notions do not accord with the deistic conception of god. To the deist sort of god there would be no point in praying. Such a god works no miracles and plays no favorites. One might cherish toward the deist god a sense of awe, even reverence, but to imagine that one might ask favors of it would be a bit naive, as if one were imagining god to be some sort of humanlike being. This would be to fail to grasp the remoteness and vastness and impersonality of the god of nature.

The first duty that Washington said nations were expected to perform toward God was "to acknowledge God." But why would nature's god, so vast, cold, and indifferent, need acknowledgment by such as we, mere passing specks in the universe? By contrast, the God of Abraham, Isaac, Jacob, and Jesus does insist that whole nations, as well as individuals, should become conscious of what he has done for them—to pay attention, to acknowledge him and heed him.

Notice also the three other duties of nations toward God: not only "to acknowledge His providence," but "to obey his will"; next, "to be grateful for his benefits"; and, finally, "to implore" his protection and favor. To pay attention to his acts of providence, to obey, to be grateful, and to implore his favor—duties such as these suggest something very like the Jewish and Christian God, and not at all the god of the scientists and deists.

The second paragraph of Washington's address also deserves comment. The president urged a whole day of prayer and thanksgiving to be set aside. And he particularly urged it to be observed with sincerity—and something more than sincerity: "our sincere and humble thanks." He urged his fellow citizens to acknowledge "the signal and manifold mercies." That word *signal* was a special favorite of Washington's (and some of the other Founders). By *signal* they seem to have meant "stand out," "flash," like a light from a lighthouse. You can't miss this signal in the darkness. It was *meant* to stand out. It is part of a pattern, a sign of favor and blessing, a sign intended to encourage a people in dark hours.

Signal mercies—those that stand out. Many such events from the War of Independence remained vivid in Washington's mind for many years afterward. It was as if he had seen the hand of God intervening in human affairs with his own eyes. He spoke next of "the favorable interpositions of his providence, which we experienced in the course and conclusion of the late war." Note the strong word *interpositions*. In other words, Providence rearranged things, intruded in their positions. And for Washington, this was not a matter of speculation. He called it a matter of "experience."

More than once, Washington commented that it would take a particularly hard-hearted man not to notice and not to be grateful for favors rendered, in such extreme circumstances, when life or death hung in the balance, and liberty's success or failure was at stake. The implication here was that God, the Almighty, the Governor of the universe, the Author of all good things, *cared* about the cause of liberty and those who committed themselves to that cause.

In his second paragraph, Washington also characterized the God he was invoking, so that the citizens of the United States would not mistake who he meant. He asked the people of the United States to devote Thanksgiving Day "to the service of that great and glorious Being, who is the beneficent Author of all the good that was, that is, or that will be." Washington's God is the Maker of all good things, in short, a God who is good, beneficent, great, and glorious, and who is to be thanked for "his kind care" of the American people, even his "protection" of them in all those years "previous to their becoming a Nation." So this is a God who watches over his favored people down the years, a God with a historical view and interposing care, a God of "signal and manifold mercies," that is, mercies that extend in every direction, as here enumerated. In addition, this God is "the Lord and Ruler of Nations." And Washington urged Americans to beseech him to do some amazing things: to pardon their sins, their national sins and their personal sins; to enable them all, in public and in private duties, to perform those duties properly and punctually; and to protect and guide all sovereigns and nations. What sort of deism was it that would expect God to keep an accounting of "sins," whatever those might have been to a deist, and far more than that, to be able to pardon sins? There is no greater attribute of God than that he is able to make sins disappear, simply wipe them away. That is an act of Spirit and Truth, not of material power.

Moreover, in asking God to protect and guide other nations, Washington singled out "especially such as have shown kindness to us." In other words, God should be favorably disposed not only to America, as shown by his signal acts on its behalf, but also toward its friends.

Just to recognize this long list as actions that God had taken on America's behalf, as Washington did, is to grasp the point that Jesus made when he instructed his followers to pray in "the Lord's Prayer": "Give us this day our daily bread." Even the humblest events in our lives are within the Father's caring. Every good thing—all the things we need—come from him.

At this point, as if to make sure that people did not imagine this "Being" as abstract and remote, Washington reminded the nation of the many discreet but crucially important human events and turns of nature that had made possible its independence and the happy formation of its Constitution and form of government. He reminded Americans that these humble realities were gifts. And Americans must, as decent creatures must, acknowledge God's care with heartfelt thanks. In short, the God of Washington reaches down into history, onto *this* battlefield, to protect *this* man and that, *this* outpost and that, and *this* turn of the tide, and *this* outcome of the war. Not a remote God, but a God present every day, in every need. A God whose "interpositions" on America's behalf Washington had experienced.

We recall Washington's gratitude to Providence for sparing him in the battle on the Monongahela led by General Braddock, though his coat was riddled with bullets, and his horses were shot from under him—a care and protection before the United States had become a nation. And as John Jay had noted in *The Federalist* (Number 2), Providence had "in a particular manner blessed it with a variety of soils and productions and watered it with innumerable streams for the delight and accommodation of its inhabitants."[3] Indeed, Providence had given "this one connected country to one united people— a people descended from the same ancestors, speaking the same language, professing the same religion, attached to the same principles of government, [and] very similar in their manners and customs." There were also its traditions of liberty under law. All these were true blessings.

And then there were "the signal interpositions" of God's providence at the Battle of Long Island and likewise at so many other battles—the capturing of the enemy's plans, sudden favorable turns in the weather, and the overcoming of many hazards (not least, premature discovery) in the bold nighttime raid across the icy Delaware.

Washington could not stop himself from mentioning, too, "the conclusion of the late war"—recalling the event at Yorktown he had spent years waiting for—the moment the enemy fell into the same trap as he himself had, when he put his vulnerable troops upon Long Island and found himself shut in a vise between two forces, escaping only by a sort of miracle. For the British fell into a similar trap on the peninsula at Yorktown, when Washington quickly snapped closed the trap by land, and the French fleet snapped it shut by sea. And the British experienced no interposing miracle.

Washington had often counted his blessings, privately and publicly (although we know more about the latter). He meant to teach the new citizenry he led the habit of doing the same. His main underlying task as first chief magistrate of the land, he knew, was to establish lasting traditions that would befit a citizenry worthy to be free, and apt to maintain its liberties.[4]

Washington had also come back from retirement, reluctantly at first, in order to help bring the new nation out of the disunity into which it had fallen—so swiftly—after the successful conclusion of the war. Many in Europe were mocking America, so lightly ruled by the king of England, and now so badly ruled by its own so-called self-government. All Washington's efforts in the field, all the sufferings of his men, were coming to seem in vain. And so he had joined the Constitutional Convention and risked his future reputation on the squabbling of the same sort of representative politicians who, after all their solemn promises, had not been able to raise funds for his army, or to treat his men honorably.

Then he saw another kind of miracle happen, the writing of a brilliant Constitution in a mere fifty-three days. And for these great blessings, too, rising out of the troubles that might have endured, he asked his people to give thanks: "for the great degree of tranquillity, union, and plenty, which we have since enjoyed, for the peaceable and rational manner in which we have been enabled to establish constitutions of government for our safety and happiness, and particularly the national One now lately instituted." From this Constitution there flowed blessings almost unparalleled among the nations of this earth: "for the civil and religious liberty with which we are blessed." It was for this, above all, that Washington had watched his amateur army fight so hard, suffer so much, and, in heavy numbers, die.

Washington did not forget those other, seemingly more secular blessings, which in his eyes also counted as gifts of the Author of all goods: "and the means we have of acquiring and diffusing useful knowledge and in general for all the great and various favors which he hath been pleased to confer upon us." Americans in those days had much to be thankful for, and knew it. Their sentiments and their ways of expressing it, led by their president, had many precedents. They imitated similar scenes in the Bible. They were not out of tune with the gratitude the small band sheltering in the tiny *Mayflower* offered upon reaching this land in 1620.

Washington's proclamation then continued: "And also that we may then unite in most humbly offering our prayers and supplications to the great Lord and Ruler of Nations and beseech him to pardon our national and other transgressions." As we have seen, it would be something of a superstition for strict deists to offer, humbly or otherwise, "prayers and supplications" to a god who is impersonal, indifferent, and quite remote from human needs or feelings. But to "beseech him to pardon our national and other transgressions" would blow the fuse of any deism worthy of its name. What "transgressions" of humans, let alone what "national transgressions," could possibly be of interest to an impersonal and remote cause of being? If one believed in sins and their forgiveness, there was no point in being a deist. One might as well be a Jew or a Christian.

But the president pressed on in the matters for which the citizens should implore God, as least as he conceived of God:

> ... to enable us all, whether in public or private stations, to perform our several and relative duties properly and punctually, to render our national government a blessing to all the People, by constantly being a government of wise, just and constitutional laws, discreetly and faithfully executed and obeyed, to protect and guide all Sovereigns and Nations (especially such as have shown kindness unto us) and to bless them with good government, peace, and concord.

In the last sentence of his proclamation, Washington asked God for one more thing, an amazing thing: "to promote the knowledge and practice of *true* religion and virtue," as if to make clear that there were *false* religions, too, and false ways of being religious, and that from these, too, Americans needed to be protected. The introduction of the concept of truth to a commitment to religion is a very notable step.

From this proclamation we learn that the God to whom Washington bade the nation pray was at one and the same time the God of all mankind, who had all in his care, and also the God who had a special kind of care for the people of the United States, both singly and as a whole. He was a God who watched over historical events and interposed his mercies among them. He forgave sins, and he was to be implored, obeyed, thanked, and honored. He was to be honored by individuals in their private capacities and also in their corporate and public capacities, as a whole nation. We may leave it to the reader to compare Washington's idea of God with the god of deism. The Psalms of David would have been familiar to Washington from his youth, since the Psalms figure prominently in the everyday liturgy of the Anglican church. We believe that an attentive reader will recognize in them the precursors of Washington's Thanksgiving reflections. Here, for instance, is Psalm 67, verses 1–6:

> God be merciful unto us, and bless us; and cause his face to shine upon us . . .
>
> That thy way may be known upon the earth, thy saving health among all nations.
>
> Let the people praise thee, O God; let all the people praise thee.
>
> O let the nations be glad and sing for joy; for thou shalt judge the people righteously, and govern the nations upon the earth . . .
>
> Let the people praise thee, O God; let all the people praise thee.
>
> Then shall the earth yield her increase; and God, even our own God, shall bless us.

THE THANKSGIVING PROCLAMATION OF 1795

There is a second Thanksgiving Proclamation that particularly bears reflection in the light of our central inquiry: Who *was* Washington's God? Let us attend to this much-neglected proclamation for briefer comment:

> *When we review the calamities which afflict so many other nations, the present condition of the United States affords much matter of consolation and satisfaction. Our exemption hitherto from foreign war, an increasing prospect of the continuance of that exemption, the great degree of internal tranquillity we have enjoyed, the recent confirmation of that tranquillity by the suppression of an insurrection which so wantonly threatened it, the happy course of our public affairs in general, the unexampled prosperity of all classes of our citizens, are circumstances which peculiarly mark our situation with indications of the Divine beneficence toward us. In such a*

state of things it is in an especial manner our duty as a people, with devout reverence and affectionate gratitude, to acknowledge our many and great obligations to Almighty God and to implore Him to continue and confirm the blessings we experience.

Deeply penetrated with this sentiment, I, George Washington, President of the United States, do recommend to all religious societies and denominations, and to all persons whomsoever within the United States to set apart and observe Thursday, the 19th day of February next, as a day of public thanksgiving and prayer, and on that day to meet together and render their sincere and hearty thanks to the Great Ruler of Nations for the manifold and signal mercies which distinguish our lot as a nation, particularly for the possession of constitutions of government which unite and by their union establish liberty with order; for the preservation of our peace, foreign and domestic; for the seasonable control which has been given to a spirit of disorder in the suppression of the late insurrection, and generally, for the prosperous course of our affairs, public and private; and at the same time humbly and fervently to beseech the kind Author of these blessings graciously to prolong them to us; to imprint on our hearts a deep and solemn sense of our obligations to Him for them; to teach us rightly to estimate their immense value; to preserve us from the arrogance of prosperity, and from hazarding the advantages we enjoy by delusive pursuits; to dispose us to merit the continuance of His favors by not abusing them; by our gratitude for them, and by a correspondent conduct as citizens and men; to render this country more and more a safe and propitious asylum for the unfortunate of other countries; to extend among us true and useful knowledge; to diffuse and establish habits of sobriety, order, morality, and piety; and finally, to impart all the blessings we possess, or ask for ourselves, to the whole family of mankind.[5]

A deist would be unlikely to see signs of "Divine beneficence" in exemption from foreign wars, internal tranquility, the suppression of an insurrection, and unexampled prosperity. We need not doubt that Washington, as well as the deist, recognized that these events had natural and human causes. Yet he clearly believed that even natural causes worked from the web of God's power and causation, in such a way that in recognizing the power of nature, one also recognized one's duty of gratitude to the powers of the Creator. Washington himself explained the relation of nature to God's action in terms of the "contingencies," "concatenation of causes," and "circumstances" through which Providence acts in human history, as we shall see in Chapter 10. Such ideas had deep roots in Christian theology and standard preaching in the Anglican church, at least since Richard Hooker (1554–1600).

In giving thanks to God at meals, for instance, one gives thanks to the farmers, millers, and bakers who brought the bread to the table, as well as to the Almighty, who blessed the harvests, tempered the weather, and fashioned the world in such a way that food on the table and mutual dependence were normal. It was not as if such causes—God and the baker—competed against each other. Although a crucial part of the bread came from the baker, the way all such things worked together was due to the sort of world that God conceived of, executed, and approved.

It is also apparent in this Thanksgiving Proclamation that we have many and varied obligations to the Almighty. Washington describes them as if such obligations are relations of duty between persons. He seemed to imagine God as a person capable of hearing prayers and, as he saw best, responding to them. For our part, Washington tells us, we ought "to acknowledge our many and great obligations to Almighty God and to implore Him to continue and confirm the blessings we experience." We already have experience of those blessings. But their continuance depends, in some way that we do not see, upon our fulfilling "our many and great obligations" to the Almighty. "Ask and it shall be given unto you," Jesus taught us (Matthew 7:7; Luke 11:9; John 16:24). Washington seems to be heeding that lesson, in urging us "to implore" the Almighty to continue the blessings for which we thank Him.

The president then urges citizens to meet together and offer "sincere and hearty thanks to the Great Ruler of Nations," a vast and great God, indeed. And why? Because of—here comes one of Washington's signature phrases again—"the manifold and signal mercies which distinguish our lot as a nation." In the case of the United States, the mercies of God, which are abundant to every nation, nonetheless here stand out, distinguish us among the nations, and discernibly make our lot special, as immigrants constantly experience. These blessings impose special obligations of thanksgiving upon us, as well as faithfulness to our duties, lest we lose such blessings.

Washington then lists our reasons for gratitude, including "the preservation of our peace . . . the seasonable control which has been given to a spirit of disorder . . . and . . . for the prosperous course of our affairs." And lest we lose these benefits, Washington rushes us onward to "beseech the kind Author of these blessings graciously to prolong them to us" and "to dispose us to merit the continuance of His favors."

And just how shall we "merit" these great goods? "By not abusing them; by our gratitude for them, and by a correspondent conduct as citizens and men." Not exactly a light task, all that.

Washington's prayers are not exactly self-centered, complacent, or arrogant prayers. They are generous, embracing the whole world in their supplications. They are self-critical, urging all fellow citizens to demean themselves humbly, and to do their duty with regularity, to mind their daily habits and those of their children, and to give thanks, constantly to give thanks. Not bad prayers at all. And to come back to the point of our inquiry: These are not the prayers of a deist, let alone a secular humanist.

THE CIRCULAR TO THE STATES OF 1783

I now make it my earnest prayer that God would have you, and the State over which you preside, in his holy protection, that he would incline the hearts of the Citizens to cultivate a spirit of subordination and obedience to Government, to entertain a brotherly affec-

tion and love for one another, for their fellow Citizens of the United States at large, and particularly for their brethren who have served in the Field, and finally, that he would most graciously be pleased to dispose us all, to do Justice, to love mercy, and to demean ourselves with that Charity, humility, and pacific temper of mind, which were the Characteristicks of the Divine Author of our Blessed Religion, and without an humble invitation of whose example in these things, we can never hope to be a happy Nation.[6]

Because of its continued popularity today, we want to touch again on this "circular," a third public prayer of Washington's that deserves reflection, a few words at a time. The circular was written by Washington while he was still the commander of the Continental Army and was addressed to the governors of all the states, since Washington was about to retire from command. Its concluding paragraph begins with these words: "I now make it my earnest prayer, that God would have you, and the State over which you preside, in his holy protection," a turn of thought that makes no sense from a strictly deist point of view. One clue is "holy protection," since no one supposes that the deist god is "holy." The second is the very notion that the deist god picks favorites in history.

What follows is not a whit more deist:

... that he would incline the hearts of the Citizens to cultivate a spirit of subordination and obedience to Government, to entertain a brotherly affection and love for one another, for their fellow Citizens of the United States at large, and particularly for their brethren who have served in the Field.

These phrases, too—about obedience to rulers, and about love—sound closer to certain passages in the Epistles of St. Paul and much more Christian than deist.[7]

The next passage is indisputably biblical in its tone and phraseology: "and finally, that he would most graciously be pleased to dispose us all, to do Justice, to love mercy." The words recall the question of the prophet Micah (6:8), who asked, "What doth the Lord require of thee, but to do justly, and to love mercy, and to walk humbly with thy God?" And then the final appeal includes this unmistakable evocation:

> ... and to demean ourselves with that Charity, humility and pacific temper of mind, which were the Characteristicks of the Divine Author of our blessed Religion, and without an humble imitation of whose example in these things, we can never hope to be a happy Nation.

Washington, it seems, meant without equivocation to point to Jesus Christ, although by indirection, by tying "Divine Author of our blessed Religion" to those traits of the Beatitudes of the Sermon on the Mount by which Christ is most distinguished among men. These very last words also call to mind Washington's advice to the Delaware chiefs, that if they would be a happy nation, they ought to learn the religion of Jesus Christ. The "Divine Author of our blessed Religion"—not just our religion but "our *blessed* Religion"—is Jesus Christ, who calls us to imitate him with humility, and to walk in his example. This, too, is far from deist.

Is it necessary for anyone in a biblically literate age to ask of which religion is it that its founder is divine, and distinguished by the following "Characteristicks": charity, humility, a pacific temper of mind, and a wish that his disciples would offer a humble imitation of his example to the world?

Deism, you say?

CONCLUDING REFLECTIONS

Looking to the record of Washington's public prayers, which in every important particular are backed up by private expressions of faith in his correspondence and personal writings, the historian who claims that Washington was a deist is flying in the face of a mountain of evidence. Yet to concede this is not to concede that Washington was quite the explicit and fully orthodox Christian that a few other historians have claimed to see. That he was not a deist is fairly clear, even quite clear. That he was a Christian is a more shadowy affirmation.

That it was not to the God of deism that President Washington was asking the nation to pray becomes even clearer when one notices *what* Washington in these prayers expected God *to do,* and what specific requests Washington recommended that his fellow citizens address to God.

It is possible, of course, that Washington was a hypocrite, that he did not believe these fantasies himself but commended them to the public only because he was a politician and believed that this was what the public wanted. In other words, he was cynical.

The truth is, however, that such public proclamations of Washington form a seamless garment with his private letters, journals, and reflections. This is the way the private man also thought and felt and acted. More than once he spent an entire day in prayer and fasting. It seems to us that this public proclamation reveals the private Washington quite simply and directly, without affectation or artifice. This is the way he was.

If such public prayers are as close as Washington was willing to come to confessing his faith in Christianity—and he did not really go much further in his private writings—then overpowering evidence for his commitment to a full-dress Christianity is not to be found in the printed record. That he was a very good man in his moral life, stayed well within the bounds of Christian moral imperatives, and fulfilled a very high measure of nearly all Christian virtues is testified to by many witnesses. From the way he lived, his stepgranddaughter and many others close to him thought it impossible to conclude that he was anything but a devoted Christian.

Still, the stated beliefs Washington lived by fell rather short of the full Christian creed. To confess the latter would have required very little of him. Yet he evaded the many invitations offered him in public and in private to do so.

To this point, then, there remains much that is not yet clear in our minds about Washington's God that we must yet inquire into.

Perhaps it suffices at this point to conclude that what we have learned from his public prayers is that his concept of God was far more biblical than deist. Yet it seems more Hebrew than Christian. His official words seem closer to the One God of the Hebrew Prophets and the psalmist than to the Father, Son, and Paraclete of, say, the fourteenth chapter of the Gospel of St. John.

Perhaps in practice many busy and practical Christian men and women have a similarly compact view of God, even if in church they do "confess" the Creed. Not much accustomed to heavy speculation or precise theological thought, they may not have given much effort to inquiring into how they actually explain what they mean by "Father, Son, and Holy Spirit" or what practical difference belief in the Trinity makes to their lives. For all practical purposes, they, too, are biblical in their faith, at times in the mode (when they think about it at all) of vaguely imagining a singular Creator, Providence, Judge, Governor—more-or-less like the Declaration of Independence. (Hence, author John Derbyshire's quip that the lazy Christian mind is reflexively "deist.") Possibly, at other times when they pray, such practical Christians may imagine the humble, pacific Divine Author of their religion, distinguished by his charity, as Washington did in his Circular to the States. Busy, practical Christians may do both of these things, without trying to examine them together, or to distinguish them, or to indulge in any theological speculation at all. Americans, de Tocqueville noted, although far more religious than Europeans, did not spend excessive time on matters of doctrine. George Washington certainly did not.

Chapter 9

A VERY PRIVATE
CHRISTIAN

Without making ostentatious professions of religion, he was a
sincere believer in the Christian faith, and a truly devout man.

—John Marshall, Fourth Chief Justice of
the U.S. Supreme Court[1]

THE QUIET SUNDAYS

Sometimes, the best evidence is the dog that doesn't bark. Dogs barked often at Thomas Jefferson during his lifetime, publicly accusing him of being a deist and, worse, an atheist—equivalent in those days to an immoralist. Such public attacks were not launched against Washington during his lifetime. He had acquired an almost mythic status as a model Christian statesman.

The inventive storyteller Parson Weems did not create this myth. It preceded his book's appearance on the scene, and Weems merely coasted on its waves, embellishing the widely shared memory of the man, and adding to it inventions that made the narrative accord with classic hero tales. Let us glance at some of the nitty-gritty details of the attacks on Jefferson and then turn to the realities of Washington's private life.

During the presidential campaign of 1800, opponents launched a bitter attack upon Thomas Jefferson, candidate of the Republican Party (as it was then called), on the grounds that he was not a

Christian. Some editors accused him vituperatively of being a deist, which some equated with atheist or quasi atheist. They asked voters how they could trust a man who had no divine Judge to hold him accountable. The main newspaper of the Federalist Party, the *Gazette of the United States*, blasted Jefferson as "an enemy to pure morals and religion, and consequently an enemy to his country and his God." The ferocity of this sentiment shows in its bombast. The editors went so far as to describe the election as one between "GOD—AND A RELIGIOUS PRESIDENT; or . . . JEFFERSON AND NO GOD!!!"

Even Alexander Hamilton, Washington's worldly Treasury Secretary, was deeply worried about a possible Jeffersonian administration. Perhaps "some legal or constitutional step" could be taken, he wrote to John Jay, "to prevent an atheist in religion, and a fanatic in politics, from getting possession of the helm of state."[2]

At no point in George Washington's long public life were such accusations leveled publicly against him, although a small number of preachers wrote letters attacking his (as they saw it) "deism." The lack of public protest of the sort that afflicted Jefferson is a kind of negative testimony to the majority view of Washington as a discreet but steady Christian.

Some critics might have been unsure of Washington's doctrinal orthodoxy and uncertain concerning the precise extent to which Washington might be Anglican, or evangelical, or Masonic. Nearly all took him as in some acceptable sense a God-fearing, Providence-adoring, thanks-giving Christian man.

As a doting stepfather to Martha's two children and stepgrandfather to four grandchildren, Washington sent away to Britain for beautifully bound and personally embossed Bibles for each of them, as well as other books on the reasons for Christianity and devotional prayers. He encouraged them in Christian faithfulness. Sunday was a day of relaxation and of rest. Washington's diaries are sometimes make references to Sunday fox hunting, horseback riding, entertaining, visiting, and writing. But it was also a quiet time, a time for some prayers and sermon reading when the weather was too inclement for trips to church. Sometimes, too, during long Sunday afternoons, the general read sermons to Martha for Sabbath observance. Some hours on Sunday were also reserved for letter writing. Julian Niemcewicz, a Polish visitor and travel chronicler, left behind a marvelous recollection on his time at Mount Vernon, in which he described how the Washingtons allowed him to entertain himself walking the grounds quietly on Sunday, while they went about their own quiet time. For example:

> 3 June. The next day, which was Sunday, the Gl. retired to write letters, this day being set aside for this activity. I went for a walk with Mr. Law. . . . In the evening, no music, not even a game of chess; it was Sunday; everyone retired around nine o'clock.[3]

There are a number of other witnesses to the fact that Washington, even as president, normally observed the Sabbath rest, marking the day as different from other days. There are similar witnesses to his habit of inviting a guest to say grace before meals, or leading it himself, except on those occasions when such a gesture might have seemed out of place.

SCHOOLED IN THE ANGLICAN FAITH

The genius of George Washington was to shape himself to become a man of high integrity and sober reserve, a man of honor and internal fortitude, who could be trusted by all Americans, of all backgrounds. It was as if he knew that he might one day have to be the only man in the whole country of whom it could be said that everybody trusted him.

Whether as general of the Continental Army, or as abiding presence over the Constitutional Convention, or as the nation's first president, he was always the most acceptable, often the unanimous, choice of his peers. Though there were several contemporaries greater than he in learning, in rhetorical skills, and in legislative ability, there was no one else whom everybody in the land could equally look up to, and as happily follow. A large part of Washington's strategy in preparing himself for his life's work was quite in keeping with his religious and family upbringing. He was well schooled in his faith and modestly collected (and read) books about faith during his whole life. He collected more than three score volumes on religion, plus hundreds of printed sermons that admiring ministers sent to him. Above all, he learned well the Anglican habits of moderation, reserve, and privacy. As he and his friends thought about such matters, his faith was no one else's business. His faith strengthened him to persevere under immense and long-lasting difficulties. Nonetheless, both his military and his political calling necessitated that this faith, however strong, be carefully couched so as never to become a point of division, contention, or separation from others. Washington schooled himself in keeping his faith out of the sight of others. Even when he sought out groups of ministers to encourage their support for the war effort or their support for the first steps in republican government under the new Constitution, he systematically evaded any of their direct questions about the meaning to him of his Christian faith.[4]

Putting ourselves in his position, we may try to imagine what he could have said that would not be off-putting, either to someone present or to strangers who might later hear of it. He always said enough, and in generic terms, to let everyone see his reliance upon the Almighty, his faith in Providence (even when its ways asked great sufferings of him and his army), and his painfully acquired belief that for most men religion is an indispensable support for faithful moral observance. But he took great care not to reveal the intimate details of his own personal beliefs, or even to suggest that his own mode of belonging should be publicly laid before others.

Just the same, it is quite remarkable how closely his private letters and private notebooks cohere with his public utterances. No one can plausibly argue (as historians have about Jefferson) that what Washington said and wrote in private about religion diverges from what he said and wrote in public. There are some differences in intimacy of tone, of course, and in some details of specificity. But not in substance. In the paintings he bought for his home, in the prayer books he bought for his grandchildren and godchildren, and in some of his personal and private practices (such as private prayer and honoring the Sabbath), one sees better the private tonality and a bit more of the confessional side of the man. These are not in the least inconsistent with his public presentation of himself. On the contrary, they lend it a certain concrete authenticity.

Quite often and openly in his private correspondence with family members and friends, Washington recounted how he had had a vivid experience of the interposition of Providence on his behalf—in saving his life at the Monongahela, in halting the headlong flight of his army at Monmouth, in bringing news of Benedict Arnold's intention to hand West Point over to the British before the plan could be executed, in bringing many causes together to make possible his total surprise of the Hessians at Trenton, and many others. His private letters revealed, if anything, a more touching piety in daily, pedestrian matters than his public statements of gratitude to God. For instance, he wrote to Richard Washington, his London merchant, who Washington felt must be a relation, on October 20, 1761:

> Since my last of the 14th. July I have in appearance been very near my last gasp; the Indisposition then spoken of Increased upon me and I fell into a very low and dangerous State. I once thought the grim King woud certainly master my utmost efforts and that I must sink—in spite of a noble struggle but thank God I have now got the better of the disorder and shall soon be restord I hope to perfect health again.[5]

Another example:

We have had one of the most severe Droughts in these parts that ever was known and without a speedy Interposition of Providence (in sending us moderate and refreshing Rains to Molifie and soften the Earth) we shall not make one oz of Tobacco this year.[6]

And, finally, one more:

As you must be convinced that whatever affects your happiness or welfare cannot be indifferent to me I need not tell you, that I was most sensibly affected by your letter of the 20th of January [about the death of your son]. Yes, my dear Sir, I sincerely condole with you the loss of a worthy, amiable, and valuable Son! . . . Time alone can blunt the keen edge of afflictions; Philosophy and our Religion hold out to us such hopes as will, upon proper reflection, enable us to bear with fortitude the most calamitous incidents of life and these are all that can be expected from the feelings of humanity; is all which they will yield.[7]

Often, as above, Washington was obliged to write to dear friends who had just lost a much-loved son or daughter to death. Invariably, however contrary to their own human feelings this must have seemed at the time, he counseled submission to the will of Providence—and not only to the *will* of Providence, but to the wisdom and *goodness* of Providence, too, however difficult that was to see at that moment. For instance, there was his letter to Henry Knox:

I have heard of the death of your promising Son with great concern, and sincerely condole with you and Mrs. Knox on the melancholy occasion. Parental feelings are too much alive in the moment of these misfortunes to admit the consolations of religion or philosophy; but I am persuaded reason will call one or both of them to your aid as soon as the keenness of your anguish is abated. He that gave, you know, has a right to take away, his ways are wise, they are inscrutable, and irresistible.[8]

It was advice that Washington would give Knox yet again, five and a half years later, after Knox had now lost three children in quick succession:

From the friendship I have always borne you, and from the interest I have ever taken in whatever relates to your prosperity and happiness, I participated in the sorrows which I know you must have felt for your late heavy losses. But it is not for man to scan the wisdom of Providence. The best he can do, is to submit to its decrees. Reason, religion and Philosophy, teaches [*sic*] us to do this, but 'tis time alone that can ameliorate the pangs of humanity, and soften its woes.[9]

Washington gave the same advice to members of his own family. When his mother died, he consoled his sister with the following words:

Awful, and affecting as the death of a Parent is, there is consolation in knowing, that Heaven has spared ours to an age, beyond which few attain, and favored her with the full enjoyment of her mental faculties, and as much bodily strength as usually falls to the lot of fourscore. Under these considerations and a hope that she is translated to a happier place, it is the duty of her relatives to yield due submission to the decrees of the Creator.[10]

Consistently sounding the same notes, as if suffering from the inscrutable blows of Providence were familiar walking ground for his own soul, Washington counseled Burwell Bassett, a brother-in-law of Martha's who had just lost a child, that the

ways of Providence being inscrutable, and the justice of it not to be scanned by the shallow eye of humanity, nor to be counteracted by the utmost efforts of human power or wisdom, resignation, and as far as the strength of our reason and religion can carry us, a cheerful acquiescence to the Divine Will, is what we are to aim.[11]

In a similar vein yet again, Washington wrote to his friend, and former general, Major General Israel Putnam upon the loss of his wife. Here, though, he made his own Christian beliefs explicit—for how could he counsel someone to behave as a Christian unless he did, too?

> Remembring [sic] that all must die, and that she had lived to an honourable age, I hope you will bear the misfortune with that fortitude and complacency of mind, that become a Man and a Christian.[12]

Eight weeks later, it was Washington's turn to receive consolation over the fatal illness of Martha's beloved daughter, Patsy. To Bassett's condolences, Washington wrote in reply:

> It is an easier matter to conceive, than to describe the distress of this Family; especially that of the unhappy Parent of our Dear Patsy Custis, when I inform you that yesterday the Sweet Innocent Girl Entered into a more happy and peaceful abode than any she has met with in the afflicted Path she hitherto has trod.[13]

The death of children near and dear to him, like the death of his father and brother and sister-in-law, inured him to sorrows near the family hearth.

Recently, one of the two Christian paintings that Washington had hanging in his main dining room at Mount Vernon has been brought back to the mansion and restored to that room. The two paintings are the Virgin Mary with her prayer book (a late-eighteenth-century work from northern Italy, by a woman artist very popular in Britain at that time) and another work whose subject is St. John. The Virgin Mary (see illustrations insert) is now hanging just inside the front door, almost the very first object on which an incoming visitor's eyes would fall, and St. John might well have hung in a balancing position further along the same wall. The special role of these two figures in Washington's own life is not known, except that he did take special care about the symbolism of objects he kept around him. These paintings would have signified a capacious sense of tradition and given the room a cosmopolitan European feeling.

Over the years, many persons sent Washington copies of sermons that they thought he might like. This was much more common in those days than today, perhaps, for the clergy were among the best-educated men of their time, with a command of Latin, Greek, and Hebrew, and sometimes also French and German. They had studied not only languages but also philosophy, history, literature, geography, and law. They typically had the best personal libraries in their locale. If anyone was searching for a copy of John Locke, for example, or Algernon Sidney, the minister was apt to have it on his shelves—most likely marked with pencil in the margins.

In the Protestant churches of those days, ministers worked very hard upon their sermons, trying to produce real works of learning and literary elegance as well as piety. Before them often sat an appreciative audience with the likes of a John Adams or James Wilson, George Mason, Benjamin Rush, or Washington himself. Interestingly enough, a number of the Founders had received a healthy share of their own education as prospective clergymen, before some of them turned to medicine, law, or other fields—this was so of Rush, Wilson, Samuel Huntington, John Witherspoon, of course, and at least a half dozen others among the Founders.

Often enough, when Washington received these sermons, he wrote back to the author in such a way that one can tell he had actually read the text for which he was expressing gratitude and had taken something from it. In a few cases, he added the sermon to his pile of favorites, a significant number of which he sent out to have bound together in hard covers. Otherwise, in his diaries or contemporaneous letters, Washington often simply noted with appreciation a fine sermon he had just heard or complained wryly about a careless or shallow one.

In addition, as previously noted, Washington was a vestryman of his local Anglican parish and contributed a significant amount of time to parish meetings. One year, under his leadership, the parish council approved and executed the move of the building from one site to another several miles away, with all the immense body of petty detail that required. During this time, he is known to have donated to the new church at Pohick both gold leaf for gilding the religious inscription on the altarpiece and "Crimson Velvet with Gold Firing" for use on the pulpit and altar.[14]

Not only did Washington attend his local church with a regularity normal for that time, but he also attended church with considerable regularity when he traveled to Philadelphia, New York, or other cities. He often attended very long ceremonies, even some in addition to the normal Sunday service. Indeed, he sometimes went to church for both morning and evening services on the same day. The same pattern appeared when, as president, he made it a point to travel to virtually every state of the union. In May 1791, while touring Charleston, South Carolina, he noted his attendance at "Crouded Churches" in the morning and afternoon.[15] Indeed, throughout his trip through the South, he ended up going to more church services than there were days of travel. It is possible that church buildings sometimes provided the most spacious rooms in which to meet other citizens, but that cannot have been true in those cities with major civic buildings such as Philadelphia's Independence Hall. Thus, this choice of locale was only partly because churches were often the most convenient and largest places of assembly. It was also because he was determined to bind religious people to the republic, and to give his support to religion, as the surest protector of the moral health of the republic.

With Benjamin Rush and most of the other Founders, Washington believed strongly that the survival of the republic depended upon strong moral habits—that is, virtues—and that for the vast majority of the people, strong moral habits depended, in turn, upon a lively sense of the judgment of God. Why was this? As Washington pronounced in his Farewell Address:

Of all the dispositions and habits which lead to political prosperity, Religion and morality are indispensable supports. . . . Let it simply be asked where is the security for property, for reputation, for life, if the sense of religious obligation *desert* the oaths, which are the instruments of investigation in Courts of Justice? . . . Reason and experience both forbid us to expect that National morality can prevail in exclusion of religious principle.[16]

Along these lines, the following were typical replies in the air at that time. Most people need the sense that "Someone" is watching them and holding them accountable when they act in secret. Some benefit by the sense that they are not merely obeying laws but heeding the wishes of a benevolent Friend. Still others need to know that, even if they have failed in their duty, there is someone who helps them begin anew. For these and other reasons, religion adds to the motives for moral behavior supplied by philosophy.

As an Anglican, Washington would have had many reasons to know well the Book of Common Prayer and from many services during his life, public and private, would have had reason to learn virtually by heart many passages from the Psalms. He would also have encountered traditional anthems and antiphons, readings from New Testament and Old, classic religious hymns, and seasonal meditations on Providence, judgment, grace, man's fallen state, and other themes. He would have heard many sermons on these subjects, too, often quite learned sermons, combining scriptural lessons with passages from Sidney, Locke, Cicero, Seneca, and other weighty writers.

These lessons would have informed his great enjoyment of his favorite among all dramatic presentations, Joseph Addison's *Cato*.[17] It was as though that single play encapsulated the basic form of his life, his love for liberty, his sense of sacrifice, his instinct for nobility and duty, his favorite virtues, even his favorite dramatic poses, gestures, and actions. Seeing the play over and over reminded him of the indissoluble connection between honor and virtue: Where one is lacking, the other must disappear. "When vice prevails, and impious men bear sway," exclaims Addison's *Cato*, "the post of honor is a private station."[18] It was a line that stuck with Washington, appearing again and again in his personal and public correspondence.[19] In his public speech, it helped him to marry his secular and his religious idealism, since despite being set in pagan times the play is filled with piety toward the divine. For instance, the epigraph quoted in Latin by Addison is from Seneca, one of Washington's favorites, and the god that Seneca describes was commonly interpreted as Jehovah— Creator, Judge, Providence:

> But lo! here is a spectacle worthy of the God as he contemplates his works; lo! here is a contest worthy of God—a brave man matched against ill-fortune, and doubly so if his also was the challenge. I do not know, I say, what nobler sight the Lord of Heaven could find on earth, should he wish to turn his attention there, than the spectacle of Cato, after his cause had already been shattered more than once, nevertheless standing erect amid the ruins of the commonwealth.[20]

It was at such moments that the private and the public man met as one. His own sincere patriotism, his faith, and his acute sense of the great role in history that Providence had in mind for the brave experiment in America welled up within him and caught fire. To live up to his public duties, assigned to him by a good Providence, Washington had to keep reaching deep into his private reserves. However taciturn he might seem to others concerning his inner life, in his soul were hard diamonds of indomitable will.

We must look now at Washington's deep and complex understanding of Providence.

THE FRUIT

Glorious indeed has been our Contest: glorious, if we consider the Prize for which we have contended, and glorious in its Issue; but in the midst of our Joys, I hope we shall not forget that, to divine Providence is to be ascribed the Glory and the Praise.

—Address to Congress on Resigning
His Commission, December 23, 1783

Chapter 10

THE SMILES OF HEAVEN
AND THE WORK
OF PROVIDENCE

The Brigadiers and Commandants of Brigades who are desired to give notice in their orders and to afford every aid and assistance in their power for the promotion of that public Homage and adoration which are due to the supreme being, who has through his infinite goodness brought our public Calamities and dangers (in all humane probability) very near to a happy conclusion.

—General Orders, February 18, 1783[1]

I am inexpressibly happy that by the smiles of divine Providence, my weak but honest endeavors to serve my country have hitherto been crowned with so much success, and apparently given such satisfaction to those in whose cause they were exerted.

The same benignant influence, together with the concurrent support of all real friends to their country, will still be necessary to enable me to be in any degree useful to this numerous and free People over whom I am called to preside.

—Letter to the Clergy of Newport,
August 17, 1790[2]

LEARNING TO UNDERSTAND PROVIDENCE

In thinking about Providence, Washington did not start from zero. As did most Virginia Episcopalians of that era, both his mother and his father had a strong sense of the workings of Providence in their own lives. Moreover, Augustine and Mary Washington passed on to George at least two well-worn books, signed by one or both of them inside the front covers. (Both can be examined among the nine hundred volumes of George Washington's original library, since 1848 in the keeping of the Boston Athenaeum.) One of these books was Sir Matthew Hale's *Contemplations Moral and Divine* (1685), and from this book Mary Washington read frequently to her grandchildren, who recalled it gratefully, and presumably to her own children before them. We know this from her grandson Robert Lewis and his son-in-law E. C. M'Guire, who wrote of it in *The Religious Opinions and Character of Washington*. Hale's book was well worn by the time Reverend M'Guire had it in his hands, quoting from it extensively.[3]

The other book was Thomas Comber's *Short Discourses upon the Whole Common-Prayer; Designed to Inform the Judgment, and Excite the Devotion of Such as Daily Use the Same*. The inside cover bears the very large signatures of Augustine Washington (inscribed "his book 1727"), Mary Washington, and then, at age thirteen, the even larger signature of George Washington.[4]

Sir Matthew Hale's lessons on humility and modesty uncannily foreshadowed how Washington would later conduct himself, as when he warned the Congress of the many gaps in his knowledge of military matters and his lack of sufficient skills to lead the army, while pledging to do his best; and how at each stage of his later life he would express publicly an awareness of his limitations. If these are in fact lessons that Washington learned at his mother's knee, or from later reading during his school days, his conduct as an adult becomes easier to understand.

It is the same way with the Comber commentary on the Book of Common Prayer. That book is intended for daily prayer, a large part of which is taken from the psalms of David. Being used for daily prayer, the psalms are so often repeated, Comber writes, "that the poorest Christians can say them by heart." But they are also used by Jews and even Muslims. They are very common prayers, indeed. One reason for his book's chapters on the Apostles' Creed, the Nicene Creed, and other basic matters of the Christian faith, Comber writes, is that "we might know to whom we pray." And the backbone of the Book of Common Prayer is Psalm 95, which, as it were, outlines the whole nature and purpose of daily prayer. Comber shows this psalm to be a profound lesson in the meaning of belief in Providence. Psalm 95 leads us through the four great movements of true prayer, which Combers defines as "the lifting up of the soul to converse with God," the daily directing of our attention to God.[5]

First, Comber writes, we place ourselves in the presence of God, recognizing that God is present at all times and in all places, and so now, with us. Then we contemplate the sovereignty of God, that he rules over all forces and all powers and all events, that he is our Father, and that he protects his children from harm and pulls them free from it "with a power inaccessible to mortal princes." Third, we remind ourselves of the compassion of God, that he desires us to pray, and that he wants to hear our prayers, and delights in helping the weak and the needy. Finally, we recognize the integrity of prayer, that we cannot merely pray, without at the same time reforming our lives. It is urgent that we not pray as hypocrites. We cannot merely be asking of God but not obeying his word, asking but not coming to him with tender and willing hearts, asking but not altering for the better the way we live. God wants no double dealing.

Presence, sovereignty, compassion, and integrity—all these are characteristics of the God to whom humans pray. General Washington's General Orders to his troops regarding prayer during time of war hit all four of these notes. Psalm 95 teaches humans that God is always with them, in their presence, with almighty power, with compassion, and with a demand for inner integrity of spirit.

Adult life taught Washington, however, that there are other lessons to be learned about Providence, even based upon this firm foundation. The progress of a Christian through life is a long and often painful struggle. Many are the hours in which God gives no comfort, and during which it seems as if there is no God at all. Some of the doubts Washington had to face were such as these: If God is truly present to all things, and truly sovereign, what happens when armies on both sides of a war pray to him? Did not the British during the War of Independence also trust Providence?

Besides, if God is present in all things and sovereign over all things, then how was Washington to behave when his plans went awry, his dreams seemed to lie in a pile of rubble, and difficulty seemed piled upon difficulty? Had Providence deserted him? Sometimes, it seemed as if there was no way to tell that Providence actually was active in his life. If whatever happens is providential, by definition, that seems meaningless.

On the first of these points, Washington held firm to the belief that one of the reasons that God created the world is to make free creatures capable of recognizing him, thanking him, and entering into conversation with him. Washington believed that God could not help being on the side of liberty, and that liberty was the American cause, a just cause, a right cause. Washington did not believe that history always comes out right, but he did believe that the Americans at least had a chance, and that they must seize it or forever be blamed for having missed it. He was willing to hazard his life for that belief.

On the second point, he understood the need for constancy. One cannot act merely the fair-weather friend, trusting in Providence when things go sunnily, despairing when the skies fill up with ominous clouds. The duty of a valiant woman, a courageous man, is to hold firm. That is the soldier's professional virtue. If there is a Providence, Providence is firm—come sun, come storm. So ought a commander of men to stand.

But there were also other lessons to learn. First, God does not act like a puppeteer, moving human beings about like so many rag dolls. God acts through human beings. He needs them to act freely, too, through their will, courage, and perseverance, standing firm during the most awful trials. When he gave thanks to Providence, Washington nearly always gave thanks to those who stuck firmly with their duties and carried out the necessary actions. Without their collaboration, he understood, Providence cannot succeed.

Second, Providence does not mean that God often, or even ordinarily, puts his fingers directly into history, interrupting or changing normal human laws. Washington did not sit around waiting for miraculous events, but neither was he surprised when, working through purely natural causes, but exactly at the right time, the Disposer of all events arranged an improbable but quite natural series of events that favored the American cause—as in the fog that descended to cover his retreat from Long Island, and the capture of the ship of munitions near Boston just as things looked exceedingly grim. Washington did not often allude directly to "miraculous" events as signs of providential action, but he did refer to improbable "concatenations" of causes that seemed, disproportionately, to favor the success of liberty.

Third, Washington learned that Providence does not mean that everything works for the best, always issuing in happy endings. He did speak of Providence as "a good Providence," of "benevolence," and of "the Smiles of Heaven." But his favorite description of Providence, appearing much more frequently than any other, is "inscrutable." Our ways are not God's ways. Providence seems frequently to be in the business of humbling us through defeat, calamity, ruin. It was often difficult for Washington to see how such disasters worked to the nation's ultimate benefit, and in such cases both philosophy and faith taught him that the right way was to submit his wisdom to that of the Almighty. And to trust. As Comber seemed to suggest in his commentary on the Book of Common Prayer, in the end, prayer is essentially a yes to the will of God. A "'Tis well." An amen.

But let us pause to reflect on these last three points, beginning with the third.

"I flatter myself that a superintending Providence is ordering every thing for the best, and that, in due time, all will end well. That it may do so, and soon, is [my] most fervent wish."[6] This text records Washington's early, more immature view. But life soon enough taught him that he must also learn to expect the worst and not be crushed by surprises that dashed his hopes. Washington recognized quickly enough that Providence often plunges humans into suffering, defeat, and inexplicable tangles of misfortune. Yet a little over a year later, he found himself exclaiming, "But alas! we are not to expect that the path is to be strewed wt. flowers. . . . That great and good Being who rules the Universe has disposed matters otherwise and for wise purposes I am perswaded."[7]

Yet in times of suffering and despair, Washington counseled himself that we ought to trust Providence in its unfathomable wisdom, even when its workings remain beyond our comprehension. As we have seen, his was not the deist god, quite tame before human reason, but the great God Jehovah whose ways are not our ways, and whose wisdom operates on a far higher and deeper wavelength than we are given access to.

To recognize the limits of our own reason is not unreasonable, as Washington saw matters. On the contrary, it is the intelligent course of action. Beyond practical reason, the mind must follow the reasons beyond its ken, in attentive submission. Washington held that sufferings and failures—even they—somehow occur under Providence, for our own instruction and betterment. For good or ill, we ought to prepare ourselves to accept the decisions of Providence. Even when endings are painful and unhappy, patience under suffering becomes us. Moreover, Washington learned that God always (or virtually always) achieves his will through the unfolding of secondary causes, that is, through normal natural agents, acting according to their own laws and potentialities. What often does happen, though, is that natural chains of causation cut across each other, so that one cancels the other out, and the outcome is unusual and unforeseen. Thus the commonsense proverb warns: Don't count your chickens before they're hatched. The Master Artist sees the unfolding of various chains of probabilities and, deftly and without violating the laws of nature that he himself established, puts his own order of beauty and wonder into them. In the process, humankind's plans and hopes and wishes often go awry. Sometimes causes whose success seems of very low probability suddenly win out.

Washington also learned to look at the action of Providence from a different angle (and thus learned the first lesson mentioned above): Suppose that God wills the vindication of the American experiment in liberty, through victory over Great Britain. God will not suddenly appear at the head of thousands of angels and drive the redcoats from the land. On the contrary, a great many American men and women will have to suffer and die, through taking up arms and enduring the brutal hardships of harsh battlefields. If God acts, it will be through humans (or other natural causes), not on his own. Humans will have to exert their own will. And humans may fail. As Washington wrote to the clergy of Newport (see above), Providence, "together with the concurrent support of all real friends to their country, will still be necessary."

Ronald Reagan used to tell a story to illustrate this point, and there are some passages in Washington that suggest considerable sympathy for Reagan's view. The story goes as follows: After long toil on a fairly desolate several acres of land near the desert, a farmer was showing off his property to his pastor. "Over here, Pastor," the farmer said with satisfaction, "for three years we carted away rocks. We tilled and retilled. We built an irrigation system. And now we get all the wheat, barley, corn and other vegetables we need."

"Praise the Lord!" the pastor exclaimed.

"And over here my wife dug out all the cactus and brambles, had good soil hauled in, and nurtured all these fruit trees and all these vineyards. Most luscious fruit you ever tasted!"

"Praise the Lord!" exclaimed the pastor, with admiration.

"But back here is the apple of our eye," the farmer exclaimed. "This was all sand before. Now it's been fertilized, and my wife is growing the best tomatoes and avocados you ever saw. And every spice and herb you could need."

To the farmer's irritation, the pastor again exclaimed, "Praise the Lord!"

"Well, I suppose it's perfectly right to praise the Lord," the farmer retorted. "But you should have seen this property when he was working it alone."

When Providence wants fruitful harvests in most of earth's climates, the work must be done by secondary agents. God may give the increase, but humans must do the labor. It was the same in regard to the War of Independence. Washington and his men had to perform seemingly insuperable labors.

All in all, Washington imagined the world around us as a "concatenation" of causes and events, events caused by earlier causes and, in turn, setting off other chains of events. This loose network of many competing bundles of causation, full of incalculable probabilities and outside chances, represents his experience of the actual hazards of life. He himself addressed patterns of seeming inevitability yielding to totally serendipitous surprises. At one extreme, he did not concede that there is pure chaos. At the other extreme, he did not envisage blind, dumb fate, inexorable and unavoidable. He discerned progress and some degree of direction (however twisting and turning, and spiraling up or down in the various eras of history). He perceived open opportunities for affecting the destiny of the nation and his own destiny. He perceived ways of shaping and determining human character—within certain limits—either this way or that, and he encouraged himself and his men constantly to become better men, and even better Christians. God acts through us, and we must live up to the purposes he proposes to us. We must seize opportunities, especially those that may never come again. If we do not, those opportunities perish forever.

Consider a few of Washington's remarks on God's use of secondary causes. Recall for a moment his early letters about the protection Providence gave him on the Monongahela (Chapters 2 and 3). Then skip ahead to the other end of his military career, to Washington's address at Princeton on August 25, 1783:

> If in the execution of an arduous Office I have been so happy as to discharge my duty to the Public with fidelity and success, and to obtain the good opinion of my fellow Soldiers and fellow Citizens; I attribute all the glory to that Supreme Being, who hath caused the several parts, which have been employed in the production of the wonderful Events we now contemplate, to harmonize in the most perfect manner, and who was able by the humblest instruments as well as by the most powerful means to establish and secure the liberty and happiness of these United States.[8]

No matter how hard a man may try, if all other necessary causes do not come together in a timely way, his efforts will come to naught. Furthermore, if Washington had seized all the glory for himself, he would have overlooked the heavy work of other auxiliary agents (his army, his officers, and many others)—and more than all that, he would have overlooked a superintending Power, bringing together at the right time all elements necessary to victory.

It is often by disappointments and defeats that Providence teaches us. For the success of independence, much evil had to be endured, many horrible wounds borne and limbs lost, much pain of body and heart absorbed. Heavy costs are levied by Providence. Washington slowly learned that under Providence not all endings are happy or all ways smooth. On the contrary, a good outcome is reached—if at all—by the way of suffering, calamity, and stress:

> A Multiplicity of circumstances, scarcely yet investigated, appears to have co-operated in bringing about the great, and I trust the happy, revolution, that is on the eve of being accomplished. It will not be uncommon that those things, which were considered at the moment as real ills, should have been no inconsiderable causes in producing positive and permanent national felicity. For it is thus

that Providence works in the mysterious course of events "from seeming evil still educing good."[9]

THE INSCRUTABILITY OF PROVIDENCE

The inscrutability of Providence was for Washington its most arresting characteristic. He kept mentioning that inscrutability. It was the characteristic of Providence he most often emphasized, as though to stress how far beyond reason, but not unreasonably, experience leads us. His point of view seemed to develop. In the early part of his career, when Providence had mostly brought him sunny endings, he gave a too-simple understanding to Alexander Pope's refrain, "Whatever is, is right."[10] It may be good in God's eyes, for purposes we cannot discern, but it certainly does not look, or feel, good in our aggrieved experience. We must recognize frankly that Providence does not exempt us from pain or failure or even disaster.

In due course, Washington also learned that, in the turmoil of the present, we cannot discern the pattern that, much later, may become clear to us. During the buildup to the War of Independence and its early struggles, who knew whether the war effort was in line for failure or for success? Then, success in war gained, who knew what the near future held? When from the point of view of the present we try to gaze into the future, we are relatively blind, just as we were in the past when we did not foresee the circumstances in which we now dwell.

Providence knows what it is doing, but we don't. Providence may even grasp the whole picture all at once from all eternity (as Anglicans used to say, in Washington's time). We, by contrast, have to plod along, step by step, with clearer vision in hindsight than in foresight:

It is indeed a pleasure, from the walks of private life to view in retrospect, all the meanderings of our past labors, the difficulties through which we have waded, and the fortunate Haven to which the Ship has been brought! Is it possible after this that it should founder? Will not the All Wise, and all powerfull director of human events, preserve it? I think he will, he may however (for wise purposes not discoverable by finite minds) suffer our indiscretions and folly to place our national character low in the political Scale; and this, unless more wisdom and less prejudice take the lead in our governments, will most assuredly be the case.[11]

In all human probability, the future will not be a time of bliss:

But, providence, for purposes beyond the reach of mortal scan, has suffered the restless and malignant passions of man, the ambitions and sordid views of those who direct them, to keep the affairs of this world in a continual state of disquietude; and will, it is to be feared, place the prospects of peace too far off, and the promised millennium at an awful distance from our day.[12]

Mere hope cannot quiet all our uncertainties:

I have, for sometime past, viewed the political concerns of the United States with an anxious, and painful eye. They appear to me, to be moving by hasty strides to some awful crisis; but in what they will result, that Being, who sees, foresees, and directs all things, alone can tell. The Vessel is afloat, or very nearly so, and considering myself as a Passenger only, I shall trust to the Mariners whose duty it is to watch, to steer it into a safe Port.[13]

In the midst of the sufferings and fallen bodies of war, Washington learned his toughest lessons about the harsh hand of Providence. Providence more than once snatched victory from Washington's army, as it did in October 1777, as this letter to John Augustine Washington shows:

But for a thick Fog [that] rendered [all] so infinitely dark at times, as not to distinguish friend from Foe at the distance of 30 Yards, we should, I believe, have made a decisive and glorious day of it. But Providence or some unaccountable something, designd it otherwise.[14]

Experiences such as this would undermine General Washington's trust in the Panglossian cheer of Alexander Pope and other melioristic philosophers. He felt how desperately weak was his situation, teetering at times on the brink of ruin. Sometimes the number of healthy soldiers on whom he could draw was down to just a few thousand. Then terms of duty expired, and men went home to their needy families and neglected farms, taking much-needed weapons and ammunition with them. The wounds of others festered and kept them from active duty. Among many more, illnesses and fevers too slowly departed. In another letter to his brother, one year earlier, he wrote as follows:

> You can form no Idea of the perplexity of my Situation. No Man, I believe, ever had a greater choice of difficulties and less means to extricate himself from them. However under a full persuasion of the justice of our Cause I cannot entertain an Idea that it will finally sink tho' it may remain for some time under a Cloud.[15]

That cloud turned out much larger and far darker than Washington had at first imagined, and it would shadow his understanding of Providence for the rest of his life. Yet with victory finally secured and the British gone from America, some five years later, General Washington distilled his reflections on the recent past in a letter to a friend:

> I can never trace the concatenation of causes which led to these events, without acknowledging the mystery and admiring the goodness of Providence. To that superintending Power alone is our retraction from the brink of ruin to be attributed.[16]

Washington, through the last decades of his life, continued to view life's events through the mysterious lens of Providence. As he got older, his understanding of Providence deepened, and his notice of its more subtle interpositions increased. He went from sensing God's direct hand in his life to appreciating the less obvious "contingencies":

> If we are to credit newspaper accounts, the flames of war in Europe are again kindling: how far they may spread, neither the Statesman or soldier can determine; as the great governor of the Universe causes contingencies which baffle the wisdom of the first, and the foresight and valor of the Second.[17]

Right up until the year of his death, 1799, Washington continued trying to puzzle things out through the eyes of Providence:

> In what such a spirit, and such proceedings will issue, is beyond the reach of short sighted man to predict, with any degree of certainty. I hope well; because I have always believed, and trusted, that that Providence which has carried us through a long and painful War with one of the most powerful Nations in Europe, will not suffer the discontented among ourselves, to produce more than a temporary interruption to the permanent Peace and happiness of this rising Empire.[18]

Having seen what he had seen of God's favorable care for this nation, Washington felt entitled to hope, but not to presume.

PROVIDENCE IN FAMILY LIFE

Yet it was not only in matters of state and matters of war and peace, but also—and perhaps most poignantly—in matters of sickness and death in the bosom of his family, and among friends, that Washington was acutely aware of the hand of Providence. He experienced many deaths in his own lifetime, of his father, his siblings, mother, stepchildren and stepgrandchildren, nephews, and nieces. Of some of these, we have records showing his devout prayers at their bedsides and his tears. Our best documentary evidence, however, is found in letters he wrote to friends on the deaths of their own children, spouses, or other loved ones. We have seen some of these in the preceding chapter. But Washington's emphases are worth revisiting again: on the inscrutability of Providence; on the pain it often puts us through; on the need to persuade one's sensibilities, as best one can, to submit to its decrees with as much equanimity as human nature will allow; and on the invitation to trust in the ultimate goodwill of Providence on our behalf—the smiles of Heaven, hidden by the clouds.

In 1778, for instance, he had written to Bryan Fairfax, who was in the midst of a severe personal blow:

The determinations of Providence are all ways wise; often inscrutable, and though its decrees appear to bear hard upon us at times is nevertheless meant for gracious purposes; in this light I cannot help viewing your late disappointment.[19]

Washington's most succinct comment on the distance of the divine knowledge from our own may have been written to his nephew in 1793: "But the will of Heaven is not be controverted or scrutinized by the children of this world."[20]

Such quotes as these suggest a humility on the part of Washington's generation (for these views were not his alone), who were quite able to imagine the immensity of the Divine Wisdom, by comparison with the relative puniness of their own. Washington, at least, was quick to concede his own ignorance, and to admit that his own receptive powers could not bear the stupendous illumination of the far vaster knowledge of the Divine. Who was he to pretend to scrutinize what was far vaster than his own capacities? Washington did not find it ignominious to admit ignorance, finitude, humility, submission. Our own age, in contrast, has been born, perhaps, under a contrary sign: "I refuse."

Another point of difference to grasp between deism and Washington's vision of Providence is that the deist tends to believe that the deity is the lawgiver of the universe, the one who is the source of its regularity, order, rationality, and predictability. But the concept of Providence does not look only at general laws and regularities. On the contrary, its most penetrating thrust is into particularities, unique persons, unrepeatable events, and inimitable circumstances. This Providence throws its light upon this person, in this place, in this situation—and into the mists of the inimitable, the irregular, the unpredictable, the unique.

It is undoubtedly true that most of the actions of Divine Providence are conducted through human agents and other natural causes, sheerly by the timing and combination of events and the intersecting lines of causation. In such moments the Divine Artist displays his greatest artistry. And yet, as if occasionally to show the humbling power of the Lord of life and the freedom of the Creator over all creation, Providence occasionally seems to achieve its will by what seems to the human eye processes greater and more complex than ordinary natural causes. In a word, miracles—or at least events so unusual that they look like miracles.

When French troops and Indian braves, riflemen who seldom missed, fired at Washington on horseback again and again and never hit him, while having picked off virtually all the other officers, one does not want to leap and claim "miracle." Yet the event does seem to reach beyond the ordinary. So it was also on Long Island, when the strange yellowish fog blew in for six long hours past daybreak in August 1776, while Washington struggled feverishly to get his men across the East River to safety. And so also when just before midnight, the wind abated and changed direction, so that the waves of the East River no longer impeded Washington's flatboats, but aided them. One does not want to insist on *miracle*. But the unusual combination of natural causes does seem to go beyond the ordinary, and to be exceedingly precisely timed. So, too, on a dozen other occasions. Natural explanations are possible. But the highly visible pattern behind these odd events tempts the mind beyond that.

Say that Washington was uncommonly lucky, if you wish. Say that he was, in war, a child of fortune. But the common understanding in which Anglicans of his day were brought up was that Divine Providence had each individual in its care every day and in all events. And that one ought to trust Providence, even in the midst of the most extreme hardships and trials. One ought to retain one's composure. One ought to fight on the more fiercely, having good hope in the outcome, even if one's efforts should end in death and defeat. For at least in that way one would die as a Christian soldier ought to die, trusting Providence to the end.

More than once during his earlier life, Washington had looked ahead to his death. Yet he always made very clear that he trusted Providence to the end:

> According to a believable anecdote, Washington asked the doctor [New York's leading physician, Samuel Bard] for a frank report on his chances [in regard to a high fever caused by a tumor in Washington's thigh]: "I am not afraid to die and therefore can bear the worst. . . . Whether tonight or twenty years hence makes no difference. I know I am in the hands of a good Providence."[21]

On another occasion, in 1790, he wrote about his confidence about a better world in the "hereafter":

> In looking forward to that awful moment when I must bid adieu to sublunary things, I anticipate the consolation, of leaving our country in a prosperous condition. And while the curtain of separation shall be drawing, my last breath will, I trust, expire in a prayer for the temporal and eternal felicity of those, who have not only endeavored to gild the evening of my days with unclouded serenity, but extended their desires to my happiness hereafter, in a brighter world.[22]

GENERAL PROVIDENCE, SPECIAL PROVIDENCE

Theologians and preachers of the founding period observed a difference between the Providence that the Creator exercises over all his creation inclusively and called this General Providence. But they noted another dimension of Providence that was even more marvelous, God's Providence over human history and the use (and abuse) of human liberty, which they called Special Providence. Special Providence is more marvelous because it exposes a profundity and deftness in God's artistry, so that without infringing upon human liberty he nonetheless achieves his purposes *through* and *around* free human actions.[23]

To reach an intellectual conception of God that protects both divine freedom and human freedom has been the object of centuries of sustained inquiry among Jewish and Christian divines, and to a more limited extent among Muslim scholars, too. Most attempts go awry because thinkers unwittingly begin with too materialistic and mechanistic a view both of "causes" and of "action"—divine action and human action, which are not of the same order. But it is not our task here to enter into those efforts over many centuries to find a metalanguage for doing justice both to humans and to God.

Washington himself did not indulge in such abstract speculation. But he certainly came to hold, in daily conduct and in his long-term expectations of life, that he and others should make the most extensive use possible of their innate capacities for initiative and responsibility. They should act, and act boldly, with full and eager hope. Providence *expects* humans to do their utmost. By contrast, humans *implore* Providence to favor the outcome of those exertions, at least by fending off the worst circumstances that might lead to failure, and if possible by sending favorable winds and tides in the flow of forthcoming events.

In any human contest, there are circumstances no human controls. It is in the happy ordering of those that the skillful hand of Providence is most especially honored.

We have noted earlier that Washington often spoke of nations, as well as individuals, as having duties before God. Among these duties are those of imploring Providence to bless the nation's projects, and of thanking Providence when those blessings become tangible in the nation's actual success. At times of success, he took frequent care to point out that to God must go the glory. Just as in times of desperate need, it was to God that prayers sped heavenward.

In the same way, Washington was among the first to espy a special Providence for the nascent United States, even before it became an independent nation. He recognized fairly early that the underlying issue was not merely independence from Great Britain in order to continue as before with a system here like the one in Britain. He saw that Providence had made the stakes much higher. There was a chance here to create a new experiment in liberty, for the benefit of the entire human race. For this experiment was to be based upon the liberty rooted in human nature, in the human capacities for reflection and choice—the very capacities that mark humans as, more than any other creature in the known universe, "made in the image of God." Such liberty is natural to humans. It does not belong to Americans alone. Therefore, the American experiment in building a system adequate to natural liberty has universal application. Washington held that in a future age that he, alas, would not live to see, peoples even in the most distant lands would repair to the example of the United States. They would find here a model adaptable to their own human nature.

Already in 1783, Washington was calling on the confederated states to raise their eyes to their new continental possibilities, "and we shall have equal occasion to felicitate ourselves on the lot which Providence has assigned us, whether we view it in a natural, a political, or a moral light."[24] In the very long and unused draft of his first inaugural address, Washington had cast his imagination still further into the future and embraced the entire globe:

Can it be imagined . . . that this Continent was not created and reserved so long undiscovered as a Theatre, for those glorious displays of divine Munificence, the salutary consequences of which will flow to another Hemisphere & extend through the interminable series of ages? Should not our souls exult in the prospect?

Here he seemed to step back for a bit, to contemplate the prospect.

Though I shall not survive to perceive with these bodily senses,[25] but a small portion of the blessed effects which our Revolution will occasion in the rest of the world; yet I enjoy the progress of human society & human happiness in anticipation.

Here Washington assigned more power to ideas and freedom of "enquiry" than some might expect, as well as a greater benevolence toward "the many":

I rejoice in the belief that intellectual light will spring up in the dark corners of the earth; that freedom of enquiry will produce liberality of conduct; that mankind will reverse the absurd position that *the many* were, made for *the few;* and that they will not continue slaves in one part of the globe, when they can become freemen in another.[26]

We have already seen that Washington had anxieties about the future. He did not consider happy prospects such as this inevitable, but only within our possibilities, if we conducted our actions well, and if Providence continued to bless our labors. Big *ifs*, indeed. Knowing the downward slope of human morals, Washington, as we have seen, often feared the worst.

In brief, Washington's views of the sort of world in which both liberty and the actions of a good Providence are possible might be stated in a short series of propositions. These might be thought "metaphysical," in the sense in which they put into words assumptions about the way the world works that seem to have been operating in the quotations we have taken in such abundance from

Washington's utterances, public and private. They have a certain commonsense ring about them. They are permeated both with the sound philosophy of Washington's favorite writers, such as Cicero, Seneca, Addison, Locke, and others, and with a profound Christian (or even Hebrew) sensibility. Those attributes, no doubt, made them seem plain good sense to well-read persons all around him, and to people of common sense who did very little reading but observed life around them with a sharp eye.

1. History is open to human initiative, imagination, and action.
2. Good intentions do not guarantee good results from human actions; much depends on many unforeseeable factors, on unpredictable circumstances, and—in a word—on the good favor of the Disposer of all events (Special Providence).
3. Much depends, too, on the excellence and efficacy of human actions.
4. Providence is not fate, nor mere fortune. It is personal both in its subject (the divine Person) and in its object (the human person), intelligent, benevolent, and efficacious. It is open—and in its freedom responsive—to personal interaction, supplication, and devoted action.
5. Providence is sovereign over all things, of nature and of history, of the external world, and of the realm of consciousness, reflection, and choice.
6. Providence is not an idol of material composition, but spirit and truth, and wishes to be addressed in spirit and in truth. Nothing is hidden from Providence, not even our most secret thoughts or desires.
7. God is benevolent, but he is also sovereign, and a just Judge, and his justice is to be feared.
8. To each nation he assigns a mission, and as to how that mission is carried out, he is a just and demanding judge, who cannot be deceived.

9. The mission assigned to America is an experiment in the system of natural liberty, of immense consequence to the entire human race. The judgment of the United States for a misuse of that liberty shall be especially severe, proportional to the importance of the task assigned it.

10. The experiment in the United States might fail; decadence in the use of liberty—not at all unprecedented even in the history of the Christian church—might bring destruction upon it. The favor of God is not unconditional, although his capacity for forgiveness and reawakening is.

11. Americans should act according to God's law in order not to turn away his favor, and in that sense to "merit" the blessings they ask, on the basis of his generous, freely granted, and undeserved promises. We do not, strictly, merit these blessings, but it would be hypocritical to ask them of God while we willfully violate his law.

Each of these propositions matches up with assumptions made manifest in Washington's words and actions. Only on the strength of background convictions such as these, or of convictions like them, do his descriptions of the actions of Providence make sense.

Chapter 11

TO DIE LIKE A
CHRISTIAN

*Thus the age in which Hamilton lived ... poses difficulties
of a special nature in defining "Christian" and in exploring
an individual's religious life.*

—Douglass Adair

WHAT IS A CHRISTIAN?
CHANGES IN DEFINITION

During the period 1780–1810, what it meant "to die like a Christian" may have been less clear than in many generations, since, as we discussed in Chapter 7, Christian life in America was in the midst of a double upheaval. The first upheaval arose from the growing professional and commercial classes, who were increasingly restless because of the tendency of some Protestants to place emphasis on Scripture alone to the disparagement of reason. The other upheaval occurred along a different fault line of American life altogether: reverberations after about 1770 from the rise of fervent new denominations of Christians—evangelicals, they would later be called, but at first simply "Baptists," "Methodists," and others—whose spirit swept like a prairie fire through the small cities and rural areas of the newly independent nation. This second upheaval demanded clear signs that a believer was not only pious, but also expressly Christian. Among these signs were openly confessing Jesus Christ as one's Lord and Savior, declaring one's full faith in his saving power alone, accepting public baptism or public confession of new faith, and perhaps even taking communion in the church. It was such tests, all of them, that Alexander Hamilton, in the end, passed.

In previous decades, all that was expected of an Anglican of the South, Professor Douglass Adair writes in his brilliant book *Fame and the Founding Fathers*, was to confess belief in Providence—or the Creator, the Governor of all things, the Almighty, the Source of all good—and to lead a moral life according to Christian norms, including some regular attendance and support of the church. Yet church obligations had to be loosely worn, since in fact there were not enough ministers to serve every church, or even every region, and in some locales a minister was available for services as infrequently as once a month. By the end of the eighteenth century, the definition of Christian thus became "especially tricky": "The period between the seventeenth and the nineteenth century is the great watershed in the modern history of religious life and belief."[1]

Thus, for several of the more prominent Founders, the two upheavals mentioned above made their identification as Christians much murkier by about the year 1800 than it had been before. Some of these believers were in considerable inner uncertainty themselves. Professor Adair points out that Alexander Hamilton, for instance, went through at least four different stages of self-identification as a Christian, and that only at the end of his life—in Adair's view—was his Christianity obviously genuine and orthodox by both older and newer standards.[2]

As it was for Hamilton's journey of faith, it is quite normal for Christians to undergo a journey or arduous voyage or time of trial as they grow in their faith. That is part of the fascination with the old classic by John Bunyan, *Pilgrim's Progress*, and even with the manuals on the "stages" of Christian life produced in every new generation. One thing faith is *not* is cut and dried. Believers often spend considerable time trying to figure out where they are in their wanderings, what it is they believe and don't believe, and invariably they are heavily tested by setbacks and sufferings to abandon the infantile forms of faith with which they began, in order to take on more mature forms. Think of St. Paul's reflection: "When I was a child, I spake as a child, I understood as a child, I thought as a child: but when I became a man, I put away childish things" (1 Corinthians 13:11). Some give up altogether. Some are gripped by a new conversion, or awakening, or rebirth, that lifts them to a form of life they hadn't known before. The changes can be quite dramatic, as they were in Hamilton's life.

THE DEATH OF ALEXANDER HAMILTON
(1755–1804)

Our task in this chapter is limited to comparing Hamilton's death with Washington's. Suffice it to say that in his youth Hamilton came from the Caribbean as a fairly devout Presbyterian—prayers on his knees every night—and continued so for a while in college in New York and in his early professional life. As he discovered others less Presbyterian in their disciplines—more Anglican, more latitudinarian—he wavered some, moving toward the deist end of the continuum. The sufferings of the army from defeat, retreat, and hard winters in military camp, which he himself lived through, and later the temptations of civilian life—the dissolutions, the selfishness, the blind pursuits—persuaded Hamilton at a third stage that a republican experiment demanded a strong moral people. For most people most of the time, and all people at crucial times, this moral constancy in turn demanded a serious return to religion. From Professor Adair's viewpoint—and in this analysis he would not be alone—this third stage is characterized by an instrumental view of religion. The real object of first priority here is politics; Hamilton made religion the instrument of politics. (This judgment of Adair's may be a bit harsh, but there seems to be truth in the notion that Hamilton was not yet ready to be serious about his relation with God.)

Only toward the end of his life, Adair discerns, perhaps after Hamilton's own son lay fallen in a duel, and Hamilton held him in his arms while for two long agonizing days the stricken lad lay dying, did Hamilton come to a deeper sense about life. Forget about the instrument of politics. What was his own tie to God? At this fourth stage, Hamilton was coming face-to-face with his Creator, quite aware of his own sinfulness, betrayals of self and others, and simple human fragility. He wanted and needed peace in his soul, a sense of standing deliberately in the truth and the good, despite his own scandalous and sometimes foolish behavior.

Just two years after his son's death, Hamilton himself was challenged to a duel by Aaron Burr and for various reasons did not see a way to refuse this challenge without losing all honor, either in faithfulness to his own words or in his courage. If he could not disown the words, he had to fight. He resolved not to shoot to kill, but to hold himself vulnerable to Burr's aim and will. In the early morning event in New Jersey, he received a shattering blow from a bullet into his hip and groin (he was standing sideways in classic duelist style). Although he knew at once the shot was fatal—there were no antibiotics in those days—in writhing pain he was hastily rowed back to Manhattan in a vain attempt to save his life.

The year was 1804; the date was July 11. It was not long after the death of his commander in chief and president, General Washington, under whom Hamilton himself had risen to the rank of general, and then to the office of Secretary of the Treasury in the first Washington administration. Most impressively of all, with James Madison and John Jay in 1787, he had authored the most successful revolutionists' handbook ever written, *The Federalist Papers*. This is the only handbook for a practical and successful government *after* a revolution, whose Founders have been honored by posterity as have virtually no others in the hundreds of revolutionary uprisings around the world since that time.[3]

Virtually the first thing Hamilton requested, on being laid in a friend's home while help was sought, was an urgent appeal to his friend the Episcopal bishop of New York, Bishop Benjamin Moore, the rector of Trinity Church, which Hamilton attended. He confessed that he knew dueling was sinful and repented it, but he begged for communion. The bishop felt he had to refuse the request, because of the scandal it would cause (regarding the duel), and because Hamilton's request seemed abrupt—he had not been a regular communicant. Hamilton then asked the same of a Presbyterian minister, another friend, who also refused him, since his church never permitted the private reception of communion, away from the congregation. The minister tried to console Hamilton that the mercy of Jesus and the graces he had won by his death on the cross would suffice to bring a penitent into spiritual communion, without the physical sign. Hamilton again confessed his abhorrence of duels, his own prior decision to waste his own shot, and his total reliance on God's mercy.

Oliver Wolcott, Jr., a good friend, stood in the next room during this exchange and reported to Bishop Moore how acute Hamilton's suffering was, and how ardent his longing. Thus, on a second visit, after eliciting Hamilton's confession of faith and reliance on his Redeemer, Bishop Moore gave him communion, satisfied with the depth of his conversion. A day later, in the presence of the bishop, with three of Hamilton's friends, his wife, and his seven children at his bedside, quietly, peacefully, and without struggle, Hamilton expired.

Days earlier, he had written a letter to his wife, Elizabeth, to be given her in case of his death. She was an emotionally frail woman, and he was at pains to give her strength:

> This letter, my very dear Eliza, will not be delivered to you, unless I shall first have terminated my earthly career; to begin, as I humbly hope from redeeming grace and divine mercy, a happy immortality.
>
> If it had been possible for me to have avoided the interview, my love for you and my precious children would have been alone a decisive motive. But it was not possible, without sacrifices which

would have rendered me unworthy of your esteem. I need not tell you of the pangs I feel, from the idea of quitting you and exposing you to the anguish which I know you would feel. Nor could I dwell on the topic lest it should unman me.

The consolations of Religion, my beloved, can alone support you; and these you have a right to enjoy. Fly to the bosom of your God and be comforted. With my last idea; I shall cherish the sweet hope of meeting you in a better world.

Adieu best of wives and best of Women. Embrace all my darling Children for me.[4]

It seems that Hamilton's death was inarguably that of a Christian. George Washington's death is not so crystal clear.

THE DEATH OF WASHINGTON

In his compelling biography of Washington, Joseph Ellis suggests that Washington did not really die as a Christian. There was no minister present. Prayers aloud were not said. From the moment he awakened very ill until barely twenty hours later when he breathed his last, Washington is not reported to have spoken of God. Notably, too, all the witnesses to his death stressed his equanimity, his calm, his clarity of reason and attention to practical detail, and most of all his remarkable consideration for everyone around him. "He died," Ellis concludes, "as a Roman Stoic rather than a Christian saint."[5]

There is not really a contradiction between being a Stoic and a Christian, of course, regarding key virtues of daily living. Vatican buildings in Rome (like the Jefferson Building of the Library of Congress in Washington, D.C.) are full of celebrations of Stoic virtues, alongside the complementary Christian virtues. St. Augustine's *City of God* (A.D. 423) is a particularly potent authority on the consonance between Christian and classical Roman (including Stoic) virtues. In it, Augustine defended Christians from the claim of the leading Roman rhetoricians of his generation that the rise of Christianity had led to the disgraceful sack of Rome by the barbarian Alaric in A.D. 410. Christians had abandoned ancient Roman virtues, they said; hence the fall of the city. No way, Augustine showed, and commended the ancient virtues one by one both on Christian and on humanistic grounds: temperance, courage, justice, prudence, modesty, candor, friendship, nobility of spirit, sobriety, steadiness of purpose, character, and the rest. Augustine set forth, indeed, a model of Christian humanism that was to inform European civilization for the next fifteen hundred years. It is a model into which George Washington comfortably fit. Washington's extraordinary kindness to others (in imitation of "the Divine Author of our blessed Religion") crowned his steadfastness in the face of death, his attention to practical duties, and his peace of conscience.

All accounts of Washington's death, in any case, stem from Tobias Lear—who was himself the practical secretary of Washington, quite discreet about personal details, and a man very busy on the day of Washington's death summoning doctors, informing family members, laying in supplies for whatever visitors might show up, and attending to a hundred other unanticipated needs for the coming days. Martha Washington was present at her husband's side for virtually every minute of his last twenty-four hours. (Her grandson reported that she prayed in silence as she sat patiently at the foot of his bed.)[6] Whatever he said during the night or whatever from her long experience with him she knew he was feeling, she kept to herself. Tobias Lear reported very little of what she said to her husband, nothing of what the two said to each other, and nothing of whatever may have passed between their eyes. In his account, Martha allowed the men—the doctors, the overseer—to attend to the general, while she stayed in the near background.

Lear did record many of Washington's last kindnesses to others, though, such as when the general urged his young servant, Christopher, to sit a while, instead of standing intently on duty. Washington also thanked Lear for lying down with him to help move his aching body. Also, noting his faithful secretary's intense desire to be of comfort to him, the general raspingly whispered, "Well, it is a debt we must pay to each other, and I hope when you want aid of this kind you will find it."[7] (In fact, Lear, having lost two wives to illness, suffered from depression in his last days but seemed happy with his third wife and successful in government service, until he surprisingly committed suicide in 1816.)[8]

The general said from the first that he was about to die from this illness; still, he made things as easy as he could for the three doctors attending him, patiently allowing them to do their duty as they saw it, holding out his arm for them to bleed, sitting up when they requested, futile as he knew their work would be. He knew what it was like for them to have a professional's conscience, and he respected that.

Yet the two most impressive facts about his death were, first, its suddenness and, then, his insistence (some of this simply by his lifetime habits) that at such a moment there must be no fuss, no demonstrativeness, no special notice.

Just two evenings before, between 7 and 8 P.M. on December 12, 1799, George Washington had been looking as good to his wife, Martha, as he ever had, ruddy in the cheeks, good-humored, vigorous. He had spent the miserable stormy day riding around the farm on his daily inspection, lashed by snow and sleet, noticing an animal pen in serious disrepair here and other jobs his overseers had overlooked here and here. At the end, he had felt the ride worthwhile, even satisfying. When Washington at last arrived home, the wind blew in with him as he came in the door, later than usual, to a dinner already being served. He was in a very cheerful mood.

The next day, the weather was too forbidding for him to go out again, and there was enough paperwork to do at his desk indoors, except that, restless as usual for a more strenuous life, Washington did slip out for an hour or two about the grounds when in the late afternoon the weather cleared. Later, at dinner, his voice was becoming notably more hoarse, but the conversation was lively and the mood convivial. Afterward, though reluctant to leave the happy circle, Martha left him and Lear by the fire reading the most recent newspapers, which had just arrived in the post, in order to attend to her granddaughter Nelly Custis Lewis upstairs, who was still room-bound after the delivery of her first child. Martha was cheerful about how well her husband looked.

At bedtime, although Lear noticed the serious hoarseness and rec-ommended some medicaments, he knew the general would refuse; he always refused to treat a cold. Washington himself seems to have had some premonitions—just the week before, he had left instruc-tions for the vault where his body would be laid after his death—but this evening he brushed Lear off and acted as though by the morning he would be fine. None of them could possibly guess that within twenty-four hours he would be dead.

As noted above, Lear recorded nothing of the personal conversa-tions between Martha and her husband and very little of conversa-tions the general might have had with his close friend of many years, Dr. James Craik. He also wrote nothing about a short walk of Washington's, perhaps on retiring to his room, to gaze for a few mo-ments on Nelly's baby, as is recorded in family letters in later years. Most haunting of all is Lear's relative silence about the abiding pres-ence of Martha, usually pictured as at the foot of the general's canopied bed, which was placed between the two curtained windows.

Did Martha know it was her husband's last day as clearly as her husband seems to have felt it? Perhaps when he awoke her in the middle of the night, she knew. Perhaps they even whispered about contingencies as they waited for daylight. It would have been like the general to make preparations. In addition, she had certainly heard (and in some cases herself forwarded) his practical instruc-tions to his staff about his final affairs.

Do wives really need to be told in order to sense the worst? Martha and George had long been great talkers about intimate things, of the soul as well as of the sentiments. Had he not read ser-mons to her on inclement Sunday afternoons, when they had not gone to church? She had every reason to believe that she was on his wavelength, and in communion with him wordlessly. It is not likely, in his consideration for others, which Lear recorded, that he did not have tender words of consideration for his Martha, which Lear did not record.

Washington's own serious deterioration began at about three in the morning of the fourteenth, when he awoke to feel his throat closing and could scarcely breathe. He thought it best to alert Martha, lest she later be shocked and frightened by finding him choking, or even dead. Darkness and cold still filled the room. He could barely speak, but he forbade her to leave the bed until the servants came to light the fires, three or four hours later, lest she catch another of her dangerous colds. She said she wanted to call Dr. Craik, their old family friend. The general whispered hoarsely that she was not to do so until daylight.

Given Martha's character and habits, it is inconceivable during those long and dark hours that she did not try to make him comfortable, perhaps lifting his head or bolstering his pillow beneath him. We are left to imagine that from time to time she hugged him or patted him or held his hand. It may well be that they talked, and that he told her of his strong sense that he would die soon, telling her not to be afraid. There is no sign that on the next day she had any doubts or fears about the outcome, and no one needed to spend time calming or comforting her. Husband and wife waited in bed in the dark some three hours or so, until the noises of the maid were heard, firing the kindling and setting out the bowls and towels. At the break of light and warmth, Martha immediately sent out urgent word for Lear and Mr. Rawlins, the overseer.

Rawlins arrived first, and the general wanted Rawlins to bleed him a little, according to the medical practice of the time, before the doctors came. At Martha's pleading, Rawlins stopped at less than half a pint, itself not a little blood. The dark liquid came thick and slow from the General's forthrightly raised and extended arm.

The doctors came at various times, three of them, old friends and attendants. For hours, they tried everything they could think of, although the two older doctors outvoted the youngest when he suggested a tracheotomy to allow air into the lungs, which at the time could barely pass through the general's swollen epiglottis. (This was the one procedure, some doctors say today, that might have saved the general.) The sudden onset of whatever the disease was the General suffered from (even today, experts are not certain) is not common, and its symptoms are all the more frightening. The patient finds himself cut off from breathing for perilous seconds, finds a little release, and then after a respite is stricken again.

Four times during the long day his attendants bled him. Since from the first moments the general told all not to worry, that this was the time for his death—"the debt we all owe"—their ministrations seemed to him secondary.

Fairly systematically he attended to his duties. It certainly seemed as if he did not fear death nor tremble at the judgment of God. He had some instructions about the farm and the other properties for Tobias Lear and Mr. Rawlins, and some requests to the former about his military papers and his letters. Otherwise, there were long hours of quiet in the house, as Martha, some of the closest servants, and a very few others attended at his side, trying from time to time to make him comfortable.

Then began the long wait. "I die hard," Washington quipped to his old friend Dr. Craik. "But I am not afraid to go." The doctor pressed his hand but did not utter a word. Then the doctor rose and sat by the fire in grief. At times all three doctors retired to the lower floor to consult, and to share their sorrow in silence.

Between five and six o'clock, with darkness already gathering outside, the three doctors again hovered over his bed. Dr. Craik asked the general if he could sit. The general weakly held out his hand, and Lear helped him sit up. Hoarsely, Washington whispered to his doctors, "I feel myself going. I thank you for your attentions; but I pray you take no more trouble about me, let me go off quietly; I cannot last long." He was allowed to lie back down again, restless and uncomfortable. He did not complain. Every so often he asked the hour. When Lear occasionally helped him to shift his weight, the general now said nothing except with notably grateful eyes, whose silent message was of great comfort to Lear. Martha sat at the foot of the bed in patience and watchfulness. She had a Bible on the bed.

At eight o'clock, the doctors gathered again at the bedside, applying a medicament to his legs and his feet and a heating blister to his throat. They did this without hope of saving him, only for comfort—perhaps more comfort to themselves than to him. When the doctors left the room, except for Dr. Craik, who again left the bed for his seat by the fireplace, Lear also slipped away for some time. He had letters to write and other duties to attend to. He returned just before ten.

At ten o'clock, Washington made several efforts to speak to Lear, who then leaned forward at his bedside, but the general could not get the words out. Then at last he succeeded, haltingly, "I am just going! Have me decently buried; and do not let my body be put into the vault less than three days after I am dead." Lear could not speak, but nodded. Washington wanted to look into Lear's eyes and then managed to force out: "Do you understand me?" This time Lear answered with a clear "Yes!" And Washington's final words were "'Tis well!"

The room sat silent a while. (Washington's words had biblical precedent in the widow's reply to the prophet Elisha.)

Martha then spoke up in a firm and collected voice. "Is he gone?" Lear could not speak but held up his hand to signal that the general was dead. In exactly the same voice as before she repeated the general's last words: "'Tis well!" Softly she added, "All is now over. I shall soon follow him! I have no more trials to pass through."

And follow him she did before two years were out. In all that period, until the months of her rapid decline just before her end, she was thoughtful, kind, and attentive to her friends and carried out her many public duties, as before. She proved herself every bit the soldier he had been.

Two letters Martha received during this period need to be recounted here. The first was from Abigail Adams, which arrived some two weeks after Washington's death. Martha had kept her composure until then, but Abigail's warmth so touched her that it took Martha two hours to get through the short note through her abundant tears. That letter, with its tangible love, broke the dam of her feelings, as she let herself go in a long, cleansing cry.[9]

Then there was also the letter from the governor of Connecticut, Jonathan Trumbull, who enclosed extracts from the letter President Washington had sent on the death of Trumbull's father, the wartime governor of Connecticut. In her response, Martha concentrated rather on her husband's extracts, echoing his views in words that reveal her state of soul. The date was January 15, 1800, one month and one day after her husband's death:

When the mind is deeply afflicted by those irreparable losses which are incident to humanity, the good Christian will submit without repining to the dispensations of divine Providence, and look for consolation to that Being who alone can pour balm into the bleeding heart, and who has promised to be the widow's God. But in the severest trials, we find some alleviation to our grief in the sympathy of sincere friends; and I should not do justice to my sensibility, was I not to acknowledge that your kind letter of condolence on the 30th of December was grateful to my feeling. I well knew the affectionate regard which my dear deceased husband always entertained for you, and therefore conceive of what you have given of what was written to you on a former melancholy occasion, is truly applicable to this. The loss is ours; the gain is his.

For myself, I have only to go with humble submission to the will of that God who giveth, and who taketh away, looking forward with faith and hope to the moment when I shall be again united with the partner of my life. But while I continue on earth, my prayers will be offered up for the welfare and happiness of my friends, among whom you will always be numbered, being, Dear Sir,

Your sincere and afflicted friend.[10]

On May 24, 1802, Martha was laid to rest beside her husband in the Mount Vernon vault he had prepared for them.

CONCLUSION

Where, then, does Washington's death fit along the continuum we mentioned at the beginning of this chapter? Safely on the Christian side, we think, for all the reasons recounted earlier in this book, and now with some final reflections, too. As we have learned, what counted as a Christian as of 1799 in Virginia was not as lucid and transparent as in earlier times. Thus, even today, not all will find his the sort of Christian death they would have wished for Washington (or for themselves). Catholics may miss any sign of longing for last communion, such as Hamilton evinced, and evangelicals may miss a confession of sin and a heartfelt turn toward the Savior. After all, the silence of Martha Washington about what she knew of her husband's last disposition, the silence of Tobias Lear about any prayerfulness (even on Martha's part, or that of the servants and doctors, or of Lear himself), and above all the grave taciturnity of Washington himself leave the spectator without the conclusive evidence the mind would seek. Still, it was a noble death and quite Christian in its entire context.

On balance, we think it right to allow Washington that degree of Christian fidelity by which he had always lived, and to which he often exhorted his own family to live, that same fidelity that in time of war he had urged upon his beloved army, and that same fidelity that as general and president he had commended to the entire nation. Since he lived his life as a Christian, it seems reasonable that the benefit of any doubt should lie with the conclusion that he died as one. Besides, death often comes—and even to saints—silent and unadorned.

Chapter 12

A CHRISTIAN?

Pro and Con

I shall only add that if he was not a Christian, he was more like one than any man of same description, whose life has been hitherto recorded.

— Timothy Dwight, President of Yale University[1]

I consider it an indispensable duty to close this last solemn act of my Official life, by commending the Interests of our dearest Country to the protection of Almighty God, and those who have the superintendence of them, to his holy keeping.

— Address to Congress on Resigning His Commission, December 23, 1783[2]

WHAT IS A CHRISTIAN?

There is said to have been an oral tradition that George Washington became a Roman Catholic during the last days of his life.[3] Yet nothing in the records of Washington's death, as we detailed in the last chapter, suggests anything like the last rites of the Catholic church. And insofar as the rumor rests on Washington's well-known friendship with the Carroll family, it is further disproved by their failure ever to hint at such a conversion. Such a revelation would have been of immense symbolic potency for the first Catholic bishop in the United States in 1799, Archbishop Carroll. His eloquent eulogy of his friend George Washington, while ranking among the most memorable of the hundreds of eulogies presented in that season, makes not the slightest hint that Washington was a Catholic. On the contrary, it avoids denominational references altogether, presenting Washington as he so often strove to present himself, namely, as a nonsectarian Christian:

> For his country's safety, he had often braved death, when clad in her most terrific form; he had familiarised himself with her aspect; at her approaching to cut the thread of his life, he beheld her with constancy and serenity; and with his last breath, as we may believe from knowing the ruling passion of his soul, he called to heaven to save his country, and recommend it to the continual protection of that Providence, which he so greatly adored. May his prayer have been heard![4]

In other words, the question "What is a Christian?" admits of many quite different answers. In America, the standard for being counted a Christian is Protestant, not Catholic. But among Protestants, too, there have been quite different measuring rods.

Standards for being counted an Anglican in late-eighteenth-century Virginia included baptism, acceptance of the Apostles' and Nicene Creeds (both of which were recited aloud by the congregation during some services each year), and some regular attendance at church—although the last might be quite attenuated without incurring "excommunication," if that word is not too foreign to express the Anglican temper. It seems quite clear that Washington easily met the standards for being considered an Anglican in good standing. One historian of the Anglican church of that period writes:

> A high assessment of church tradition had not always characterized Anglican thought in America. A latitudinarian mood lingered

throughout the eighteenth century, supplemented by the new confidence in rationality that defined the post-Newtonian intellectual culture. Especially in the early South, some Episcopalians viewed their church as a "temple of reason" besieged by sectarian irrationality. Bishop James Madison (1749–1812) of Virginia and Bishop Samuel Provoost (1742–1815) of New York cultivated such an image of intellectual tolerance that their critics suspected them of deist sympathies.[5]

In other words, George Washington was well within the mainstream of at least one vein of Anglicanism for his time (latitudinarianism) and may actually have held beliefs, and preferred rituals, more conservative than that. The historian continues:

The lofty regard for reason and natural theology in latitudinarian circles found full expression in the pedagogy of Scottish-born William Smith (1727–1803). . . . Smith exemplified the casual attitude toward church tradition in the latitudinarian strain. He led the effort during the 1780s to omit from the proposed prayer book of the post-Revolutionary Episcopal Church two of the ancient creeds (the Nicene and the Athanasian), to drop from the Apostles' Creed any reference to Christ's descent into hell, and to remove any reference to baptismal regeneration.[6]

Clearly, the theological temperament of William Smith seems miles away from Washington's. Washington did not even support his fellow Founder from Virginia James Madison in his "Remonstrance," much less is there evidence that he would bring himself to side with such radicals as William Smith. Indeed, one thing Washington didn't like about theologians (and nearly all clergymen in those days took theology quite seriously) was that so often theologians put others down as less than Christian. It seemed to Washington, as to most Americans, that true religion is better served by steady deeds than by correct definitions on technical points.

All in all, many of Washington's contemporaries, such as his good friend John Marshall, regarded him as a model Christian. On the other side, a minority pointed to two worrisome signs. Washington nearly always refrained from taking communion at the appointed time at Sunday services, and he almost systematically abstained from public declarations of his faith, even when presented with a perfect occasion to do so, and even when actually prompted or point-blank questioned. As noted earlier in this book, Paul F. Boller, Jr., in his book on Washington's religion, gives an extended treatment of one such example of Washington's deliberate evasiveness under questioning.[7] Washington was faithful enough in his public practice, going to church on all sorts of occasions and in many different cities as he traveled. But why was he so reticent in public about his exact affiliation, so unwilling to make public witness to his particular beliefs? It is a puzzle, even for those who defend his good faith as a Christian.

This reticence especially troubled clergymen strongly affected by the evangelical revivals that swept across America with increasing power after about 1780. The standards for being counted a "true" Christian by the evangelical preachers placed far more emphasis on a public declaration of faith, spurred by the vivid personal experience of being born again into the grace of God, acutely conscious of and repentant for one's previous sins.

Given the personal power of this encounter with the divine, it is hard for evangelicals to think of those Christians who have not shared in it as real Christians. In their own lives, they see now, *they* were not true Christians before they had this powerful experience. Studying Washington's life carefully, many of them fail to see signs of this outpouring of personal testimony. His reticence was, by their lights, too phlegmatic and made him seem untouched by true conversion. It was hard for them to see him as a Christian. In fact, certain members of the clergy made a career of undercutting Washington's reputation as a Christian, such as the Reverend Bird Wilson, an Episcopalian minister from Albany, New York: "I have diligently perused every line that Washington ever gave to the public, and I do not find one expression in which he pledges himself as a believer in Christianity. I think anyone who will candidly do as I have done, will come to the conclusion that he was a deist and nothing more."[8]

The argument over whether, and to what degree, Washington was a Christian is visible even in the hundreds of eulogies pronounced upon the occasion of his death, and seems to have been renewed decade after decade—and still goes on today.

Which side is correct? If we look merely at the external structure of the argument as it is actually carried out, the underlying assumption of all parties is Washington's long and historic reputation of having been a model Christian. Added to this tradition have been a number of myths—about his being caught on his knees at prayer at Valley Forge, for instance. In many homes across the country a print of this famous scene has a place of honor, and in others, Washington's "Prayer," adapted from his Circular Letter to the States, has such a place.

Dissenters, however, strip the Circular Letter of the small additions that put it in prayer form and show that the legend of the prayer at Valley Forge has no historical footing. It appears to have been made up by the early popular biographer (hagiographer perhaps, legend writer really) Parson Weems, as a story that vividly illustrated his point about Washington's reliance on Providence. The dissenters also raise nagging questions about Washington's failure to declare himself openly for Jesus Christ and to profess specifically Christian beliefs in a public forum (and, it seems, even in private).

A CHRISTIAN STATESMAN

For some decades after Washington's death, however, when many people still remembered having seen him, his reputation was sky-high, and not only as a victorious general and first president, but as a good man and, more, a Christian statesman. There was a kind of

"Apotheosis of Washington," as the painter in the Capitol Building imagined it. While the dissenters poked holes in this view, by and large those who came down on the positive side of the argument proceeded as though their view represented the common sense of the matter. They spent most of their time rebutting the most egregious allegations of the dissenters. But they did make some new points.

A few things about Washington's faith do seem especially telling. One was the fact that Washington was godfather to at least eight young children in his close circle. To become a godfather or godmother for another person is to take on a public and solemn role in the rite of baptism, whereby the adult agrees to monitor the growth of the godchild in her long education in the Christian faith that life itself supplies—through the trials, doubts, sufferings, and occasional exhilaration that constitute a "pilgrim's progress."

On several occasions, when invited, Thomas Jefferson declined to take on such responsibilities, pleading that to do so would give a false impression of his own religious standing. By contrast, Washington, who was quite capable of avoiding hypocrisy by declining to take part in a communion service of which he did not feel worthy, agreed to undertake this task at least eight times, for members of his own family or the families of friends. Similarly, he took special care and delight in furnishing his own stepchildren and stepgrandchildren (from Martha's first marriage) with bound prayer books and other books about religion, often nicely embossed with their own names.

In a similar way, as mentioned earlier, during his lifetime, Thomas Jefferson was often publicly opposed as a secret atheist. Yet on this front, George Washington had virtually no serious opposition making the sorts of charges launched against Jefferson. Even those who questioned whether Washington was as fully Christian as they would have liked him to be did not portray him as an anti-Christian, in the way that a good many attacked Jefferson. For what it's worth, people of Washington's day almost universally took him to be at least a friend to Christianity, and to some significant degree a good Christian. If some number found him insufficiently Christian by their tests, many others figured they themselves couldn't pass those tests either. However that may be, the public accepted Washington as a Christian, even a model Christian, in a way that a very large proportion of it never accepted Jefferson and made the latter's election in 1800 perilously close.

Again, even though there was not a sufficient number of ministers to appear at Pohick Church (or at other Anglican churches throughout rural Virginia) every Sunday, Washington's own attendance was remarkably regular. More striking still was his regularity in going to church in New York and Philadelphia when the affairs of government took him to those cities, as well as on his presidential trips to visit all the states of the union.

Moreover, the record shows not only that Washington attended church with some regularity (taking account of the fact that on some Sundays each month a minister was not available), but also that he attended the vestry's business meetings with regularity and often took the lead in projects to improve the church or its functioning. In fact, he did double duty in this role, serving also as vestryman for Fairfax Parish in Alexandria (ten miles from Mount Vernon), as well as nearer to Mount Vernon at Pohick Church in Truro Parish (only seven miles away).[9]

One of the overlooked features of Washington's regular attendance at Anglican services, however, is the weekly use in them of the Book of Common Prayer, with its often eloquent and lengthy recitation of the basic tenets of the Christian faith, its invocations of the Trinity, and its tender accounts of the birth, passion, and death of the Son of God. In addition, at least once a month Washington would have heard, with implied consent, and possibly even recited aloud with all the others, the words of the Apostles' or the Nicene Creed. It would be very strained, indeed, to maintain that Washington did not have a habitual familiarity with the great tenets of the Christian faith, or that he had not given them any personal sanction at all by his constant attendance, without dissent, while they were being pronounced by the whole believing body in his presence. There is not the slightest sign that he felt in his public life that he was betraying these beliefs, or in the least being hypocritical about them. Indeed, by various sly allusions to "the Divine Author of our blessed Religion" and "the light of Revelation," from time to time, he subtly indicated the direction of his personal faith, without thrusting it upon others.

With his armies in the field, Washington was if anything even more insistent on the need for regular communal prayer and the sincere participation in it of all. He often warned that they could not expect the favor of God's help in their cause unless they lived in a way worthy of it. He even exhorted them, once or twice, to fight as true Christian soldiers. Their desperate need for the help of Providence was his constant, insistent theme.

Among his troops, in Massachusetts, he banned Guy Fawkes Day, lest the army seem to exclude Catholics from the union—and give offense to the Catholic powers whose alliance the newly independent nation was seeking. He was especially tender, as president, in his addresses to the Hebrew Congregations of Newport, Rhode Island, and Savannah, Georgia. As president, he made a point of responding to all the distinct religious groups that wrote to him, and also to some major Masonic lodges. He wanted all to feel part of the republic, and to know that they had in him a tribune.

THE CRITICS' COMPLAINT

Those who write that Washington was not a serious Christian heap upon his head, it seems, an exceedingly heavy burden of hypocrisy. Innuendo of that sort does not seem to square with his universal reputation for integrity, candor, and thoughtful conduct.

Still, against the affirmation that Washington was a Christian, even some Anglican preachers, with others, alleged the following negatives (and perhaps others):

He never, it seems, took communion at those Sunday services at which it was offered.

He almost invariably stood during prayers (as others did, as well), rather than knelt.

Even when asked to do so, he refused to declare his specific beliefs in public fora.

In private correspondence, as in public utterances, he very rarely used the name of Jesus Christ, and he did not use Christian names for God, such as Redeemer, Savior, Trinity, or Incarnate Lord.

His death seemed more Stoic than Christian—no minister attended; no prayers were said.

His taciturnity about Christian themes gives rise to the suspicion that he was rather more like Jefferson, a Unitarian, in sympathy at least.

Unquestionably, he believed in God, had a special awareness of and gratitude for the role of Providence in his life and the life of America, held religion (for most people) indispensable for the maintenance of republican virtue, and even did all he could to enhance the work of chaplains in the military and ministers (of all religions) in the daily life of the republic—but nearly all of this seems more Stoic than specifically Christian. His view of Providence was Greek or Roman, as if it were a synonym of *fate*.

All these objections have a grain of truth in them. Still, they are consistent with Washington's being a serious Christian who believed that he had a public vocation that required some tact regarding his private confessional life. Naturally, the public role should not contradict (or make a mockery of) the private convictions that governed his known character and practice.

It is not at all unusual for public men in pluralistic American life to maintain a notable reserve about their private convictions. They do not burden the public with declarations of their deepest beliefs, whose general force they trust their actions will sufficiently reveal. In the public forum, they happily give to Caesar what is Caesar's; and in the private forum, to God what is God's. More than most such men, however, Washington often insisted publicly that nations, as well as individuals, have duties to the Creator, and that nations, as well as individuals, must give him public thanks and even publicly beg his pardon for the sins of citizens of all ranks. In this practice, Washington disagreed with Jefferson and Madison. When Madison urged him to sign his "Remonstrance" against Governor Patrick Henry's scheme for a voluntary tax to pay the salary of ministers, Washington demurred.

Although not very frequently, but all the same with great power, Washington was far more public in his declarations of faith than many who would come after him. Washington reached beyond the Constitution to swear his oath of office upon the Bible; he even kissed the Bible upon taking the oath. It is also due to Washington's example that all who came after him in the office of the president have on many public occasions invoked the continued blessings of God upon the nation. With memory still vivid with actual evidences of the "signal interpositions" of Providence in their lives, in nearly every important national speech of his life, Washington recognized with fervent gratitude the manifold blessings visibly showered upon Americans by "the Smiles of Providence."

TESTIMONIES TO HIS FAITH

It may be worth citing here at the end a few lines from the reflections by serious observers near the time of Washington's death. We found particularly striking these lines, first, some from a chaplain who served in Henry Knox's brigade and often observed Washington in his army life, then some from another friendly eulogist, and finally some from members of Washington's family. All these are notable for the modesty of their claims and their judiciousness.

First, here are the comments of the Reverend Alexander MacWhorter, a Presbyterian minister from Newark, New Jersey, who had been a chaplain with the brigade of General Knox and rendered this judgment on the nationally declared Day of Mourning, December 27, 1799, barely two weeks after the death of his commander in chief:

General Washington was a uniform professor of the Christian religion. He steadily discountenanced vice; abhorred the principles of infidelity, and the practice of immorality. He was a constant and devout attendant upon divine worship. In the army he kept no chaplain of his own, but attended divine services with his brigades, in rotation, as far as conveniency would allow, probably to be an example to his officers, and encourage his soldiers to respect religion. He steadily attended the worship of God when president. He was not in this respect like too many, who practically declare themselves superior to honoring their Maker in the offices of religion. He firmly believed in the existence of God and his superintending providence. This appears in almost all his speeches. He was educated in the Episcopal Church, and always continued a member thereof, and was an ornament to the same. He was truly of the catholic faith, and considered the distinction of the great denominations of Christianity rather as shades of difference, than anything substantial or essential to salvation.[10]

Another reverend, Eliab Stone, in Reading, Massachusetts, offered four "proofs" that Washington had lived and died a Christian: On his inauguration day, he promised never to do secular business on the Sabbath, and he never did. He was regular and constant in his attendance at public worship, and his manner was unfailingly "serious and engaged." He "maintained daily intercourse with Heaven by prayer," regularly maintained family prayer, and throughout the War of Independence "he is known to have observed stated seasons of retirement for secret devotion." Finally, both in private and in public communications, he expressed "his deep sense of a superintending providence, and of his own dependence upon the divine care and direction."[11]

Note, however, the date of Stone's eulogy, February 22, 1800. This date is well before the apparently imaginary story of a Quaker witness to the general's private prayer at Valley Forge was told in clever detail by Parson Weems, inserted for the first time only in the seventeenth edition of his early biography of Washington, in 1817.[12] Even if Parson Weems's story is unreliable, as considerable evidence indicates,[13] the "knowledge" that Washington slipped off for private prayer had currency. If true, it would not have been out of character with the piety of his private letters. If true, it would have put Washington's appeals to his officers and soldiers for public and private prayer on the solid foundation of his own example and would have saved him from any feeling of acting as a hypocrite.

The Rev. Stone's report of some knowledge about Washington's recourse to private prayer during the war (and not only during the war) is backed up by many others, including some in Washington's own family. When his stepdaughter, Martha Parke "Patsy" Custis was dying in 1773, Washington's sister-in-law, Hannah Bushrod Washington, later described him to his stepgranddaughter, Nelly, as having prayed "most fervently, most affectingly" at Patsy's bedside. His wife's daughter-in-law, Eleanor Calvert Custis Stuart, related that he kneeled by Patsy's bed and "solemnly recited the prayers for the dying—while tears rolled down his cheeks, & his voice was often broken by sobs."[14]

CONCLUSION

This much must be said. If it was George Washington's intention to maintain a studied ambiguity (and personal privacy) regarding his own deepest religious convictions, so that all Americans, both in his own time and for all time to come, might feel free to approach him on their own terms—and might also feel like full members of the new republic, equal with every other—that is an intention, if such it was, he abundantly fulfilled. Nowadays, the most atheist professor, the rebel from any church, the Mason, and with them the devout Baptist, the serious Catholic, and the active Presbyterian, along with the academic or the lawyer committed to Stoic philosophy who wears even less overlay of religion than Washington, and perhaps even such other American immigrants as Buddhists, Hindus, and Muslims (secular and religious)—all find it possible to repair to Washington as to a figure with whom to identify in spirit.

He was a rare person, open, tolerant, respectful of the consciences of all, faithful to his own tradition without any condescension toward those of others, taciturn about his own personal convictions in order not to throw anyone else off balance—taciturn not because he did not love his own traditions but, on the contrary, because he understood them in an enlarged and authentic sense. A practical man, he had not, as James Madison once remarked of him, "ever attended to the arguments for Christianity, and for the different systems of religion."[15] But about the core questions of the Jewish and Christian religion—the sovereignty of God over all the contingencies of history, and the commandments to love both God and neighbor, the recognition of human weakness in humbleness, and the obligation to be thankful for all the manifold blessings of the Almighty (bearing down upon no people on earth more than the much-blessed Americans)—about all these things, Washington was so secure in his faith and practice as not to have to say much at all. One could look at what he did.

We said at the beginning of this inquiry that we would try to meet three questions, and we believe we have.

First, was Washington a deist? Although we recognize that the term *deism* covers a broad continuum, from breakaway nonbelievers to philosophically minded bishops and Christian laity, the evidence seems to us overwhelming that Washington was not a deist, certainly not at the extremist end of the spectrum. He held as a matter of daily practice and frequent prayer the Jewish and Christian view of God, that is, that God interposes his actions in the affairs of history and all through the daily governance of the universe, not by disrupting the laws of nature but by deftly and artistically using the openings discernible in the dazzling array of life's daily contingencies. It was not against nature for a nor'easter to gather and batter Long Island, but when it did so on August 28 and 29, 1776, and when behind it came an unusual but not unnatural fog that lasted almost exactly as many hours as necessary for Washington to complete his withdrawal from the island—that was not unnatural, either, but it certainly turned out to be a very deft touch of divine artistry indeed.

Washington instructed his men—and later the whole nation—to pray for God's continuing interventions on behalf of the preservation and the prospering of freedom on earth; he asked them also to pray that God would forgive the sins of citizens of all ranks. He prayed to his God as the same God to whom the ancient Israelites had prayed, and as the same to whom Jesus addressed the Lord's Prayer: "Our Father who art in heaven . . . give us this day our daily bread . . . and deliver us from evil."

Those who call Washington a deist mean to contrast being a deist with being a Christian. If the proper name of the deist god was Jehovah, as was true of Washington's God, theirs isn't much of a contrast. The truth is, Washington spoke too much of Providence and the interpositions of God's actions in contingent human affairs to count as a deist in the intended "scientific" sense. He had no use for a watchmaker god indifferent to the affairs of humans, including the fate of freedom in the United States, and universally.

Washington's God had freedom in mind when he made the world. Freedom was one of the Creator's prime architectural principles in designing the world. That is why Washington's God credibly favored the experiment in freedom here in the United States, just as the God Jehovah favored the Hebrews in their liberation from Egypt. The evidence simply does not allow the description of Washington as a deist, unless with so many qualifiers that the name is deprived of its intended sting.

The second question we said we would address is the meaning of the term *Providence*. Should it be understood as *fate* or *fortune* as the Greeks and Romans used those terms? We conclude that the evidence does not allow that. Washington did not think that the outcome of the War of Independence was inexorably fixed in some tragic and inescapable way. Nor did he hold that the God whose name is Jehovah is whimsical and childish in his passions like the gods of the ancient world. Washington distinguished clearly between false gods and the true God. One of the key differences in this distinction is the recognition of full, total, and universal sovereignty even over the *existence* of all things. Another is the recognition that from one active, insightful Mind comes not only all being, but the very notion of truth. We speak of the "true" God, because truth matters; it is of a wholly different order from falsehood, as is the true God from false gods.

It is worth pointing out that Washington differed from Jefferson in turning toward the Hebrew idea of God, instead of the eighteenth-century idea of the watchmaker. Jefferson himself seems to have wavered on what he meant by *providence,* but his providence was usually consistent with the deist idea of god—simply a governor of all things, like the designer of the spring and the wheels of a watch. Washington's idea is much closer to that of the Greeks and Romans, but enlarged by the biblical sense of creation and history, whereas Jefferson's seems closer to the mechanics of the European Enlightenment. Jefferson thought he was much smarter than Washington on these matters and predicted that most Americans would be Unitarian within decades. Jefferson pictured an uncomplicated rational man, inhabiting a moral universe. Washington's vision seems richer in its instinct for the inscrutability of Providence and both human neediness and nobility of soul. Jefferson's seems commendable for its simplicity and clarity. That may be why we admire better Jefferson's play of mind, but Washington's character.

Finally, there is the question whether Washington used Christianity only for civil and political purposes, while secretly maintaining a sort of deistic skepticism about the biblical faith. This notion allows atheists to cozy up to Washington, too. To that extent, we suppose, since the nation's founder ought to be accessible to everybody, Washington's reticence serves a good purpose. Still, for reasons recounted above, the preponderance of the evidence falls fairly heavily on the side of Washington's bona fides as a Christian. Anglican Christianity is what he professed. Anglican Christianity is what he acted out.

Christian preachers of many faiths recognized in him a model Christian. As we have seen, a family in-law published much evidence of how the family regarded him as a Christian.[16] His forebears were Christian, his progeny were Christian. His dearest friend, who thought they were two in one soul, his wife, Martha, a quite devout Christian, was certain they were one in mind above all in their mutual confidence in eternal life together. His last words, and her first words on learning that he was gone, were "'Tis well!"—in itself an almost perfect "Amen."

Since there are so many individual consciences, with so many inner turns and twists, we are reluctant even to attempt to judge the inner drama in which others are engaged, including Washington. Since this deficiency seemed to his own church not to thrust him beyond the pale nor, among those who knew him best, to diminish his reputation as a model Christian, we are inclined to side with that judgment. If we were with St. Peter, we, too, would be inclined to wave Washington through. We would have him stand among the long, long ranks of faithful Christians, however many others (in God's mercy) may also be there.

Whatever others may say, for the authors of this book it would be a happy event if all presidents conducted themselves, to at least the extent that Washington did, as good Christians (or good Jews, or persons of conscience), in private life and in public.

On this point, the first editor of *The Writings of George Washington* (1837, in twelve volumes) and later the president of Harvard,

Jared Sparks, Unitarian though he was, seems to us to have said it well enough:

> If a man, who spoke, wrote, and acted as a Christian through a long life, who gave numerous proofs of his believing himself to be such, and who was never known to say, write, or do a thing contrary to his professions, if such a man is not to be ranked among the believers of Christianity, it would be impossible to establish the point by any train of reasoning. How far he examined the grounds of his faith is uncertain, but probably as far as the large portion of Christians, who do not make theology a special study; and we have a right to presume, that a mind like his would not receive an opinion without a satisfactory reason. He was educated in the Episcopal Church, to which he always adhered; and my conviction is, that he believed in the fundamental doctrines of Christianity as usually taught in that Church, according to his understanding of them; but without a particle of intolerance, or disrespect for the faith and modes of worship adopted by Christians of other denominations.[17]

What we already have in Washington's example is sufficient for the giving of great gratitude to that blessed Providence, who gave our nation so admirable, if so human, a father.

APPENDIX 1

Selected Writings of George Washington

Orders to His Troops
Wartime Proclamations, Declarations, and Circular Letters
Unused Notes for the First Inaugural
Selections from the First Inaugural
Correspondence with Various Congregations
First Declaration of Thanksgiving
Second Declaration of Thanksgiving
Unused Notes for the Farewell Address
Selections from the Farewell Address

ORDERS TO HIS TROOPS

Washington told his men they could not pray for the favor of Providence unless they also acted as Christian soldiers. His words to his troops reflect not only his public beliefs about God and our actions, but also his private beliefs. He was no hypocrite. He held himself to the same standard.

The men are to parade at beating the long roll to-morrow morning at 10 o'clock; and be marched as usual to the Fort, to attend Divine Service. The Officers to be present at calling the roll, and see that the men do appear in the most decent manner they can.[1]

The General most earnestly requires, and expects, a due observance of those articles of war, established for the Government of the army, which forbid profane cursing, swearing and drunkeness; And in like manner requires and expects, of all Officers, and Soldiers, not engaged on actual duty, a punctual attendance on divine Service, to implore the blessings of heaven upon the means used for our safety and defence.[2]

The General orders, that Day [i.e., July 20, 1775, a day of "public humiliation, fasting, and prayer," as ordered by the Continental Congress] to be religiously observed by the Forces under his Command, exactly in manner directed by the proclamation of the Continental Congress: It is therefore strictly enjoin'd on all Officers and Soldiers, (not upon duty) to attend Divine Service, at the accustomed places of worship, as well in the Lines, as the Encampments and Quarters; and it is expected, that all those who go to worship, do take their Arms, Ammunitions and Accoutrements and are prepared for immediate Action if called upon.[3]

The Church to be cleared to morrow, and the Rev'd Mr. Doyles will perform Divine Service therein at ten Oclock.[4]

I also give it in Charge to you to avoid all Disrespect to or Contempt of the Religion of the Country and its Ceremonies. Prudence, Policy, and a true Christian Spirit, will lead us to look with Compassion upon their Errors without insulting them. While we are contending for our own Liberty, we should be very cautious of violating the Rights of Conscience in others, ever considering that God alone is the Judge of the Hearts of Men, and to him only in this Case, they are answerable.[5]

As the Contempt of the Religion of a Country by ridiculing any of its Ceremonies or affronting its Ministers or Votaries has ever been deeply resented, you are to be particularly careful to restrain every Officer and Soldier from such Imprudence and Folly and to punish every Instance of it. On the other Hand, as far as lays in your power, you are to protect and support the free Exercise of the Religion of the Country and the undisturbed Enjoyment of the rights of Conscience in religious Matters, with your utmost Influence and Authority.[6]

As the Commander in Chief has been apprized of a design form'd for the observance of that ridiculous and childish custom of burning the Effigy of the pope [i.e., "Pope's Day," as Guy Fawkes Day was known in the colonies]—He cannot help expressing his surprise that there should be Officers and Soldiers in this army so void of common sense, as not to see the impropriety of such a step at this Juncture; at a Time when we are solliciting, and have really obtain'd, the friendship and alliance of the people of Canada, whom we ought to consider as Brethren embarked in the same Cause. The defence of the general Liberty of America: At such a juncture, and in such Circumstances, to be insulting their Religion, is so monstrous, as not to be suffered or excused; indeed instead of offering the most remote insult, it is our duty to address public thanks to these our Brethren, as to them we are so much indebted for every late happy Success over the common Enemy in Canada.[7]

All Officers, and Soldiers, are strictly enjoined to pay all due reverance, and attention on that day, to the sacred duties due to the Lord of hosts, for his mercies already received, and for those blessings, which our Holiness and Uprightness of life can alone encourage us to hope through his mercy to obtain.[8]

The General commands all officers, and soldiers, to pay strict obedience to the Orders of the Continental Congress, and by their unfeigned, and pious observance of their religious duties, incline the Lord, and Giver of Victory, to prosper our arms.[9]

As the Troops are to be exempt from all duties of fatigue to morrow, the regiments are to parade on their regimental parades, and to be marched from thence a little before Ten, to hear divine service from their respective chaplains.[10]

To be well prepared for an engagement is, under God (whose divine Aid it behoves us to supplicate) more than one half the battle.[11]

Let us therefore rely upon the goodness of the Cause, and the aid of the Supreme Being, in whose hand Victory is, to animate and encourage us to great and noble Actions.[12]

The Colonels or commanding officers of each regiment are directed to procure Chaplains accordingly; persons of good Characters and exemplary lives—To see that all inferior officers and soldiers pay them a suitable respect and attend carefully upon religious exercises. The blessing and protection of Heaven are at all times necessary but especially so in times of public distress and danger.[13]

That the Troops may have an opportunity of attending public worship, as well as take some rest after the great fatigue they have gone through; The General in future excuses them from fatigue duty on Sundays (except at the Ship Yards, or special occasions) until further orders. The General is sorry to be informed that the foolish, and wicked practice, of profane cursing and swearing (a Vice heretofore little known in an American Army) is growing into fashion; he hopes the officers will, by example, as well as influence, endeavour to check it, and that both they, and the men will reflect, that we can have little hopes of the blessing of Heaven on our Arms, if we insult it by our impiety, and folly; added to this, it is a vice so mean and low, without any temptation, that every man of sense, and character, detests and despises it.[14]

All the troops in Morristown, except the Guards, are to attend divine worship to morrow morning at the second Bell; the officers commanding Corps, are to take especial care, that their men appear clean, and decent, and that they are to march in proper order to the place of worship.[15]

All the troops in town (not on duty) to attend divine service to morrow, agreeable to the orders of the 12th. Instant.[16]

All the troops in, and about Morristown (those on duty excepted), are to attend divine service, to morrow morning.[17]

All the troops in, and near Morristown, (except on duty) to attend divine service, to morrow morning.[18]

Let Vice, and Immorality of every kind, be discouraged, as much as possible, in your Brigade; and as a Chaplain is allowed to each Regiment, see that the Men regularly attend divine Worship.[19]

It is much to be lamented, that the foolish and scandalous practice of profane Swearing is exceedingly prevalent in the American Army—Officers of every rank are bound to discourage it, first by their example, and then by punishing offenders—As a mean to abolish this, and every other species of immorality—Brigadiers are enjoined, to take effectual care, to have divine service duly performed in their respective brigades.[20]

[The General] has full confidence that in another Appeal to Heaven with the blessing of providence, which it becomes every officer and soldier humbly to supplicate, we shall prove successful.[21]

All Chaplains are to perform divine service tomorrow, and on every succeeding Sunday, with their respective brigades and regiments, where the situation will possibly admit of it. And the commanding officers of corps are to see that they attend; themselves, with officers of all ranks, setting the example. The Commander in Chief expects an exact compliance with this order, and that it be observed in future as an invariable rule of practice—And every neglect will be considered not only a breach of orders, but a disregard to decency, virtue and religion.[22]

Divine Service to be performed to morrow, in all the regiments which have chaplains.[23]

The General has his happiness completed relative to the successes of our northern Army. On the 14th. instant, General Burgoyne, and his whole Army, surrendered themselves prisoners of war. Let every face brighten, and every heart expand with grateful Joy and praise to the supreme disposer of all events, who has granted us this signal success. The Chaplains of the army are to prepare short discourses, suited to the joyful occasion to deliver to their several corps and brigades at 5 O'clock this afternoon—immediately after which, Thirteen pieces of cannon are to be discharged at the park of artillery, to be followed by a feu-de-joy with blank cartridges, or powder, by every brigade and corps of the army.[24]

The Commander in Chief directs that divine Service be performed every Sunday at 11 O'Clock in those Brigades to which there are Chaplains; those which have none to attend the places of worship nearest to them. It is expected that Officers of all Ranks will by their attendence set an Example to their men.

While we are zealously performing the duties of good Citizens and soldiers we certainly ought not to be inattentive to the higher duties of Religion. To the distinguished Character of Patriot, it should be our highest Glory to add the more distinguished Character of Christian. The signal Instances of providential Goodness which we have experienced and which have now almost crowned our labours with complete Success, demand from us in a peculiar manner the warmest returns of Gratitude and Piety to the Supreme Author of all Good.[25]

Divine Service is to be performed tomorrow in the several Brigades or Divisions. The Commander in Chief earnestly recommends that the troops not on duty should universally attend with that seriousness of Deportment and gratitude of Heart which the recognition of such reiterated and astonishing interpositions of Providence demand of us.[26]

In justice to the zeal and ability of the Chaplains, as well as to his own feelings, the Commander in chief thinks it a duty to declare the regularity and decorum with which divine service is now performed every sunday, will reflect great credit on the army in general, tend to improve the morals, and at the same time, to increase the happiness of the soldiery, and must afford the most pure and rational entertainment for every serious and well disposed mind.[27]

WARTIME PROCLAMATIONS, DECLARATIONS, AND CIRCULAR LETTERS

Washington made very plain that God and religion are indispensable to nations. To be worthy of his favor, we owe the Creator fasting, humiliation, and prayer.

Thursday the seventh Instant, being set apart by the Honourable the Legislature of this province [i.e., Massachusetts], as a day of fasting, prayer, and humiliation, "to implore the Lord, and Giver of all victory, to pardon our manifold sins and wickedness's, and that it would please him to bless the Continental Arms, with his divine favour and protection"—All Officers, and Soldiers, are strictly enjoined to pay all due reverance, and attention on that day, to the sacred duties due to the Lord of hosts, for his mercies already received, and for those blessings, which our Holiness and Uprightness of life can alone encourage us to hope through his mercy to obtain.[28]

The Continental Congress having ordered, Friday the 17th. Instant to be observed as a day of "fasting, humiliation and prayer, humbly to supplicate the mercy of Almighty God, that it would please him to pardon all our manifold sins and transgressions, and to prosper the Arms of the United Colonies, and finally, establish the peace and freedom of America, upon a solid and lasting foundation"———The General commands all officers, and soldiers, to pay strict obedience to the Orders of the

Continental Congress, and by their unfeigned, and pious observance of their religious duties, incline the Lord, and Giver of Victory, to prosper our arms.[29]

The Honorable the Congress having recommended it to the United States to set apart Thursday the 6th. day of May next to be observed as a day of fasting, humiliation and prayer, to acknowledge the gracious interpositions of Providence; to deprecate deserved punishment for our Sins and Ingratitude, to unitedly implore the Protection of Heaven; Success to our Arms and the Arms of our Ally: The Commander in Chief enjoins a religious observance of said day and directs the Chaplains to prepare discourses proper for the occasion; strictly forbidding all recreations and unnecessary labor.[30]

When we consider the magnitude of the prize we contended for, the doubtful nature of the contest, and the favorable manner in which it has terminated, we shall find the greatest possible reason for gratitude and rejoicing; this is a theme that will afford infinite delight to every benevolent and liberal mind, whether the event in contemplation, be considered as the source of present enjoyment or the parent of future happiness; and we shall have equal occasion to felicitate ourselves on the lot which Providence has assigned us, whether we view it in a natural, a political or moral point of light.

The Citizens of America, placed in the most enviable condition, as the sole Lords and Proprietors of a vast Tract of Continent, comprehending all the various soils and climates of the World, and abounding with all the necessaries and conveniencies of life, are now by the late satisfactory pacification, acknowledged to be possessed of absolute freedom and Independency; They are, from this period, to be considered as the Actors on a most conspicuous Theatre, which seems to be peculiarly designated by Providence for the display of human greatness and felicity; Here, they are not only surrounded with every thing which can contribute to the completion of private and domestic enjoyment, but Heaven has crowned all its other blessings, by giving a fairer oppertunity for political happiness, than any other Nation has ever been favored with. Nothing can illustrate these observations more forcibly, than a recollection of the happy conjuncture of times and circumstances, under which our Republic assumed its rank among the Nations; The foundation of our Empire was not laid in the gloomy age of Ignorance and Superstition, but at an Epocha when the rights of mankind were better understood and more clearly defined, than at any former period, the researches of the human mind, after social happiness, have been carried to a great extent, the Treasures of knowledge, acquired by the labours of Philosophers, Sages and Legislatures, through a long succession of years, are laid open for our use, and their collected wisdom may be happily applied in the Establishment of our forms of Government; the free cultivation of Letters, the unbounded extension of Commerce, the progressive refinement of Manners, the growing liberality of sentiment, and above all, the pure and benign light of Revelation, have had ameliorating influence on mankind and increased the blessings of Society. At this auspicious period, the United States came into existence as a Nation, and if their Citizens should not be completely free and happy, the fault will be intirely their own.

Such is our situation, and such are our prospects: but notwithstanding the cup of blessing is thus reached out to us, notwithstanding happiness is ours, if we have a disposition to seize the occasion and make it our own; yet, it appears to me there is an option still left to the United States of America, that it is in their choice, and depends upon their conduct, whether they will be respectable and prosperous, or contemptable and miserable as a Nation.[31]

I now make it my earnest prayer, that God would have you, and the State over which you preside, in his holy protection, that he would incline the hearts of the Citizens to cultivate a spirit of subordination and obedience to Government, to entertain a brotherly affection and love for one another, for their fellow Citizens of the United States at large, and particularly for their brethren who have served in the Field, and finally, that he would most graciously be pleased to dispose us all, to do Justice, to love mercy, and to demean ourselves with that Charity, humility and pacific temper of mind, which were the Characteristicks of the Divine Author of our blessed Religion, and without an humble imitation of whose example in these things, we can never hope to be a happy Nation.[32]

UNUSED NOTES FOR THE FIRST INAUGURAL

Washington's poetic musings on our new nation, and the "searcher of hearts."

If the blessings of Heaven showered thick around us should be spilled on the ground or converted to curses, through the fault of those for whom they were intended, it would not be the first instance of folly or perverseness in short-sighted mortals. The blessed Religion revealed in the word of God will remain an eternal and awful monument to prove that the best Institutions may be abused by human depravity; and that they may even, in some instances be made subservient to the vilest purposes. Should, hereafter, those who are entrusted with the management of this government, incited by the lust of power and prompted by the Supineness or venality of their Constituents, overleap the known barriers of this Constitution and violate the unalienable rights of humanity: it will only serve to shew, that no compact among men (however provident in its construction and sacred in its ratification) can be pronounced everlasting and inviolable, and if I may so express myself, that no Wall of words, that no mount of parchm[en]t can be so formed as to stand against the sweeping torrent of boundless ambition on the one side, aided by the sapping current of corrupted morals on the other.[33]

I feel the consolatory joys of futurity in contemplating the immense deserts, yet untrodden by the foot of man, soon to become fair as the garden of God, soon to be animated by the activity of multitudes & soon to be made vocal with the praises of the *Most High*. Can it be imagined that so many peculiar advantages, of soil &

climate, for agriculture & for navigation were lavished in vain—or that this Continent was not created and reserved so long undiscovered as a Theatre, for those glorious displays of Divine Munificence, the salutary consequence of which shall flow to another Hemisphere & extend through the interminable series of ages? Should not our Souls exult in the prospect? Though I shall not survive to perceive with these bodily senses, but a small portion of the blessed effects which our Revolution will occasion in the rest of the world; yet I enjoy the progress of human society & human happiness in anticipation. I rejoice in a belief that intellectual light will spring up in the dark corners of the earth; that freedom of enquiry will produce liberality of conduct; that mankind will reverse the absurd position that *the many* were, made for *the few*; and that they will not continue slaves in one part of the globe, when they can become freemen in another.[34]

After a consciousness that all is right within and an humble hope of approbation in Heaven—nothing can, assuredly, be so grateful to a virtuous man as the good opinion of his fellow citizens Tho' the partiality of mine led them to consider my holding the Chief Magistracy as a matter of infinitely more consequence than it really is; yet my acceptance must be ascribed rather to an honest willingness to satisfy that partiality, than to an overweening presumption upon my own capacity. Whenever a government is to be instituted or changed by the Consent of the people, confidence in the person at the head of it is, perhaps, more peculiarly necessary. . . . I solemnly assert and appeal to the searcher of hearts to witness the truth of it, that my leaving home to take upon myself the execution of this Office was the greatest personal sacrifice I have ever, in the course of my existence, been called upon to make.[35]

SELECTIONS FROM THE FIRST INAUGURAL

Washington's official text highlights his reliance on the "propitious smiles of Heaven."

Since there is no truth more thoroughly established, than that there exists in the oeconomy and course of nature, an indissoluble union between virtue and happiness, between duty and advantage, between the genuine maxims of an honest and magnanimous policy, and the solid rewards of public prosperity and felicity: Since we ought to be no less persuaded that the propitious smiles of Heaven, can never be expected on a nation that disregards the eternal rules of order and right, which Heaven itself has ordained: And since the preservation of the sacred fire of liberty, and the destiny of the Republican model of Government, are justly considered as deeply, perhaps as finally staked, on the experiment entrusted to the hands of the American people.[36]

I shall take my present leave; but not without resorting once more to the benign parent of the human race, in humble supplication that since he has been pleased to favour the American people, with opportunities for deliberating in perfect tranquility, and dispositions for deciding with unparellelled unanimity on a form of Government, for the security of their Union, and the advancement of their happiness; so his divine blessing may be equally *conspicuous* in the enlarged views, the temperate consultations, and the wise measures on which the success of this Government must depend.[37]

CORRESPONDENCE WITH VARIOUS CONGREGATIONS

In writing to various religious congregations throughout the country, Washington wanted all religious communities to feel welcome in this new nation, and to recognize the critically important role they play in it.

To the United Baptist Churches in Virginia

If I could have entertained the slightest apprehension that the Constitution framed in the Convention, where I had the honor to preside, might possibly endanger the religious rights of any ecclesiastical society, certainly I would never have placed my signature to it; and if I could now conceive that the general government might ever be so administered as to render the liberty of conscience insecure, I beg you will be persuaded that no one would be more zealous than myself to establish effectual barriers against the horrors of spiritual tyranny, and every species of religious persecution. For you, doubtless, remember that I have often expressed my sentiment, that every man, conducting himself as a good citizen, and being accountable to God alone for his religious opinions, ought to be protected in worshipping the Deity according to the dictates of his own conscience.

While I recollect with satisfaction that the religious society of which you are members, have been, throughout America, uniformly, and almost unanimously, the firm friends to civil liberty, and the persevering promoters of our glorious revolution; I cannot hesitate to believe that they will be the faithful supporters of a free, yet efficient general government. Under this pleasing reflection I rejoice to assure them that they may rely on my best wishes and endeavors to advance their prosperity.[38]

To the General Assembly of Presbyterian Churches

While I reiterate the professions of my dependence upon Heaven as the source of all public and private blessings; I will observe that the general prevalence of piety, philanthropy, honesty, industry, and oeconomy seems, in the ordinary course of human affairs, particularly necessary for advancing and confirming the happiness of our country. While all men within our territories are protected in worshipping the Deity according to the dictates of their consciences; it is rationally to be expected from them in return, that they will be emulous of evincing the sanctity of their professions by the innocence of their lives and the beneficence of their actions; for no man, who is profligate in his morals, or a bad member of the civil community, can possibly be a true Christian, or a credit to his own religious society.

I desire you to accept my acknowledgments of your laudable endeavors to render men sober, honest, and good Citizens, and the obedient subjects of a lawful government.[39]

To the Annual Meeting of Quakers

Government being, among other purposes, instituted to protect the persons and consciences of men from oppression, it certainly is the duty of rulers, not only to abstain from it themselves, but, according to their stations, to prevent it in others.

The liberty enjoyed by the people of these states of worshipping Almighty God agreeably to their consciences, is not only among the choicest of their *blessings*, but also of their *rights*. While men perform their social duties faithfully, they do all that society or the state can with propriety demand or expect; and remain responsible only to their Maker for their religion, or modes of faith, which they may prefer or profess.

Your principles and conduct are well known to me; and it is doing the people called Quakers no more than justice to say, that (except their declining to share with others the burden of the common defense) there is no denomination among us, who are more exemplary and useful citizens.

I assure you very explicitly, that in my opinion the conscientious scruples of all men should be treated with great delicacy and tenderness; and it is my wish and desire, that the laws may always be as extensively accommodated to them, as a due regard to the protection and essential interests of the nation may justify and permit.[40]

To the Hebrew Congregations of Philadelphia, New York, Charleston, and Richmond

The liberal sentiment towards each other which marks every political and religious denomination of men in this country stands unrivalled in the history of nations. The affection of such people is a treasure beyond the reach of calculation; and the repeated proofs which my fellow citizens have given of their attachment to me, and approbation of my doings form the purest source of my temporal felicity. The affectionate expressions of your address again excite my gratitude, and receive my warmest acknowledgements.

The power and goodness of the Almighty were strongly manifested in the events of our late glorious revolution, and his kind interposition in our behalf has been no less visible in the establishment of our present equal government. In war he directed the sword and in peace he has ruled in our councils, my agency in both has been guided by the best intentions, and a sense of the duty which I owe my country: and as my exertions hitherto have been amply rewarded by the approbation of my fellow-citizens, I shall endeavor to deserve a continuance of it by my future conduct.[41]

To the Roman Catholics in the United States of America

The prospect of national prosperity now before us is truly animating, and ought to excite the exertions of all good men to establish and secure the happiness of their country, in the permanent duration of its freedom and independence. America, under the smiles of a Divine Providence, the protection of a good government, and the cultivation of manners, morals, and piety, cannot fail of attaining an uncommon degree of eminence, in literature, commerce, agriculture, improvements at home and respectability abroad.

As mankind become more liberal they will be more apt to allow that all those who conduct themselves as worthy members of the community are equally entitled to the protection of civil government. I hope ever to see America among the foremost nations in examples of justice and liberality. And I presume that your fellow-citizens will not forget the patriotic part which you took in the accomplishment of their Revolution, and the establishment of their government; or the important assistance which they received from a nation in which the Roman Catholic faith is professed.

I thank you, gentlemen, for your kind concern for me. While my life and my health shall continue, in whatever situation I may be, it shall be my constant endeavour to justify the favourable sentiments which you are pleased to express of my conduct. And may the members of your society in America, animated alone by the pure spirit of Christianity, and still conducting themselves as the faithful subjects of our free government, enjoy every temporal and spiritual felicity.[42]

To the Hebrew Congregation of Newport

The citizens of the United States of America have a right to applaud themselves for having given to mankind examples of an enlarged and liberal policy—a policy worthy of imitation. All possess alike liberty of conscience and immunities of citizenship.

It is now no more that toleration is spoken of as if it were the indulgence of one class of people that another enjoyed the exercise of their inherent natural rights, for, happily, the Government of the United States, which gives to bigotry no sanction, to persecution no assistance, requires only that they who live under its protection should demean themselves as good citizens in giving it on all occasions their effectual support.

It would be inconsistent with the frankness of my character not to avow that I am pleased with your favorable opinion of my administration and fervent wishes for my felicity.

May the children of the stock of Abraham who dwell in this land continue to merit and enjoy the good will of the other inhabitants—while every one shall sit in safety under his own vine and fig tree and there shall be none to make him afraid.

May the father of all mercies scatter light, and not darkness, upon our paths, and make us all in our several vocations useful here, and in His own due time and way everlastingly happy.[43]

To the Hebrew Congregation of the City of Savannah, Georgia

I rejoice that a spirit of liberality and philanthropy is much more prevalent than it formerly was among the enlightened nations of the earth, and that your brethren will benefit thereby in proportion as it shall become still more extensive; happily the people of the United States have in many instances exhibited examples worthy of imitation, the salutary influence of which will doubtless extend much farther if gratefully enjoying those blessings of peace which (under the favor of heaven) have been attained by fortitude in war, they shall conduct themselves with reverence to the Deity and charity toward their fellow-creatures.

May the same wonder-working Deity, who long since delivered the Hebrews from their Egyptian oppressors, planted them in a promised land, whose providential agency has lately been conspicuous in establishing these United States as an independent nation, still continue to water them with the dews of heaven and make the inhabitants of every denomination participate in the temporal and spiritual blessings of that people whose God is Jehovah.[44]

FIRST DECLARATION OF THANKSGIVING

Reading much like a prayer, this declaration of Washington's is explicit in its demands on all citizens for thanks and gratitude to God—an active and involved God who can "bless" us.

Whereas it is the duty of all Nations to acknowledge the providence of Almighty God, to obey his will, to be grateful for his benefits, and humbly to implore his protection and favor, and Whereas both Houses of Congress have by their joint Committee requested me "to recommend to the People of the United States a day of public thanks-giving and prayer to be observed by acknowledging with grateful hearts the many signal favors of Almighty God, especially by affording them an opportunity peaceably to establish a form of government for their safety and happiness." Now therefore I do recommend and assign Thursday the 26th. day of November next to be devoted by the People of these States to the service of that great and glorious Being, who is the beneficent Author of all the good that was, that is, or that will be. That we may then all unite in rendering unto him our sincere and humble thanks, for his kind care and protection of the People of this country previous to their becoming a Nation, for the signal and manifold mercies, and the favorable interpositions of his providence, which we experienced in the course and conclusion of the late war, for the great degree of tranquillity, union, and plenty, which we have since enjoyed, for the peaceable and rational manner in which we have been enabled to establish constitutions of government for our safety and happiness, and particularly the national One now lately instituted, for the civil and religious liberty with which we are blessed, and the means we have of acquiring and diffusing useful knowledge and in general for all the great and various favors which he hath been pleased to confer upon us. And also that we may then unite in most humbly offering our prayers and supplications to the great Lord and Ruler of Nations and beseech him to pardon our national and other transgressions, to enable us all, whether in public or private stations, to perform our several and relative duties properly and punctually, to render our national government a blessing to all the People, by constantly being a government of wise, just and constitutional laws, discreetly and faithfully executed and obeyed, to protect and guide all Sovereigns and Nations (especially such as have shown kindness unto us) and to bless them with good government, peace, and concord. To promote the knowledge and practice of true religion and virtue, and the encrease of science among them and Us, and generally to grant unto all Mankind such a degree of temporal prosperity as he alone knows to be best.[45]

SECOND DECLARATION OF THANKSGIVING

Not as obviously a "prayer" as the First Declaration, this one is in some ways more "moralizing" in its recommendations for "public thanksgiving and prayer" as Washington worries about the calamities that could strike our fledgling nation.

When we review the calamities which afflict so many other nations, the present condition of the United States affords much matter of consolation and satisfaction. Our exemption hitherto from foreign war, an increasing prospect of the continuance of that exemption, the great degree of internal tranquillity we have enjoyed, the recent confirmation of that tranquillity by the suppression of an insurrection which so wantonly threatened it, the happy course of our public affairs in general, the unexampled prosperity of all classes of our citizens, are circumstances which peculiarly mark our situation with indications of the Divine beneficence toward us. In such a state of things it is in an especial manner our duty as a people, with devout reverence and affectionate gratitude, to acknowledge our many and great obligations to Almighty God and to implore Him to continue and confirm the blessings we experience. Deeply penetrated with this sentiment, I, George Washington, President of the United States, do recommend to all religious societies and denominations, and to all persons whomsoever, within the United States to set apart and observe Thursday, the 19th day of February next, as a day of public thanksgiving and prayer, and on that day to meet together and render their sincere and hearty thanks to the Great Ruler of Nations for the manifold and signal mercies which distinguish our lot as a nation, particularly for the possession of constitutions of government which unite and by their union establish liberty with order; for the preservation of our peace, foreign and domestic; for the seasonable control which has been given to a spirit of disorder in the suppression of the late insurrection, and generally, for the prosperous course of our affairs, public and private; and at the same time humbly and fervently to beseech the kind Author of these blessings graciously to prolong them to us; to imprint on our hearts a deep and solemn sense of our obligations to Him for them; to teach us rightly to estimate their immense value; to preserve us from the arrogance of prosperity, and from hazarding the advantages we enjoy by delusive pursuits; to dispose us to merit the continuance of His favors by not abusing them; by our gratitude for them, and by a correspondent conduct as citizens and men; to render this country more and more a safe and propitious asylum for the unfortunate of other countries; to extend among us true and useful knowledge; to diffuse and establish habits of sobriety, order, morality, and piety, and finally, to impart all the blessings we possess, or ask for ourselves, to the whole family of mankind.[46]

UNUSED NOTES FOR THE FAREWELL ADDRESS

Washington continues as "nursing father"—chiding all citizens lest they seem ungrateful for the "beneficence" offered them in such abundance.

That as the allwise dispensor of human blessings has favored no Nation of the Earth with more abundant, and substantial means of happiness than United America, that we may not be so ungrateful to our Creator; so wanting to ourselves; and so regardless of Posterity, as to dash the cup of beneficence which is thus bountifully offered to our acceptance.[47]

SELECTIONS FROM THE FAREWELL ADDRESS

Although never actually spoken, this address is a masterpiece of Washington's final public opinions on government and the new nation. Its memorable axiom that "religion and morality are indispensable supports" to free republics remains an important message.

Of all the dispositions and habits which lead to political prosperity, Religion and morality are indispensable supports. In vain would that man claim the tribute of Patriotism, who should labour to subvert these great Pillars of human happiness, these firmest props of the duties of Men & citizens. The mere Politician, equally with the pious man ought to respect & to cherish them. A volume could not trace all their connections with private and public felicity. Let it simply be asked where is the security for property, for reputation, for life, if the sense of religious obligation desert the oaths, which are the instruments of investigation in Courts of Justice? And let us with caution indulge the supposition, that morality can be maintained without religion. Whatever may be conceded to the influence of refined education on minds of peculiar structure, reason and experience both forbid us to expect that National morality can prevail in exclusion of religious principle.[48]

Observe good faith and justice towds. all Nations. Cultivate peace and harmony with all. Religion and morality enjoin this conduct; and can it be that good policy does not equally enjoin it? It will be worthy of a free, enlightened, and, at no distant period, a great Nation, to give to mankind the magnanimous and too novel example of a People always guided by an exalted justice and benevolence. Who can doubt that in the course of time and things the fruits of such a plan would richly repay any temporary advantages wch. might be lost by a steady adherence to it? Can it be, that Providence has not connected the permanent felicity of a Nation with its virtue? The experiment, at least, is recommended by every sentiment which ennobles human Nature. Alas! is it rendered impossible by its vices?[49]

APPENDIX 2

Washington's Names for Providence

For me, it is enough to have seen the divine Arm visibly outstretched for our deliverance, and to have recd the approbation of my Country, and my Conscience on account of my humble instrumentality in carrying the designs of **Providence** *into effect; but for my gallant Associates in the Field, who have so essentially contributed to the establishment of our Independence and national glory, no rewards can be too great.*

George Washington
"To the Legislature of New Jersey,"
December 6, 1783, WGW 27:261

"Almighty"[1]
"Almighty and Merciful Sovereign of the Universe"[2]
"Almighty Being who rules over the Universe"[3]
"Almighty God"[4]
"Almighty Ruler of the Universe"[5]
"Allwise disposer of events"[6]
"Allwise Providence "[7]
"All-Powerful Guide"[8]
"All-Powerful Providence"[9]
"All-wise and Most Gracious Providence"[10]
"All-wise and Uncontrollable Providence"[11]
"All Wise and Powerful Being"[12]
"All Wise, and all Powerfull Director of Human Events"[13]
"All wise Creator"[14]
"Allwise Dispensor of human blessings"[15]
"All-wise Disposer of [circumstances]"[16]
"Author of All Blessing"[17]
"Author of All Good"[18]
"Author of the Universe"[19]

"That Being, in whose hands are all of Human Events"[20]
"That Being, who is powerful to save, and in whose hands is the fate of nations"[21]
"That Being who sees, foresees, and directs all things"[22]
"Beneficent Being"[23]
"Beneficent Author of all good that was, that is, or that will be"[24]
"Benign Parent of the Human Race"[25]
"Bounteous Providence"[26]
"Bountiful Providence"[27]
"Creator"[28]
"Deity"[29]
"Director of human events"[30]
"Divine Arm"[31]
"Divine Author of life and felicity"[32]
"Divine Author of our blessed Religion"[33]
"Divine Being"[34]
"Divine Beneficence"[35]
"Divine Blessing"[36]
"Divine Goodness"[37]
"Divine governmt."[38]
"Divine Providence"[39]
"Eye of Omnipotence"[40]
"Father of All Mercies"[41]
"Giver of Life"[42]
"Giver of Victory"[43]
"God"[44]
"God of Armies"[45]
"Good Providence"[46]
"Governor of the Universe"[47]
"Gracious and All Kind Providence"[48]
"Gracious God"[49]
"Gracious Providence"[50]
"Grand Architect of the Universe"[51]
"Great and Glorious Being"[52]
"Great and Good Being"[53]
"Great Arbiter of the universe"[54]
"Great Author of all the care and good"[55]
"Great Author of every public and private good"[56]
"Great Author of the Universe"[57]
"Great Creator"[58]
"Great Director of Events"[59]
"Great Disposer of Human Events"[60]
"Great governor of the Universe"[61]
"Great power above"[62]

"Great Ruler of events"[63]
"Great Ruler of Nations"[64]
"Great Ruler of the Universe"[65]
"Great Searcher of human hearts"[66]
"Greatest and Best of Beings"[67]
"Heaven"[68]
"Indulgent Providence"[69]
"Infinite Goodness"[70]
"Invisible Hand"[71]
"Infinite Wisdom"[72]
"Jehovah"[73]
"Judge of the Hearts of Men"[74]
"Jesus Christ"[75]
"Kind Author"[76]
"Kind Providence"[77]
"Lord"[78]
"Lord and Giver of All Victory"[79]
"Lord and Ruler of Nations"[80]
"Lord of Hosts"[81]
"Maker"[82]
"Name of That Being, from Whose Bountiful Goodness We are Permitted to Exist and Enjoy the Comforts of Life"[83]
"Omnipotent Being"[84]
"Overruling Providence"[85]
"Power"[86]
"Providence"[87]
"Pure and Benign Light of Revelation"[88]
"Sovereign Arbiter of Nations"[89]
"Sovereign Dispenser of life and health"[90]
"Superintending Power"[91]
"Superintending Providence"[92]
"Supreme Arbiter of Human Events"[93]
"Supreme Architect of the Universe"[94]
"Supreme Author of All Good"[95]
"Supreme Being"[96]
"Supreme Dispenser of every Good"[97]
"Supreme Disposer"[98]
"Supreme Ruler of Nations"[99]
"Supreme Ruler of the Universe"[100]
"Wise disposer of all Events"[101]
"Wonder-working Deity"[102]

ACKNOWLEDGMENTS

First of all, our warmest thanks to Jim Rees, Executive Director of the Museum and Visitors' Center at Mount Vernon, who first invited us to take on this project, and whose support has been invaluable. We also warmly thank Mary Thompson, historian at Mount Vernon, who has been working on George Washington's religion for years longer than we have, and whose forthcoming study, "*In the Hands of a Good Providence,*" is a book far more substantial and detailed than ours. Her generous spirit in allowing us to draw upon her work is rare and precious in the annals of scholarship. Dawn Bonner from Mount Vernon donated her time and creativity in assembling the assortment of illustrations. Similarly, we are grateful to Gerald E. Kahler of Williamsburg, who graciously shared with us his distinguished thesis on the almost four hundred eulogies given after George Washington's death, successfully presented for a graduate degree at the College of William and Mary.

Closer to home, we are enormously in the debt of Christopher Levenick, a graduate student in history at the University of Chicago and currently the W. H. Brady Fellow at the American Enterprise Institute. Over two years, he devoted a sizable portion of his time and his formidable historical skills to building up our files on the religion of George Washington, proposing many novel arguments, warning us away from errors great and small, and helping with vital distinctions. Looking back on it, we find his help to have been indispensable and wonder how we could have gone forward without him, especially since he came to our assistance quite serendipitously—"from the hands of a good Providence," we think.

In addition, we have had the assistance on this project of extraordinary interns at the American Enterprise Institute over the last three years, notably Laura Niver, who had worked for Jana on Capitol Hill and who got our files started in a solid fashion; Tim Foley from Georgetown; Stephen White fresh from the University of Dallas; Joe Manzari of the University of California at San Diego; Jeffrey Morris just after his graduation from Yale; Jonathan Fluger as a freshman at Princeton; and Jonathan Murray from the University of Alabama.

Until early September 2005, Michael Leaser was most cheerfully the linchpin of the office, performing many of the chores of keeping the manuscript typed in a uniform way and managing the flow of paper and people. In the last few months before publication, Kyle Vander Meulen took up these tasks brilliantly.

We are grateful to Loretta Barrett, our creative and most supportive literary agent, and to our great editor at Perseus Books, Liz Maguire, who believed we could do it in a time frame we thought impossible—and whose warm, prodding assistance helped prove she was right.

We are also undyingly grateful to those friends and more distant colleagues in inquiry who gave their most precious time to read and criticize early drafts of this manuscript, saving us from untold errors, and guiding us to overlooked materials: Gordon Wood, author of *The Creation of the American Republic 1776–1787* and *The Radicalism of the American Revolution*; James H. Hutson, who, in addition to serving as chief of the Manuscript Division at the Library of Congress, edited *Religion and the War Republic* and wrote *The Forgotten Features of the Founding*; and Matthew Spalding, the author of *A Sacred Union of Citizens*. Each of these authors swiftly read parts of the manuscript and gave valuable criticisms and suggestions.

We must, however, single out C. Robert Leith, instructor of history at Ohio University Southern Campus, and especially Frank E. Grizzard Jr., author of *The George Washington Encyclopedia* and *The Ways of Providence: Religion and George Washington*. Both gave painstaking, detailed, and truly creative criticisms. They also proposed numerous additions, some of which have been included. Their herculean generosity made this a far better book. Only the limitations of the joint authors of this "detective story" are responsible for the errors that remain.

Finally, we must extend our love and thanks to our beautiful and smart wife and mother, Karen Laub Novak—without whom, for us, nothing is possible.

With great gratitude to all!

Michael and Jana Novak
October 2005

NOTES

LIST OF ABBREVIATIONS USED IN THE NOTES

DGW: Diaries of George Washington.
PGW: *The Papers of George Washington.*
WGW: *The Writings of George Washington.*

PREFACE

1. Frank E. Grizzard, Jr., *The Ways of Providence: Religion and George Washington* (Buena Vista, Va.: Mariner, 2005), pp. 19–24.

2. James H. Hutson, "Forum—Thomas Jefferson's Letter to the Danbury Baptists: A Controversy Rejoined," *William and Mary Quarterly,* Vol. 49, No. 4 (1999), pp. 775–790.

CHAPTER 1

1. Letter from Abigail Adams to her sister, Mary Smith Cranch, December 22, 1799, Philadelphia, quoted in Peter Hannaford, *The Essential George Washington: Two Hundred Years of Observations on the Man, the Myth, the Patriot* (Bennington, Vt.: Images from the Past, 1999), pp. 5–6.

2. Douglas Southall Freeman, *George Washington: Planter and Patriot,* Vol. 3 (New York: Scribner's, 1951), p. 6; James Thomas Flexner, *George Washington: The Forge of Experience (1732–1775)* (Boston: Little, Brown, 1965), pp. 191–192.

3. Hannaford, *Essential George Washington,* pp. 5–6.

4. Hannaford, *Essential George Washington,* p. 12.

5. See William B. Allen, ed., *George Washington: A Collection* (Indianapolis, Ind.: Liberty Fund, 1988), pp. 463–465, esp. p. 464.

6. Hannaford, *Essential George Washington,* p. 30.

7. Ibid., p. 23.

8. According to recent research, this still may have been the largest in North America and produced unusually tasty blends. See, e.g., Albert Eisle, "Resurrecting

George Washington's Booze," *The Hill,* June 9, 2005 (http://www.hillnews.com/TheHill/Features/CapitalLiving/060905.html).

9. See account in Garry Wills, *Cincinnatus: George Washington and the Enlightenment* (Garden City, N.Y.: Doubleday, 1984), pp. 52–53.

10. Mary V. Thompson, "In the Hands of a Good Providence," manuscript in the Library of Mount Vernon (publication forthcoming).

11. Ibid., pp. 26–27. See also Chapter 2, "Birth and Education," in Mason Locke Weems, *A History of the Life, Death, Virtues, and Exploits of George Washington* (Philadelphia: Lippincott, 1918). Mason Locke Weems (1759–1825) was an Anglican parson (hence his nickname, Parson Weems) and itinerant bookseller who had an extraordinary gift for enrapturing audiences with his storytelling abilities and, in another mood, regaling them with laughter until they shook and hooted. His brief biography of Washington, hardly a hundred pages long, went through edition after edition after its first publication in 1800. He dedicated the volume—expressly designed to stir readers with the desire to emulate Washington's piety, virtue, patriotism, and heroic action—to Martha Washington and took pains to interview as many members of the Washington family, neighbors, and early associates as he could. For certain, no other biographer has as many stories about Washington's earliest years. Nonetheless, for more than a century, it has been fashionable for historians heavily to discount Weems's biography, because it is so manifestly pious, filled with exclamation marks, and even saccharine in its sentiments of admiration (bordering on flattery of the family). It is modeled on ancient biographies of heroes, perhaps even fables of the heroes, so that the reader is never sure whether its stories have a basis in historical fact or are simply tales of moral "types" and "models," intended to inspire. Even in the latter instance, though, these stories do tend to highlight the very virtues that the most sober critics of Washington admit to admiring, for example, his honesty, tender care for morals and manners, and confidence in Providence. It is certain that various members of the Washington family, well into the nineteenth century, were still repeating the anecdotes that Weems made famous, such as the stories of the cherry tree and the cabbage seeds. The family seemed to accept his anecdotes. Without necessarily committing themselves to the literal truth of the details of these stories, they repeated them as signposts pointing toward Washington's real virtues. The best edition of Weems available today is Marcus Cunliffe (Cambridge, Mass.: Belknap Press of Harvard University Press, 1962), and the rather florid but arresting tales of Washington's childhood are at pages 6–16. Each of the three main stories stresses the loving eagerness of Augustine Washington to teach his son the importance of sharing, honesty, and attention to his "true father," the Almighty, Providence. Quite clearly, the father is the focal point of these stories, the son merely the pupil. The stories are all the more affecting and believable because of that device. For our part, we do not judge these stories to be factual; there is insufficient evidence for them. On the other hand, it is not right to deprive ourselves of pointers that the Washington family accepted as verisimilitude, as did many readers of those early years who had known George Washington quite well. We do not, in other cases, disavow the "poetic truth" embodied in certain anecdotes about

people, and in this case family approval seems to warrant something a little stronger than mere poetic truth, if not quite so strong as literal truth. It seems to us that Weems's interviews of those who knew the young Washington deserve some credibility. It is too bad that his treatment of his own research weakens our willingness to take his words at full face value.

12. Flexner, *Forge of Experience* pp. 191–192; Freeman, *Planter and Patriot,* Vol. 3, p. 6.

13. Ibid.

14. Garry Wills, *Cincinnatus,* p. xxii; Freeman, *Planter and Patriot,* Vol. 3, p. 293.

15. David D. Kirkpatrick,"Putting God Back into American History," *New York Times,* February 27, 2005.

16. Of course, "lukewarm" could be intended as an insult: See, e.g., Revelation 3:15–16, "I know your deeds, that you are neither cold nor hot. I wish you were either one or the other! So, because you are lukewarm—neither hot nor cold—I am about to spit you out of my mouth."

17. Seneca, *De Providentia,* II.9. Washington had Seneca (in English) in his personal library.

18. Thompson, "In the Hands," pp. 35–43; Paul F. Boller, *George Washington and Religion* (Dallas: Southern Methodist University Press, 1963), pp. 39–43.

19. Paul K. Longmore, *The Invention of George Washington* (Berkeley: University of California Press, 1989), p. 182.

20. Flexner, *Forge of Experience,* pp. 191–192; Freeman, *Planter and Patriot,* Vol. 3, p. 6.

21. James Thomas Flexner, *George Washington in the American Revolution, 1775–1783* (Boston: Little, Brown, 1967, 1968), p. 203.

22. Letter from Edward Thornton to James Bland Burges (a member of Parliament and undersecretary to the secretary of state for the Foreign Department), April 2, 1792, quoted in Hannaford, *Essential George Washington,* pp. 75–76.

23. Letter from Thomas Jefferson to Dr. Walter Jones, January 2, 1814, quoted in Hannaford, *Essential George Washington,* p. 42.

24. Edmund S. Morgan, *The Genius of George Washington* (New York: Norton, 1980), pp. 3–25.

CHAPTER 2

1. "George Washington Bicentennial News," *Alexandria* [Virginia] *Gazette,* November 1932 (Vol. 2, No. 2), in Peter Hannaford, *The Essential George Washington* (Bennington, Vt.: Images from the Past, 1999), p. 60.

2. Mary V. Thompson, "In the Hands of a Good Providence" p. 25, in which she cites Jack D. Warren, Jr., "The Childhood of George Washington," *Northern Neck of Virginia Historical Magazine,* Vol. 49, No. 1 (December 1999), pp. 5786–5787.

3. James Thomas Flexner, *Washington: The Indispensable Man* (New York: Signet, 1984), p. 3.

4. Thompson, "In the Hands," pp. 29–30

5. Flexner, *Indispensible Man*, p. 37.

6. "'Nursing fathers' appears in the 23rd verse of the 49th chapter of the book of Isaiah, which in the King James Version of the Bible (1611) reads: 'And kings shall be thy nursing fathers, and their queenes thy nursing mothers: they shall bow downe to thee with their face toward the earth, and licke up the dust of thy feete, and thou shalt know that I am the LORD; for they shall not be ashamed that waite for me.'" James Hutson, *Forgotten Features of the Founding* (Lanham, Md.: Rowman & Littlefield, 2003), p. 46.

7. "General Orders," July 9, 1776, WGW 5:245–246: "The Colonels or commanding officers of each regiment are directed to procure Chaplains accordingly; persons of good Characters and exemplary lives—To see that all inferior officers and soldiers pay them a suitable respect and attend carefully upon religious exercises. The blessing and protection of Heaven are at all times necessary but especially so in times of public distress and danger—The General hopes and trusts, that every officer and man, will endeavour so to live, and act, as becomes a Christian Soldier defending the dearest Rights and Liberties of his country."

8. "General Orders," September 26, 1780, WGW 20:95.

9. "To Colonel Lewis Nicola," May 22, 1782, WGW 24:273.

10. Josiah Quincy, ed., *Journals of Major Samuel Shaw, The First American Consul at Canton* (Boston: Wm. Crosby and H. P. Nichols, 1847), pp. 103–105.

11. Andrew A. Lipscomb and Albert Ellery Bergh, eds., "To George Washington, 1784," *The Writings of Thomas Jefferson*, Memorial Edition, Vol. 4 (Washington, D.C., 1903–1904), p. 218. Also in Julian P. Boyd, ed., *The Papers of Thomas Jefferson*, Vol. 7 (Princeton, N.J.: Princeton University Press, 1950–ongoing), p. 106.

12. "To Major General Henry Knox," February 20, 1784, WGW 27:341–342.

13. "To Boinod and Gaillard," February 18, 1784, WGW 27:338.

14. For a brilliant exposition, see Chapter 2, "The Dinner," in Joseph Ellis, *Founding Brothers* (New York: Knopf, 2000), pp. 48–80.

15. Flexner, *Indispensible Man*, p. 370.

CHAPTER 3

1. "To John Augustine Washington," July 18, 1755, WGW 1:152.

2. Christopher Gist, *Journals*, ed. William M. Darlington (Pittsburgh, Pa., 1893), pp. 84–86. This book was republished in January 2002 by Heritage Books in Maryland. Quoted in James Thomas Flexner, *George Washington: The Forge of Experience (1732–1775)*, (Boston: Little, Brown, 1965), p. 74.

3. Flexner, *Forge of Experience*, p. 59.

4. "Journey to the French Commandant," 1753, WGW 1:23.

5. Flexner, *Forge of Experience*, p. 67.

6. Gist, *Journals*, p. 84.

7. James Thomas Flexner, *Washington: The Indispensable Man* (New York: Signet, 1984), p. 13.

8. "To John Augustine Washington," May 31, 1754, WGW 1:70.

9. Flexner, *Forge of Experience,* p. 92.

10. Flexner, *Indispensable Man,* p. 108.

11. "To John Augustine Washington," July 18, 1755, WGW 1:152. The 1784–1785 change is as follows: "oppertunity of contradicting the first and of assuring you that I have not as yet, composed the latter. But by the all powerful dispensams. [*sic*] of Providence, I have been protected beyond all human probability and expectation for I had 4 Bullets," etc.

12. William J. Federer, *America's God and Country: Encyclopedia of Quotations* (Coppel, Tex.: Fame Publishing), p. 637.

13. "Biographical Memoranda," WGW 29:44.

14. "Biographical Memoranda," WGW 29:45.

15. "To Robert Jackson," August 2, 1755, WGW 1:155.

16. WGW 1:152n. The Rev. Samuel Davies, at that time a clergyman in Hanover County, preached an August 17 sermon to one of these companies, which was printed in Philadelphia and London and was entitled *Religion and Patriotism the Constituents of a Good Soldier.* After applauding the patriotic spirit and military ardor, which had begun to manifest themselves, the preacher added the quote in the text.

17. "Biographical Memoranda," WGW 29:47.

18. "To Rev. William Gordon," May 13, 1776, WGW 37:526.

CHAPTER 4

1. "To Brigadier General Thomas Nelson," August 20, 1778, WGW 12:343.

2. "To Rev. William Gordon," March 9, 1781, WGW 21:332.

3. Thomas Paine, *Thomas Paine: Collected Writings,* ed. Eric Foner (New York: Library of America, 1995), p. 91.

4. "To Martha Washington," June 18, 1775, WGW 3:294.

5. "To Burwell Bassett," June 19, 1775, WGW 3:297.

6. "To [Governor] Robert Dinwiddie," November 9, 1756, WGW 1:505

7. "To John Blair [president of the Virginia Council]," April 17, 1758, WGW 2:178.

8. "General Orders," July 4, 1775, WGW 3:309.

9. "General Orders," November 14, 1775, WGW 4:87.

10. "General Orders," September 13, 1777, WGW 9:211.

11. "General Orders," October 20, 1781, WGW 23:247.

12. John Witherspoon, "The Dominion of Providence over the Passions of Men," May 17, 1776, in Ellis Sandoz, ed., *Political Sermons of the American Founding Era: 1730–1805* (Indianapolis, Ind.: Liberty Fund, 1991), pp. 546–547.

13. "To Joseph Reed," November 30, 1775, WGW 4:130.

14. "To Joseph Reed," January 14, 1776, WGW 4:243.

15. "From Rev. William Gordon to Samuel Wilcon," April 6, 1776, *Proceedings of the Massachusetts Historical Society,* Vol. 60 (October 1926–June 1927), p. 363.

16. David McCullough, *1776* (New York: Simon & Schuster, 2005), p. 96.

17. "To Joseph Reed," March 7, 1776, WGW 4:380.

18. "From Abigail Adams to John Adams," March 16, 1776, in *Adams Family Correspondence*, Vol. 1 (Cambridge, Mass.: Belknap Press, 1963), p. 360.

19. "To Josiah Quincy," March 24, 1776, WGW 4:421–422.

20. "General Orders," July 2, 1776, WGW 5:211–212.

21. "To Lund Washington," August 19, 1776, WGW 5:458.

22. George F. Scheer and Hugh F. Rankin, eds., *Rebels and Redcoats: The American Revolution Through the Eyes of Those Who Fought and Lived It* (New York: Da Capo Press, 1957), p. 168.

23. McCullough, *1776*, p. 186.

24. Scheer and Rankin, eds., *Rebels and Redcoats*, p. 171.

25. "To Andrew Lewis," October 15, 1778, WGW 13:79.

26. "General Orders," September 3, 1776, WGW 6:8.

CHAPTER 5

1. "General Orders," August 3, 1776, WGW 5:367.

2. "Letter to the President of Congress," April 18, 1776, WGW 4:489.

3. *The Federalist Papers*, ed. Clinton Rossiter (New York: Mentor, 1961), p. 72.

4. David Hackett Fischer, *Washington's Crossing* (New York: Oxford University Press, 2004), pp. 5–6. Beginning with the Boston campaign, Washington's practice appears to have varied according to the character of the unit in question. Some would never brook physical punishment, whereas other units could not be disciplined without it. The gentleman Whigs of the Baltimore Cadets, for instance, one of the best regiments in the army and deadly serious about soldiering, claimed immunity from corporal punishment and served by personal contract (p. 29). Some of the units from western Virginia and western Pennsylvania, with their long rifles and hunting shirts and independent ways, at times needed uncompromising punishment to set an example. David McCullough explains how rough punishment sometimes was in his magisterial book *1776* (New York: Simon & Schuster, 2005), p. 32.

5. Edmund S. Morgan, *The Genius of George Washington* (New York: Norton, 1980), pp. 3–25.

6. Gerald Edward Kahler, *Washington in Glory, America in Tears,* unpublished dissertation (College of William and Mary, Williamsburg, Va., 2003), p. 394.

7. For example, he ordered his troops: "The Commander in Chief earnestly recommends that the troops not on duty should universally attend with that seriousness of Deportment and gratitude of Heart which the recognition of such reiterated and astonishing interpositions of Providence demand of us." ("General Orders," October 20, 1781, WGW 23:247.)

8. Fischer, *Washington's Crossing*, p. 25. David McCullough describes the same scene as a snowball fight, see *1776*, p. 61.

9. "To the President of Congress," April 10, 1778, WGW 11:240.

10. Fischer, *Washington's Crossing*, pp. 7–30.

11. "To the Committee of Congress with the Army," January 29, 1778, WGW 10:363.

12. "To John Banister," April 21, 1778, WGW 11:286.

13. "To the Secretary for Foreign Affairs," August 1, 1786, WGW 28:503.

14. "General Orders," August 3, 1776, WGW 5:367.

15. "To Brigadier General William Smallwood," May 26, 1777, WGW 8:129.

16. "General Orders," June 28, 1777, WGW 8:308.

17. "General Orders," May 2, 1778, WGW 11:342–343.

18. Reinhold Niebuhr, "Why the Church Is Not Pacifist," in *Christianity and Power Politics* (New York: Archon Books, [1940] 1969), pp. 14–15.

19. Niebuhr, "Why the Church," pp. 17–18.

CHAPTER 6

1. "To Colonel Benedict Arnold," September 14, 1775, WGW 3:492.

2. Gordon S. Wood, *The American Revolution: A History* (New York: Modern Library Paperback, 2003), pp. 129–130.

3. "Speech to the Delaware Chiefs," May 12, 1779, WGW 15:55.

4. "In the meantime, it will be a desirable thing for the protection of the Union to co-operate, as far as circumstances may conveniently admit, with the disinterested endeavours of your Society to civilize and Christianize the Savages of the Wilderness" ("To the Directors of the Society of United Brethren for Propagating the Gospel Among the Heathen," [sometime after July 10, 1789], WGW 30:355n).

5. Mary V. Thompson, "In the Hands of a Good Providence," pp. 63–65.

6. Thompson, "In the Hands," p. 76.

7. Ibid., pp. 75–76.

8. The most judicious treatment of how often Washington received communion is found in ibid., pp. 106–118.

9. "To Reverend G. W. Snyder," September 25, 1798, WGW 36:452.

10. "The faithful who enroll in Masonic associations are in a state of grave sin and may not receive Holy Communion." See the "Declaration on Masonic Associations," the Congregation for the Doctrine of the Faith, November 26, 1983, Acta Apostolica Sedis, Vol. 76 (1984), p. 300; Documenta 54.

11. "Freemasonry," writes Robert Micklus, was "first and foremost a form of clubbing in an age of clubbing. . . . In an age when clubbing really was the thing to do, being a Freemason—to Freemasons, at least—was as much a part of the social fabric of eighteenth-century life as being a member of a club such as Hamilton's Tuesday Club," in J. A. Leo Lemay, ed., *Deism, Masonry, and the Enlightenment* (Newark: University of Delaware Press, 1987), p. 128. In addition, Steven C. Bullock says that American Masons "identified their order with the values of virtue, learning, and religion," *Revolutionary Brotherhood: Freemasonry and the Transformation of the American Social Order, 1730–1840* (Chapel Hill: University of North Carolina Press, 1996), p. 138. At the Boston Athenaeum, the senior author inspected the commemorative booklet for the one hundredth anniversary of

Washington's induction into the Masons, held before a crowd of almost six thousand, at which the opening prayer concluded, "Through our Lord Jesus Christ. Amen." Robert B. Folger, Address Delivered to the Members of Benevolent Lodge, No. 192, November 4, 1852, in Honor of the Memory of George Washington, an Active Member of the Ancient and Honorable Order of Free and Accepted Masons (New York: C. Shields, 1852).

12. For a comprehensive account of bishops, priests, and prominent lay Episcopalians affiliated with the Masons, see Richard A. Rutyna and Peter C. Steward, The History of Freemasonry in Virginia (Lanham, Md.: University Press of America, 1998), pp. 167–171.

13. "Circular to the States," June 8, 1783, WGW 26:496. In some reproductions, the exact words of Washington are preceded by the traditional form of a public prayer in church, recast with the preface "Almighty God" and the closing, "Through Jesus Christ our Lord." Neither of those phrases occurs in the original text, and insofar as they purport to quote Washington verbatim, such renditions are erroneous.

14. See, for example, Mason Locke ("Parson") Weems, The Life of George Washington, 8th ed. (Philadelphia: Printed for the Authors, 1809); Edward C. M'Guire, The Religious Opinions and Character of Washington (New York: Harper, 1836); William J. Johnstone, George Washington, The Christian (New York: Abingdon Press, 1919); Janice T. Connell, Faith of Our Founding Father: The Spiritual Journey of George Washington (New York: Hatherleigh Press, 2004).

15. See, for example, Franklin Steiner, The Religious Beliefs of Our Presidents (Girard, Kans.: Haldeman-Julius, 1936); Garry Wills, Cincinnatus: George Washington and the Enlightenment (Garden City, N.Y.: Doubleday, 1984); Isaac Kramnick and R. Laurence Moore, The Godless Constitution: The Case Against Religious Correctness (New York: Norton, 1996).

16. The literature on the Second Great Awakening is vast and rich, but perhaps the finest treatment of the split between American Protestantism's head and heart can be found in Alan Heimert's magisterial Religion and the American Mind: From the Great Awakening to the American Revolution (Cambridge: Harvard University Press, 1966).

17. The senior author of this book remembers being made quite uncomfortable by this familiarity, since in his own Catholic upbringing, the name Jesus was almost never voiced except privately; it was reserved for private prayer. Voiced aloud, it sounded to a Catholic ear a bit effeminate—or at least too intimate for use with others. Among ourselves, Christ—the formal title for Messiah—was spoken of with manly affection. ("Are you a follower of Christ?" "Do you love Christ?") "Christ," but seldom, in public, "Jesus."

18. Walter A. McDougall, Freedom Just Around the Corner: A New American History (1585–1828) (New York: HarperCollins, 2004), p. 327.

19. Ibid., p. 325.

20. Sydney E. Ahlstrom, A Religious History of the American People (New Haven, Conn.: Yale University Press, 1973), p. 573.

21. Paul F. Boller, *George Washington and Religion* (Dallas: Southern Methodist University Press, 1963), pp. 80–82.

22. Avery Cardinal Dulles, "The Deist Minimum," *First Things,* Vol. 149 (January 2005), p. 25. Note the affinities Dulles alludes to between Christianity and Stoicism. Some historians argue Washington was not a Christian but a Stoic, as if these were radically different alternatives.

23. "It was the implicit belief in some form of imposition, with its consequent exactness, that constituted the motive force in scientific research. Why should educated men have believed that there was anything to find out?" Alfred North Whitehead, *Adventures of Ideas* (New York: Mentor Books, 1955), p. 118. John Adams, Washington's vice president, thought in very much the same terms when he wrote, "I will insist that the Hebrews have done more to civilize men than any other nation. If I were an atheist, and believed in blind eternal fate, I should still believe that fate had ordained the Jews to be the most essential instrument for civilizing the nations. If I were an atheist of the other sect, who believe or pretend to believe that all is ordered by chance, I should believe that chance had ordered the Jews to preserve and propagate to all mankind the doctrine of a supreme, intelligent, wise, almighty sovereign of the universe, which I believe to be the great essential principle of all morality, and consequently of all civilization," quoted in Russell Kirk, *The Roots of American Order* (Wilmington, Del.: ISI Books, 2003), p. 17.

24. "Vernunft . . . ist die höchste Hur, die der Teufel hat," from "Martin Luther's Last Sermon in Wittenberg . . . 17 January 1546," in *Dr. Martin Luthers Werke, Kritische Gesamtsusgabe,* Vol. 51 (Weimar: Herman Boehlaus Nachfolger, 1914), p. 126.

25. "For reason is the greatest enemy that faith has: it never comes to the aid of spiritual things, but—more frequently than not—struggles against the Divine Word, treating with contempt all that emanates from God," *The Table-Talk of Martin Luther,* CCCLIII, trans. William Hazlitt (Philadelphia: Lutheran Publication Society), p. 116.

26. John Calvin, *Institutes of the Christian Religion,* 3.2.7, trans. Henry Beveridge.

27. Edward, Lord Herbert of Cherbury, *De Veritate,* in *Deism: An Anthology,* ed. Peter Gay (Princeton: D. Van Nostrand, 1968).

28. On this point, see Henry F. May's classic account of what he calls the "moderate enlightenment," in *The Enlightenment in America* (New York: Oxford University Press, 1976), pp. 3–101.

29. "Paine was particularly disturbed about the widespread atheism in France and set out to combat it. . . . He intended *The Age of Reason* to reawaken faith in God, especially in France where one of the aftermaths of revolution was skepticism and negation. He called for a return to simplicity in worship. He related the political rights of man to the religious rights of man," in Norman Cousins, *In God We Trust: The Religious Beliefs and Ideas of the American Founding Fathers* (New York: Harper, 1958), pp. 391, 393. See also Harvey J. Kaye, *Thomas Paine and the Promise of America* (New York: Hill & Wang, 2005).

30. Cousins, *In God We Trust*, p. 390.

31. Dulles, "Deist Minimum," pp. 28–29.

32. "Deism," *Westminster Dictionary of Christian Theology*, p. 148.

33. Jefferson's redacted New Testament has been reproduced many times. The standard scholarly edition was edited by Dickinson W. Adams in the first volume of the Second Series of the *Papers of Thomas Jefferson* (Princeton, N.J.: Princeton University Press, 1983). Edwin Gaustad adds helpful biographical perspective in Chapter 5 of *Sworn on the Altar of God* (Grand Rapids, Mich.: Eerdmans, 1996), pp. 123–131.

34. See, for example, Jefferson's letter to Benjamin Rush: "To the corruptions of Christianity I am indeed opposed; but not to the genuine precepts of Jesus himself. I am a Christian, in the only sense he wished any one to be; sincerely attached to his doctrines, in preference to all others; ascribing to himself every *human* excellence; & believing he never claimed other," in *Jefferson: Writings*, ed. Merrill D. Peterson (New York: Library of America, 1984), p. 1122. See also in the same book Jefferson's letter to Charles Thomson, in which Jefferson says of his own redacted New Testament, "A more beautiful or precious morsel of ethics I have never seen; it is a document in proof that I am a real Christian, that is to say, a disciple of the doctrines of Jesus," p. 1373.

35. "Deism," *The Dictionary of the History of Ideas*, Vol. 1 (New York: Scribner's, 1973), p. 646.

36. Michael Novak, *On Two Wings: Humble Faith and Common Sense at the American Founding* (San Francisco: Encounter Books, 2002).

37. "To the Ministers, Elders, Deacons, and Members of the Reformed German Congregation of New York," November 27, 1783, WGW 27:249.

38. "Proposed Address to Congress," [April 1789?], WGW 30:299.

39. "To George Mason," October 3, 1785, WGW 28:285.

40. "Religion and the Common Good: Washington on Church and State," in Daniel Dreisbach, Mark D. Hall, and Jeffrey H. Morrison, eds., *The Founders on God and Government* (Lanham, Md.: Rowman & Littlefield, 2004), pp. 1–22. An earlier version of the essay appeared as "George Washington on Religious Liberty," in the *Review of Politics,* Vol. 65, No. 1 (Winter 2003), pp. 11–33.

41. "Catalogue of Books for Master Custis Referred to on the Otherside, Viz.," WGW 2:515.

42. "It seems to have been reserved to the people of this country, by their conduct and example, to decide *the important question*, whether societies of men are really capable or not of establishing good government from *reflection* and *choice,*" in *The Federalist Papers* (Number 1), ed. Clinton Rossiter (New York: Mentor, 1961), p. 1.

43. "We shall be left nearly in a state of Nature, or we may find by our own unhappy experience, that there is a natural and necessary progression, from the extreme of anarchy to the extreme of Tyranny; and that arbitrary power is most easily established on the ruins of Liberty abused to licentiousness," in "Circular to the States," June 8, 1783, WGW 26:489.

44. "Circular to the States," June 8, 1783, WGW 26:485.

45. "Circular to the States," June 8, 1783, WGW 26:484–485.

46. "Circular to the States," June 8, 1783, WGW 26:485.

47. "Undelivered First Inaugural Address: Fragments," [April–June 1789?], PGW *Pres. Series* 2:152–158.

48. "To Joseph Hopkinson," May 27, 1798, WGW 36:274.

49. "Letter to the Hebrew Congregation of Newport," in W. B. Allen, ed., *George Washington: A Collection* (Indianapolis, Ind.: Liberty Fund, Inc., 1988), pp. 547–548. See Appendix 1 for full text.

50. "To the Society of Quakers," October 1789, PGW *Pres. Series,* 4:266. Far from merely flattering the Quakers, Washington in this irenical talk also displayed his displeasure about the Quaker refusal "to provide for the common defense" of these very rights. See Appendix 1.

51. December 13, 1790, PGW *Pres. Series,* 7:61–62.

52. "To the Members of the New Church in Baltimore," [January 27, 1793], WGW 32:315.

CHAPTER 7

1. WGW 15:180.

2. John Witherspoon, "The Dominion of Providence over the Passions of Men," in Ellis Sandoz, ed., *Political Sermons of the American Founding Era: 1730–1805* (Indianapolis, Ind.: Liberty Fund, 1991), pp. 529–558.

3. "Let us pause, my fellow-citizens, for one moment over this melancholy and monitory lesson of history; and with the tear that drops for the calamities brought on mankind by their adverse opinions and selfish passions, let our gratitude mingle an ejaculation to Heaven for the propitious concord which has distinguished the consultations for our political happiness," in *The Federalist Papers* (Number 20), ed. Clinton Rossiter (New York: Mentor, 1961), p. 137.

4. PGW, *Pres. Series,* 7:61–62.

5. "Letter to the General Convention of Bishops, Clergy, and Laity of the Protestant Episcopal Church in New York, New Jersey, Pennsylvania, Delaware, Maryland, Virginia, and North Carolina," August 19, 1789, WGW 30:383n.

6. The selections listed come from the following letters: "To the Emperor of Germany," May 15, 1796, WGW 35:46; "Proclamation," August 17, 1776, WGW 5:445; "General Orders," May 2, 1778, WGW 11:342–343; "To George Washington Parke Custis [stepgrandson of Washington]," November 28, 1796, WGW 35:283; "Circular to the States," June 8, 1783, WGW 26:496; "To Thomas McKean," November 15, 1781, WGW 23:343; "To the Hebrew Congregation of Newport, Rhode Island," August 18, 1790, PGW *Pres. Series,* 6:285; "To George Washington Parke Custis [stepgrandson of Washington]," November 28, 1796, WGW 35:283; "Thanksgiving Proclamation," October 3, 1789, WGW 30:427–428; "Circular to the States," June 8, 1783, WGW 26:496; "General Orders," February 27, 1776, WGW 4:355; "To the Hebrew Congregation of Newport,

Rhode Island" [August 18, 1790], PGW *Pres. Series,* 6:285; "To the Ministers, Elders, and Deacons of the Reformed Church of Schenectady," June 30, 1782, WGW 24:391; "To Reverend Jonathan Boucher," May 21, 1772, WGW 3:84.

7. "Letter from John Adams to Abigail Adams," September 16, 1774, *Adams Family Correspondence,* ed. L. H. Butterfield (Cambridge, Mass.: Belknap Press, 1963).

8. "Letter to the Hebrew Congregation of the City of Savannah," Georgia, [undated] *George Washington: A Collection* (Indianapolis, Ind.: Liberty Fund, 1988), p. 549.

9. *Thanksgiving Day Proclamation of October 26, 1781,* in *Journals of the Continental Congress 1774–1789,* ed. Worthington Chauncy Ford and Gaillard Hunt (Washington, D.C.: U.S. Government Printing Office, 1904–1937), pp. 1074–1076.

10. "Letter to Brigadier General Thomas Nelson," August 20, 1778, WGW 12:343.

11. "Letter to Reverend William Gordon," July 8, 1783, WGW 27:50.

12. Mary V. Thompson, "In the Hands of a Good Providence" (publication forthcoming), pp. 94–96.

13. James Thomas Flexner, *George Washington in the American Revolution (1775–1783),* (Boston: Little, Brown, 1968), p. 13.

14. "Letter to David Humphreys," March 23, 1793, WGW 32:398.

15. "Letter to Reverend Israel Evans," March 13, 1778, WGW 11:78. This sermon was among the favorites that Washington had bound in hard covers for his library. The copy in the Boston Athenaeum is signed by Washington and bears pen marks that might be his.

16. See, for example, "To Burwell Bassett," April 25, 1773, WGW 3:133; "To John Augustine Washington," February 24, 1777, WGW 7:198; "To Bryan Fairfax," March 1, 1778, WGW 11:3; "To Reverend William Gordon," July 8, 1783, WGW 27:50; "To the Secretary of War," September 8, 1791, WGW 31:360; "To Elizabeth Parke Custis Law," March 30, 1796, WGW 35:1; "To Thaddeus Kosciuszko," August 31, 1797, WGW 36:22.

17. "To Governor Jonathan Trumbull," April 15, 1784, WGW 27:399.

18. "To William Tudor," August 18, 1788, WGW 30:55.

19. "To John Augustine Washington," January 27, 1793, WGW 32:315.

20. Joseph J. Ellis, *His Excellency: George Washington* (New York: Knopf, 2004), p. 151.

21. The first dictionary we checked was Webster's New International (2nd ed., 1960), which gives the following two definitions of *providence:* (a) "divine guidance or care" and (b) "God, conceived of as guiding men with his prescience, love, care, or intervention." The second dictionary we consulted was the Oxford English Dictionary (Oxford University Press, 1971), which also give two relevant definitions: (a) "the foreknowing and beneficent care and government of God (or of nature, etc.); divine direction, control or guidance" and (b) "hence applied to the Deity as exercising prescient and beneficent power and direction." The uses of

providence by Flexner, Freeman, Ellis, and others, therefore, seem out of step with common usage today, and they would seem to have been even more so in the period 1770–1799.

22. "Letter to Martha Washington," June 18, 1775, WGW 3:293–294.

23. Langdon Gilkey, late of the Divinity School at the University of Chicago, who has written wisely about Christianity in America, provides an excellent account of the difference between fate and providence when, quoting St. Augustine, he writes, "'[Let not astrologers] be imposing Fate on the Maker of heaven, the Creator and Ruler of the Stars. For even if fate were from the stars, the Maker of the stars could not be subject to their destiny.' Neither Christ, nor you, nor I, Augustine goes on to say, is subject to fate," in *Maker of Heaven and Earth* (Garden City, N.Y.: Doubleday Anchor Books [1959] 1969), pp. 23–24. Providence is sovereign over fate, not on an equal plane with it. In the same way, Washington prayed—not to fate, which would have been pointless—but to Providence.

24. James Thomas Flexner, *George Washington: The Forge of Experience (1732–1775)* (Boston: Little, Brown, 1965), p. 245n.

25. Douglas Southall Freeman, *George Washington: Young Washington,* Vol. 2 (New York: Scribner's, 1948), p. 397.

26. Flexner, *Forge of Experience,* p. 244; James Thomas Flexner, *George Washington: Anguish and Farewell (1793–1799)* (Boston: Little, Brown, 1972), p. 490.

27. "Letter to Martha Washington," June 18, 1775, WGW 3:293–294.

28. Flexner, *Anguish and Farewell,* p. 490.

29. An Anglican preacher of the era wrote: "Never perhaps had a human being a more vivid sense than Washington of that great truth which lies at the bottom of all our religion and all our joys; I mean, the belief in a particular Providence," citing then the divine care of the swallows (Matthew 10:29–42); see Mason Locke Weems, *A History of the Life and Death, Virtues and Exploits of General George Washington; Dedicated to Mrs. Washington* (Philadelphia: Lippincott, 1918). See also Thomas Comber's reflections on providence, passim, in *Short Discourses upon the Whole Common Prayer* (1684) and notably: "[There is] no clearer acknowledgement of our Dependance [*sic*] upon God, nor more effectual means to procure all good Things, than publick or Common Prayer," and "Pray without ceasing: at least at all hours."

30. See also F. F. Bruce, *The Gospel of John* (Grand Rapids, Mich.: Eerdmans, 1983), p. 299.

31. Flexner, *Anguish and Farewell,* p. 490.

32. "To Joseph Reed," March 7, 1776, WGW 4:380. Washington is referring to Alexander Pope's renowned *Essay on Man,* Epistle 1.x. 289–294: "All nature is but art, known to thee; / all chance, direction, which thou canst not see; / All discord, harmony, not understood; / All partial evil, universal good; / And, spite of pride, in erring reason's spite; / One truth is clear, whatever is, is right."

33. "Letter to Lund Washington," May 29, 1779, WGW 15:180.

34. Jared Sparks, *The Writings of George Washington,* Vol. 12 (New York: Harper, 1852), p. 406.

35. "Speech to the Delaware Chiefs," May 12, 1779, WGW 15:55.

36. E. C. M'Guire, *The Religious Opinions and Character of Washington,* 2nd ed. (New York: Harper & Brothers, 1847), pp. 17ff., 158ff.; also Philip Slaughter, historian of the Diocese of Virginia, in *Christianity: The Key to the Character and Career of General Washington: Discourse to the Mt. Vernon Ladies' Association, May 30, 1886,* especially pp. 32–33. In our judgment, M'Guire and Slaughter wrote less as historians than as proponents, and their citations and interpretations need to be read critically. M'Guire's testimony is important as a reflection of the thinking of the Washington family (and the women friends of Betty, Washington's sister) about the religion of their most famous relative. Slaughter is significant for covering the lore of Washington's own church, the Anglican Church of Virginia. These factors may bias the case made by both. On the other hand, if the Anglicans disowned Washington, or the family tried to "explain him away" as a religious aberration, then Washington's reputation, then and now, would look very different indeed.

37. Thus did Washington record in his diary for 1774: "June 1st. Went to Church & fasted all day." DGW 3:254.

38. Slaughter, *Christianity: The Key to the Character and Career of General Washington,* p. 30.

39. Freeman, *Young Washington,* pp. 387–388.

40. "Circular to the States," June 8, 1783, WGW 26:496.

41. "Circular to the States," June 8, 1783, WGW 26:485.

CHAPTER 8

1. "First Inaugural Address," April 30, 1789, WGW 30:293.

2. WGW 30:427–428.

3. *The Federalist Papers* (Number 2), ed. Clinton Rossiter (New York: Mentor, 1961), p. 6.

4. Matthew Spalding, *A Sacred Union of Citizens: George Washington's Farewell and the National Character* (New York: Rowman & Littlefield, 1998); see especially Chapter 2, "Establishing the National Character," pp. 9–47.

5. "Proclamation of Thanksgiving and Prayer," February 17, 1795, in *Messages and Papers of the Presidents,* ed. William Richardson (Washington, D.C.: U.S. Government Printing Office, 1902), pp. 171–172.

6. "Circular to the States," June 8, 1783, WGW 26:496.

7. See, for example, Romans 13:1–14; 1 Corinthians 13:4–7.

CHAPTER 9

1. John Marshall, *The Life of George Washington* (Indianapolis, Ind.: Liberty Fund, 2000), p. 466.

2. Edwin Gaustad, *Sworn on the Altar of God: A Religious Biography of Thomas Jefferson* (Grand Rapids, Mich.: Eerdmans, 1996), p. 92.

3. Julian Ursyn Niemcewicz, *Under Their Vine and Fig Tree: Travels Through America, 1797–1799, 1805* (Elizabeth: New Jersey Historical Society, 1965), p. 99.

4. Paul F. Boller, Jr., *George Washington and Religion* (Dallas: Southern Methodist University Press, 1963), pp. 80–91.

5. "To Richard Washington," October 20, 1761, WGW 2:371.

6. "To Robert Cary and Company," June 20, 1762, WGW 2:379.

7. "To Benjamin Lincoln," February 11, 1788, WGW 29:412–413.

8. "To the Secretary of War," September 8, 1791, WGW 31:360.

9. "To Henry Knox," March 2, 1797, WGW 35:408–409.

10. "To Elizabeth Washington Lewis," September 13, 1789, WGW 30:76.

11. "To Burwell Bassett," April 25, 1773, WGW 3:133.

12. "To Major General Israel Putnam," October 19, 1777, WGW 9:400–401.

13. "To Burwell Bassett," June 20, 1773, WGW 3:138.

14. Donald Jackson, ed., *The Diaries of George Washington*, Vol. 3 (Charlottesville: University Press of Virginia, 1976–1979), pp. 113n, 234n–235n.

15. DGW 6:132.

16. "Farewell Address, September 19, 1796," WGW 35:229.

17. James Thomas Flexner, *George Washington in the American Revolution (1775–1783)*, Vol. 2 (Boston: Little, Brown, 1968), p. 30.

18. *Cato*, Act 4, Scene 4, lines 141–142. See *Cato: A Tragedy, and Selected Essays* [of Joseph Addison], ed. Christine Dunn Henderson and Mark E. Yellin (Indianapolis, Ind.: Liberty Fund, 2004), p. 87.

19. "To the Secretary of War," July 27, 1795, WGW 34:251; "To David Humphreys," June 12, 1796, WGW 35:92; "To Alexander Hamilton," June 26, 1796, WGW 35:103.

20. Seneca, *De Providentia*, II.9. The editors of the Liberty Fund edition of Addison's *Cato* note that Addison omits the phrase "and doubly so if his also was the challenge" from the Latin.

CHAPTER 10

1. "General Orders," February 18, 1783, WGW 26:136.

2. "Letters to the Clergy of Newport," August 17, 1790, WGW 31:93n.

3. E. C. M'Guire, *The Religious Opinions and Character of Washington*, 2nd ed. (New York: Harper & Brothers, 1847).

4. Thomas Comber, *Short Discourses upon the Whole Common-Prayer; Designed to Inform the Judgment, and Excite the Devotion of Such as Daily Use the Same*, 4th ed. (London: 1712).

5. Ibid., p. 40.

6. "To Landon Carter," October 27, 1777, WGW 9:453–454.

7. "To Joseph Reed," November 27, 1778, WGW 13:348.

8. "To the Inhabitants of Princeton and Neighborhood, Together with the President and Faculty of the College," August 25, 1783, WGW 27:116.

9. "To William Tudor," August 18, 1788, WGW 30:55. "From seeming evil still educing good" is a line from the Scottish poet James Thomson's (1700–1748) poem "Hymn on a Review of the Seasons."

10. "Letter to Joseph Reed," March 7, 1776, WGW 4:380. Washington wrote: "I will not lament or repine at any act of Providence because I am in a great measure a convert to Mr. Pope's opinion, that whatever is, is right."

11. "To Governor Jonathan Trumbull," April 15, 1784, WGW 27:399.

12. "To the Earl of Buchan," May 26, 1794, WGW 33:383.

13. "To the Secretary of War," November 17, 1799, WGW 37:428–429.

14. "To John Augustine Washington," October 18, 1777, WGW 9:397.

15. "To John Augustine Washington," December 18, 1776, WGW 6:398–399.

16. "To Annis Boudinot Stockton," August 31, 1788, WGW 30:76.

17. "To David Humphreys," February 7, 1785, WGW 28:66.

18. "To Reverend Bryan, Lord Fairfax," January 20, 1799, WGW 37:94–95.

19. "To Bryan Fairfax," March 1, 1778, WGW 11:3.

20. "To George Augustine Washington," January 27, 1793, WGW 32:315.

21. James Thomas Flexner, *George Washington and the New Nation (1783–1793)* (Boston: Little, Brown, 1970), p. 212.

22. *George Washington: In His Own Words,* ed. Maureen Harrison and Steve Gilbert (New York: Barnes & Noble Books, 1997), p. 309.

23. A succint treatment of the ideas of General Providence and Special Providence can be found in Stephen H. Webb, *American Providence: A Nation with a Mission* (New York: Continuum, 2004); see especially pp. 13–14, 33.

24. "Circular Letter to the States," June 8, 1783, WGW 26:484.

25. "Perceive with these bodily senses" presumably as distinguished from perception after death.

26. "Fragments of the Discarded First Inaugural Address, April 1789," in W. B. Allen, *George Washington: A Collection* (Indianapolis, Ind.: Liberty Fund, 1988), p. 456.

CHAPTER 11

1. Douglass Adair, "Was Alexander Hamilton a Christian Statesman?" in *Fame and the Founding Fathers: Essays by Douglass Adair* (Indianapolis, Ind.: Liberty Fund, 1998), pp. 200–226; see especially pp. 205 ff.

2. Adair, "Was Alexander Hamilton," pp. 206 ff.

3. Hannah Arendt, *On Revolution* (New York: Penguin Putnam, [1963] 1990).

4. *The Papers of Alexander Hamilton*, Vol. 26, ed. Harold C. Syrett (New York: Columbia University Press, 1961–1987), p. 293.

5. Joseph Ellis, *His Excellency: George Washington* (New York: Knopf, 2004), p. 269.

6. Mary V. Thompson, "In the Hands of a Good Providence" (publication forthcoming), pp. 227–228.

7. Tobias Lear, "The Last Illness and Death of George Washington," in Raymond Brighton, *The Checkered Career of Tobias Lear* (Portsmouth, N.H.: Portsmouth Marine Society, 1985). Available online at the website of Lear's hometown: http://seacoastnh.com/Famous_People/Tobias_Lear.

8. Ibid.; see the "biography section" on the website.

9. Harrison Clark, *All Cloudless Glory: The Life of George Washington*, Vol. 2 (Washington, D.C.: Regnery, 1996), p. 427.

10. Ibid.

CHAPTER 12

1. Gerald Edward Kahler, *Washington in Glory, America in Tears: The Nation Mourns the Death of George Washington, 1799–1800*, unpublished Ph.D. dissertation, (College of William and Mary, Williamsburg, Va., 2003), p. 341.

2. "Address to Congress on Resigning His Commission," December 23, 1783, WGW 27:285.

3. Janice T. Connell, *Faith of Our Founding Father: The Spiritual Journey of George Washington* (New York: Hatherleigh Press, 2004).

4. "Eulogy on George Washington," in *Prose and Poetry of America*, ed. Julian L. Maline and Wilfred M. Mallon (Syracuse, N.Y.: L. W. Singer, 1949), p. 435.

5. E. Brooks Holifield, *Theology in America: Christian Thought from the Age of the Puritans to the Civil War* (New Haven, Conn.: Yale University Press, 2003), p. 242.

6. Ibid., p. 242.

7. Paul F. Boller, Jr., *George Washington and Religion* (Dallas: Southern Methodist University Press, 1963), pp. 80–91.

8. Ibid., p. 16.

9. Mary V. Thompson, "In the Hands of a Good Providence," manuscript in the Library of Mount Vernon (publication forthcoming), p. 63.

10. Kahler, p. 339.

11. Ibid.

12. Mason Locke Weems, *A History of the Life and Death, Virtues and Exploits of General George Washington* (Philadelphia: Lippincott, 1918). Available online at http://xroads.virginia.edu/~CAP/gw/chap13.html.

13. Frank E. Grizzard, Jr., *The Ways of Providence* (Charlottesville, Va.: Mariner, 2005), pp. 23–24.

14. "Several members of Washington's domestic household have left credible remarks on the subject of George Washington and prayer, which should not be easily dismissed." Thompson, "In the Hands," pp. 122–124. Thompson cites the evidence of Eleanor ("Nelly") Parke Custis (Washington's stepgranddaughter), Hannah Bushrod (sister-in-law), Eleanor Calvert Custis (daughter-in-law), Major George Lewis (nephew), and Robert Lewis (nephew).

15. Boller, *George Washington*, p. 89.

16. E. C. M'Guire, *The Religious Opinions and Character of Washington*, 2nd ed. (New York: Harper, 1847).

17. Jared Sparks, ed., *The Writings of George Washington*, Vol. 12 (Boston, Mass.: American Stationers' Company, 1837), p. 411.

APPENDIX 1

1. "After Orders," September 25, 1756, WGW 1:473.

2. "General Orders," July 4, 1775, WGW 3:309.

3. "General Orders," July 16, 1775, WGW 3:341.

4. "General Orders," August 5, 1775, WGW 3:403.

5. "To Colonel Benedict Arnold," September 14, 1775, WGW 3:492.

6. "Instructions to Colonel Benedict Arnold," September 14, 1775, WGW 3:495–496.

7. "General Orders," November 5, 1775, WGW 4:65.

8. "General Orders," February 27, 1776, WGW 4:355.

9. "General Orders," May 15, 1776, WGW 5:43.

10. "General Orders," May 16, 1776, WGW 5:50.

11. "General Orders," June 30, 1776, WGW 5:206.

12. "General Orders," July 2, 1776, WGW 5:211.

13. "General Orders," July 9, 1776, WGW 5:245.

14. "General Orders," August 3, 1776, WGW 5:367.

15. "General Orders," April 12, 1777, WGW 7:407.

16. "General Orders," April 19, 1777, WGW 7:442.

17. "General Orders," May 17, 1777, WGW 8:77.

18. "General Orders," May 24, 1777, WGW 8:114.

19. "To Brigadier General William Smallwood," May 26, 1777, WGW 8:129.

20. "General Orders," May 31, 1777, WGW 8:152–153.

21. "General Orders," September 13, 1777, WGW 9:211.

22. "General Orders," June 28, 1777, WGW 8:308.

23. "General Orders," July 5, 1777, WGW 8:531.

24. "General Orders," October 18, 1777, WGW 9:390–391.

25. "General Orders," May 2, 1778, WGW 11:342.

26. "General Orders," October 20, 1781, WGW 23:247.

27. "General Orders," March 22, 1783, WGW 26:250.

28. "General Orders," March 6, 1776, WGW 4:369.

29. "General Orders," May 15, 1776, WGW 5:43.

30. "General Orders," April 12, 1779, WGW 14:369.

31. "Circular to the States," June 8, 1783, WGW 26:484–486.

32. "Circular to the States," June 8, 1783, WGW 26:496.

33. "Fragments of the Discarded First Inaugural Address" [April 1789] in W. B. Allen, ed., *George Washington: A Collection* (Indianapolis, Ind.: Liberty Fund, 1988), pp. 453–454.

34. "Fragments of the Discarded First Inaugural Address" [April 1789], in Allen, *George Washington,* p. 456.

35. "Fragments of the Discarded First Inaugural Address" [April 1789], in Allen, *George Washington,* pp. 456–457.

36. "The First Inaugural Address" [April 30, 1789], WGW 30:294–295.

37. "The First Inaugural Address" [April 30, 1789], WGW 30:296.

38. "To the United Baptist Churches in Virginia" [May 1789], in Allen, *George Washington*, p. 532.

39. "To the General Assembly of Presbyterian Churches" [May 1789], in Allen, *George Washington*, p. 533.

40. "To the Annual Meeting of Quakers" [September 1789], in Allen, *George Washington*, pp. 533–534.

41. "To the Hebrew Congregations of Philadelphia, New York, Charleston, and Richmond" [December 1790], WGW 31:185–186.

42. "To the Roman Catholics in the United States of America" [March 15, 1789], in Allen, *George Washington*, pp. 546–547.

43. "To the Hebrew Congregation of Newport" [August 1789], in Allen, *George Washington*, pp. 547–548.

44. "To the Hebrew Congregation of the City of Savannah, Georgia," in Allen, *George Washington*, p. 549.

45. "Thanksgiving Proclamation," October 3, 1789, WGW 30:427–428.

46. "Proclamation of Thanksgiving and Prayer," February 17, 1795, in James D. Richardson, ed., *A Compilation of the Messages and Papers of the Presidents of the United States, 1789–1897* (Washington, D.C.: Published by the Authority of Congress, 1898–1899), pp. 171–172.

47. "Farewell Address [First Draft]," May 15, 1796, WGW 35:56.

48. "Farewell Address," September 19, 1796, WGW 35:229.

49. "Farewell Address," September 19, 1796, WGW 35:231.

APPENDIX 2

1. "To Colonel Benedict Arnold," December 5, 1775, WGW 4:149.

2. "To the Emperor of Germany," May 15, 1796, WGW 35:46.

3. "First Inaugural Address," April 30, 1789, WGW 30:293.

4. "Circular to the States," June 8, 1783, WGW 26:496.

5. "General Orders," May 5, 1778, WGW 11:354.

6. "To the Major and Brigadier Generals," September 8, 1775, WGW 3:483; "To Major General Henry Knox," September 12, 1782, WGW 25:150n; "To the Attorney General," August 26, 1792, 32:136; "To William Pearce," May 25, 1794, WGW 33:375.

7. "To the Massachusetts Senate and House of Representatives," August 10, 1783, WGW 27:93; "To William Augustine Washington," February 27, 1798, WGW 36:171.

8. "To Major General Henry Knox," February 20, 1784, WGW 27:341.

9. "To Mrs. Martha Custis," July 20, 1758, WGW 2:242.

10. "To the Legislature of New Jersey," December 6, 1783, WGW 27:261.

11. "To Burwell Bassett," April 24, 1796, WGW 35:27.

12. "To Reverend Israel Evans [Chaplain to Poor's New Hampshire Brigade]," March 13, 1778, WGW 11:78.

13. "To Governor Jonathan Trumbull," April 15, 1784, WGW 27:399.

14. "To Doctor James Anderson," July 25, 1798, WGW 36:365.

15. "Farewell Address," May 15, 1796, WGW 35:56.

16. "To Joseph Reed," February 1, 1776, WGW 4:300.

17. "To the Citizens and Inhabitants of the Town of Baltimore," September 8, 1781, WGW 23:109.

18. "Seventh Annual Address," December 8, 1795, WGW 34:386.

19. "To Reverend Samuel Langdon," September 28, 1789, WGW 30:416.

20. "To the Inhabitants of Canada," September 1775, WGW 3:478.

21. "Answer to an Address from the Massachusetts Legislature" [March 28, 1776], WGW 4:44.

22. "To the Secretary of War," November 17, 1799, WGW 37:428.

23. "To the Mayor, Corporation, and Citizens of Alexandria," April 16, 1789, WGW 30:287.

24. "Thanksgiving Proclamation," October 3, 1789, WGW 30:427.

25. "First Inaugural Address," April 30, 1789, WGW 30:296.

26. "To the Grand Lodge of Ancient, Free, and Accepted Masons of the Commonwealth of Massachusetts," April 24, 1797, WGW 35:339.

27. "To John Augustine Washington," July 4, 1778, WGW 12:157; "To Robert R. Livingston," January 31, 1781, WGW 21:164.

28. "To George Washington Parke Custis [stepgrandson of Washington]," November 28, 1796, WGW 35:283.

29. "To the United Baptist Churches of Virginia," May 1789, PGW, *Pres. Series*, 2:424.

30. "To Governor Jonathan Trumbull," May 15,1784, WGW 27:399

31. "To the Legislature of New Jersey," December 6, 1783, WGW 27:261.

32. "To the Clergy of Different Denominations Residing in and near the City of Philadelphia" [March 3, 1797], WGW 35:417.

33. "Circular to the States," June 8, 1783, WGW 26:496.

34. "Answer to an Address of the Massachusetts Legislature," July 4, 1775, WGW 3:308.

35. "Proclamation of Thanksgiving and Prayer," February 17, 1795, in James D. Richardson, ed., *A Compilation of the Messages and Papers of the Presidents of the United States, 1789–1897* (Washington, D.C.: Published by the Authority of Congress, 1898–1899), pp. 171–172.

36. "To the Inhabitants of Princeton and Neighborhood, Together with the President and Faculty of the College," August 25, 1783, WGW 27:116; "First Inaugural Address," April 30, 1789, WGW 30:296.

37. "General Orders," May 5, 1778, WGW 11:354.

38. "To Major General John Armstrong," March 26, 1781, WGW 21:378.

39. "To Governor Jonathan Trumbull," July 18, 1775, WGW 3:344; "General Orders," November 28, 1775, WGW 4:119; "General Orders," February 27, 1776, WGW 4:355; "To Major General Philip Schuyler," July 11, 1776, WGW 5:258; "General Orders," October 15, 1777, WGW 9:377; "To George Plater and

Thomas Cockey Dey," November 23, 1781, WGW 23:358; "Answer to the Address of Congress," March 21, 1782, WGW 24:83; "To Chevalier de la Luzerne," June 5, 1782, WGW 24:314; "To the Magistrates and Military Officers of Schenectady," June 30, 1782, WGW 24:390; "To Reverend John Rodgers," June 11, 1783, WGW 27:1; "To the Magistrates and Inhabitants of the Borough of Elizabeth," August 21, 1783, WGW 27:113; "To the Ministers, Elders, and Deacons of the Two United Dutch Reformed Churches of Hackensack and Schalenburgh and to the Inhabitants of Hackensack," November 10, 1783, WGW 27:239; "To Governor Arthur Fenner," June 4, 1790, WGW 31:48; "To Gouvernor Morris," August 14, 1790, WGW 31:93n; "Fourth Annual Address to Congress," November 4, 1792, WGW 32:212; "To John Doughty," September 23, 1793, WGW 33:93; "To the Pennsylvania House of Representatives," February 17, 1797, WGW 35:393.

40. "To the Massachusetts Senate and House of Representatives," August 10, 1783, WGW 27:93.

41. "To the Hebrew Congregation of Newport, Rhode Island" [August 18, 1790], PGW, *Pres. Series*, 6:285.

42. "To Burges Ball," September 22, 1799, WGW 37:372.

43. "General Orders," May 15, 1776, WGW 5:43.

44. "To Henry Lee," September 22, 1788, WGW 30:95, 98; "To John Augustine Washington," November 6, 1776, WGW 6:247; WGW passim.

45. "To Edmund Pendleton," April 12, 1777, WGW 7:394; "To Landon Carter," April 15, 1777, WGW 7:414; "Farewell Orders," November 2, 1783, WGW 27:227.

46. "To Edmund Pendleton," November 1, 1779, WGW 17:51; "To Pierre Charles l'Enfant," April 28, 1788, WGW 29:481; "To Jonathan Trumbull," July 20, 1788, WGW 30:22.

47. "To David Humphreys," February 7, 1785, WGW 28:66; "To Benjamin Lincoln," June 29, 1788, WGW 30:11.

48. "To the President of Congress," July 10, 1776, WGW 5:247.

49. "To David Humphreys," December 26, 1786, WGW 29:125; "To the Members of the New Church in Baltimore," January 27, 1793, WGW 32:314.

50. "To Brigadier General John Sullivan," June 13, 1776, WGW 5:133; "To the Legislature of New Jersey," December 6, 1783, WGW 27:261; "To the Mayor, Corporation, and Citizens of Alexandria," April 16, 1789, WGW 30:287; "First Annual Address to Congress," January 8, 1790, WGW 30:491; "Proclamation," September 25, 1795, WGW 33:508; WGW passim.

51. "To [Elkanah] Watson & Cassoul," August 10, 1782, WGW 24:497.

52. "Thanksgiving Proclamation," October 3, 1789, WGW 30:427.

53. "To Joseph Reed," November 27, 1778, WGW 13:348.

54. "General Orders," August 12, 1776, WGW 5:423.

55. "To Landon Carter," May 30, 1778, WGW 11:492.

56. "First Inaugural Address," April 30, 1789, WGW 30:293.

57. "To Reverend Samuel Langdon," September 28, 1789, WGW 30:416.

58. "To the American Philosophical Society," December 13, 1783, WGW 27:270.

59. "To William Ramsay, John Fitzgerald, Robert Hooe, and the Other Inhabitants of Alexandria," November 19, 1781, WGW 23:356.

60. "To Governor Jonathan Trumbull," June 11, 1780, WGW 18:511; "To Major General Henry Knox," February 20, 1784, WGW 27:341.

61. "To David Humphreys," February 7, 1785, WGW 28:66; "To Benjamin Lincoln," June 29, 1788, WGW 30:11.

62. "To Henry Knox," September 20, 1795, WGW 34:310.

63. "To Marquis de Lafayette," September 10, 1791, WGW 31:363; "To David Humphreys," March 23, 1793, WGW 32:398; "To Samuel Bishop," August 24, 1793, WGW 33:59; "To Jonathan Williams," March 2, 1795, WGW 34:130.

64. "Proclamation of Thanksgiving and Prayer," February 17, 1795, in Richardson, *Messages and Papers,* pp. 171–172.

65. "To the Inhabitants of Richmond," August 28, 1793, WGW 33:72.

66. "To Charles Pettit," August 16, 1788, WGW 30:42; "To Reverend William Gordon," December 23, 1788, WGW 30:169.

67. "To the Learned Professions of Philadelphia," December 13, 1783, WGW 27:269.

68. "To Major General Horatio Gates," January 4, 1778, WGW 10:263, 264; "Circular to the States," June 8, 1783, WGW 26:484, 485, 490; "To Baron Van Der Capellen De Pol," August 2, 1783, WGW 27:75; "To the Patriotic Society of Enkhuysen," August 2, 1783, WGW 27:76–77; "Sixth Annual Address to Congress," November 19, 1794, WGW 34:28.

69. "To the Ministers, Elders, and Deacons of the Reformed Dutch Church at Albany," June 28, 1782, WGW 24:390.

70. "General Orders," February 15, 1783, WGW 26:136.

71. "First Inaugural Address," April 30, 1789, WGW 30:293; "To Philip Schuyler," May 9, 1789, WGW 30:317.

72. "To the Massachusetts Senate and House of Representatives," August 10, 1783, WGW 27:93; "To Thomas Nelson," August 3, 1788, WGW 30:34.

73. "To the Hebrew Congregations of the City of Savannah, Georgia," in W. B. Allen, ed., *George Washington: A Collection* (Indianapolis, Ind.: Liberty Fund 1988), p. 549.

74. "To Colonel Benedict Arnold," September 14, 1775, WGW 3:492.

75. "Speech to the Delaware Chiefs," May 12, 1779, WGW 15:55.

76. "Proclamation of Thanksgiving and Prayer," February 17, 1795, in Richardson, *Messages and Papers,* pp. 171–172.

77. "To John Adams," April 15, 1776, WGW 4:484; "To Benjamin Franklin," May 20, 1776, WGW 5:65; "To Brigadier General John Sullivan," June 16, 1776, WGW 5:151; "To the President of Congress," July 10, 1776, WGW 5:247; "To Major General Philip Schuyler," August 13, 1776, WGW 5:431; "To the Inhabitants of the City of New London," September 2, 1793, WGW 33:81; "To Reverend James Madison," September 23, 1793, WGW 33:97; "To Jonathan Williams,"

March 2, 1795, WGW 34:130; "To the President of the United States," July 13, 1798, WGW 36:329.

78. "Letter to Lund Washington," August 19, 1776, WGW 5:458.

79. "General Orders," February 27, 1776, WGW 4:355.

80. "Thanksgiving Proclamation," October 3, 1789, WGW 30:428.

81. "General Orders," March 6, 1776, WGW 4:369.

82. "To the Annual Meeting of Quakers," September 1789, in Allen, *George Washington,* p. 533; "To Reverend Bryan, Lord Fairfax," January 20, 1799, WGW 37:95.

83. "General Orders," July 29, 1779, WGW 16:13.

84. "To [Secretary of War] James McHenry," July 31, 1788, WGW 30:30.

85. "To President Joseph Reed," October 18, 1780, WGW 20:213; "To the Members of the New Church in Baltimore," January 27, 1793, WGW 32:31.

86. "Orders and Instructions to Major General Israel Putnam," March 29, 1776, WGW 4:444; "To Doctor Thomas Ruston," August 31, 1788, WGW 30:79.

87. "To Landon Carter," October 27, 1777, WGW 9:453; "To John Gabriel Tegelaar," August 2, 1783, WGW 27:74; WGW passim.

88. "Circular to the States," June 8, 1783, WGW 26:485.

89. "Eighth Annual Address to Congress," December 7, 1796, WGW 35:320.

90. "To the Trustees of the Public School of Germantown," [November 6, 1793], WGW 33:149.

91. "To Annis Boudinot Stockton," August 31, 1788, WGW 30:76.

92. "To Colonel Thomas McKean," August 13, 1776, WGW 5:428; "To Landon Carter," October 27, 1777, WGW 9:454; "General Orders," November 30, 1777, WGW 10:123; "To Marquis de Chastellux," August 18, 1786, WGW 28:524; "To the Massachusetts Senate and House of Representatives," August 10, 1783, WGW 27:93.

93. "To the General Assembly of Georgia" [sometime after December 22, 1789], WGW 30:481n.

94. "To the Brothers of Ancient York Masons Lodge No. 22 [of Alexandria, Virginia]" [April 1, 1797], WGW 35:426.

95. "General Orders," May 2, 1778, WGW 11:343.

96. "To Reverend William Gordon," May 13, 1776, WGW 37:526; "General Orders," July 2, 1776, WGW 5:211; "To the Ministers, Elders, and Deacons of the Reformed Church of Schenectady," June 30, 1782, WGW 24:391; "General Orders," February 15, 1783, WGW 26:135; "To the Inhabitants of Princeton and Neighborhood, Together with the President," August 25, 1783, WGW 27:116; "To the Mayor, Recorder, Aldermen, and Common Council of Annapolis," December 22, 1783, WGW 27:281; "Reply to the French Minister," January 1, 1796, WGW 34:414.

97. "To Major General Philip Schuyler," January 27, 1776, WGW 4:281.

98. "General Orders," October 18, 1777, WGW 9:391; "General Orders," June 30, 1778, WGW 12:131; "To Marquis de Chastellux," August 18, 1786, WGW 28:523.

99. "To the Senate and House of Representatives," November 19, 1794, WGW 34:37.

100. "To the Ministers, Elders, Deacons, and Members of the Reformed German Congregation of New York," November 27, 1783, WGW 27:249; "Eighth Annual Address to Congress," December 7, 1796, WGW 35:320.

101. "To the Inhabitants of the Island of Bermuda," September 6, 1775, WGW 3:475.

102. "To the Hebrew Congregation of the City of Savannah, Georgia," in Allen, *George Washington,* p. 549.

SELECTED BIBLIOGRAPHY

PRIMARY SOURCES, ONLINE AND IN PRINT

Fitzpatrick, John C., ed., *Writings of George Washington*, 39 vols. (Washington, D.C., 1931–1939). Available online at http://etext.lib.virginia.edu/washington/fitzpatrick/.

Jackson, Donald, and Dorothy Twohig, eds., *The Diaries of George Washington*, 6 vols. (Charlottesville, Va.: University of Virginia Press, 1976–1979). Available online at http://memory.loc.gov/ammem/gwhtml/gwintro.html.

Abbot, W. W., Dorothy Twohig, and Philander D. Chase, eds., *The Papers of George Washington: Colonial Series*, 10 vols. (Charlottesville, Va.: University of Virginia Press, 1983–1995).

_____. *The Papers of George Washington: Revolutionary War Series*, 12 vols. (Charlottesville, Va.: University of Virginia Press, 1985—).

Abbot, W. W., and Dorothy Twohig, eds., *The Papers of George Washington: Confederation Series*, 6 vols. (Charlottesville, Va.: University of Virginia Press, 1992–1997).

_____. eds., *The Papers of George Washington: Retirement Series*, 4 vols. (Charlottesville, Va.: University of Virginia Press, 1998–1999).

_____. *The Papers of George Washington: Presidential Series*, 11 vols. (Charlottesville, Va.: University of Virginia Press, 1987—).

Allen, W. B., ed., *George Washington: A Collection* (Indianapolis, Ind.: Liberty Fund, 1988).

The Journal of Major George Washington: Facsimile Edition (Williamsburg, Va: Colonial Williamsburg Foundation, 1985).

Harrison, Maureen, and Steve Gilbert, eds., *George Washington in His Own Words* (New York: Barnes & Noble, 1997).

BIOGRAPHIES AND STUDIES

Freeman, Douglas Southall, *George Washington: A Biography*, 7 vols. (New York: Scribner's, 1948–1957). Volume 7 completed by John A. Carroll and Mary W. Ashburn. A one-volume abridgment was edited by Richard Harwell as *Washington* (New York: Scribner's 1968).

Flexner, James Thomas, *George Washington*, 4 vols. (Boston: Little, Brown, 1965–1972). Flexner distilled the essence of the series in his one-volume biography, *Washington: The Indispensable Man* (New York: Signet [1969] 1984).

Clark, Harrison, *All Cloudless Glory*, 2 vols. (Washington, D.C.: Regnery, 1995–1996).

McCullough, David, *1776* (New York: Simon & Schuster, 2005).

Ellis, Joseph J., *His Excellency George Washington* (New York: Knopf, 2004).

Fischer, David Hackett, *Washington's Crossing* (Oxford and New York: Oxford University Press, 2004).

Boller, Paul F., Jr., *George Washington and Religion* (Dallas, Tex.: Southern Methodist University Press, 1963).

Grizzard, Frank E., Jr., *The Ways of Providence: Religion and George Washington* (Buena Vista, Va.: Mariner, 2005).

_____. *George! A Guide to All Things Washington* (Buena Vista, Va: Mariner, 2005).

Morgan, Edmund S., *The Genius of George Washington* (New York and London: Norton, 1980).

Weintraub, Stanley, *General Washington's Christmas Farewell: A Mount Vernon Homecoming, 1783* (New York: Plume, 2004).

Wills, Garry, *Cincinnatus: George Washington and the Enlightenment* (Garden City, N.Y.: Doubleday, 1984).

Langguth, A. J., *Patriots: The Men Who Started the American Revolution* (New York: Simon & Schuster, 1988).

Gallagher, John J., *The Battle of Brooklyn 1776* (Edison, N.J.: Castle Books, 2002).

Schecter, Barnet, *The Battle for New York: The City at the Heart of the American Revolution* (New York: Walker, 2002).

Gregg, Gary L., II, and Matthew Spalding, eds., *Patriot Sage: George Washington and the American Political Tradition* (Wilmington, Del.: ISI, 1999).

Spalding, Matthew, and Patrick J. Garrity, *A Sacred Union of Citizens: George Washington's Farewell Address and the American Character* (Lanham, Md.: Rowman & Littlefield, 1996).

Hannaford, Peter, ed., *The Essential George Washington: Two Hundred Years of Observations on the Man, the Myth, the Patriot* (Bennington, Vt.: Images from the Past, 1999).

Muñoz, Vincent Phillip, "George Washington and Religious Liberty," *Review of Politics*, Vol. 65, No. 1 (2003), pp. 11–33.

Thompson, Mary V., "In the Hands of a Good Providence" (in manuscript, publication forthcoming). This manuscript, of extraordinary use to us, is not yet in print. We hope that it will be in print within a year or two.

Kahler, Gerald E., *Washington in Glory, America in Tears: The Nation Mourns the Death of George Washington, 1799–1800,* Ph.D. dissertation, College of William and Mary, 2003. Also of good use to us was Kahler's study of Washington's eulogies, which was accepted as a thesis at the College of William and Mary and is available through their library in Williamsburg, Virginia. Within a year or two, this, too, should be in print.

INDEX